COLLINS BTO
GUIDE TO
RARE BRITISH
BIRDS

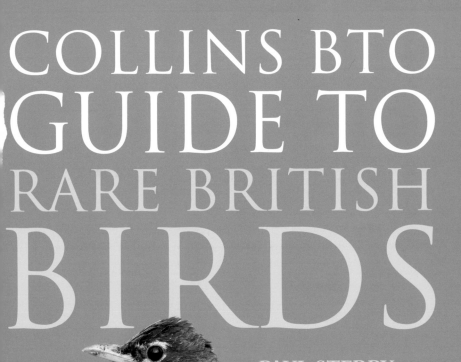

PAUL STERRY
PAUL STANCLIFFE

BTO
British Trust for
Ornithology
Looking out for birds

This edition published in 2015 by William Collins,
an imprint of HarperCollins Publishers

1 London Bridge Street
London SE1 9GF

WilliamCollinsBooks.com

First published in 2015

20 19 18 17 16 15
10 9 8 7 6 5 4 3 2 1

A catalogue record for this book is available from the British Library.

ISBN 978-0-00-755154-5 (hardback)
ISBN 978-0-00-755156-9 (paperback)

William Collins uses papers that are natural, renewable and recyclable products made
from wood grown in sustainable forests. The manufacturing processes conform to the
environmental regulations of the country of origin.

Acknowledgements
Paul Sterry would like to thank Andrew Cleave, Rob Read, David and Namrita Price-Goodfellow,
Shane O'Dwyer, Susi Bailey and his publisher Myles Archibald for their encouragement and help with
the creation of this book. In addition, the following people, in alphabetical order, helped with
photography: Steve Castle; Mark and Susie Groves of Island Sea Safaris; Karl Hughes; Chrissie Kelley of
Pensthorpe Natural Park; Joe Pender of Sapphire Pelagics; and Graham Vick.
Paul Stancliffe would like to thank Jeff Baker and Mike Toms for their help and support; Ieuan Evans
for his interest and wise words when needed; Andy Mason for the many shared birds; Dave Smith for
sharing his boundless knowledge; his girls, Abigail, Lily and Hazel for their beauty, inspiration and endless
patience; and of course the BTO for allowing him to indulge in his passion.

Edited and designed by D & N Publishing, Baydon, Wiltshire
Colour reproduction by Paul Sterry, Nature Photographers Ltd
Printed and bound in Hong Kong by Printing Express

CONTENTS

AIM AND SCOPE OF THE BOOK

This book is the companion volume to the *Collins BTO Guide to British Birds*. It covers all the rare and scarce birds that had occurred in Britain and Ireland, in the main, four times or more, at the time of writing. At the end of the book, 'The Rarest of the Rare' section lists all the species that had occurred here, in the main, three times or fewer at the time of writing; taken in combination, every species of wild bird that has ever occurred in Britain gets a mention.

SCIENTIFIC NAMES

In most cases the scientific names used in this book follow guidelines provided by the British Ornithologists' Union (BOU). However, with a few North American birds, the BOU name differs from that used by the American Ornithologists' Union (AOU). In most of these cases this book uses AOU nomenclature for North American species; in a few instances both BOU and AOU names are given, the latter shown in brackets. Furthermore, in a few cases the global birdwatching community is also at variance with BOU naming; here, alternative names are shown in brackets too.

Species descriptions comprise the bulk of the book, and the text and photographs describe and illustrate the key features needed to identify these birds with confidence. Where space allows, comparisons are made with confusion species. With species whose identification it aids, mention is made of vocalisation. In the main, calls are written phonetically but these can be used only as a rough guide: we all hear and describe sounds in subtly different ways and inevitably the given descriptions are subjective. Readers should listen to sound recordings to develop their recognition skills; a list of recommended products appears in the 'Further Reading' section at the end of the book.

The photographs have been chosen carefully to show key features that are described in the accompanying text; they also give clues to the usual habitat favoured by the bird and its typical posture. Most birds depicted are adults and these are not labelled as such if the plumage does not vary seasonally. The majority of the photographs appear in print in this book for the first time.

Throughout the book there are feature pages entitled 'ID Key Features'. These provide a quick guide to a group of species or families; they describe the structural and behavioural features that an observer should concentrate on initially when they come across an unfamiliar bird. Where relevant, these feature pages also highlight identification pitfalls.

Unlike its companion volume, *Collins BTO Guide to British Birds*, maps are not included in this title. They are of little relevance when dealing with rare and scarce birds in Britain and Ireland: by their very nature, vagrant birds can turn up almost anywhere. However, where a part of Britain or Ireland is noteworthy for the occurrence of a given species, then the region in question is mentioned in the text.

TEREK SANDPIPER

Xenus cinereus | TR | LENGTH 22–25cm

scientific name | BTO code | average size (tip of bill to tip of tail)

What's in a name?

BROAD-BILLED SANDPIPER

Limicola falcinellus | OA | LENGTH 15–17cm

Slightly smaller than, but superficially similar to, a Dunlin (*Calidris alpina*) but with some plumage features reminiscent of a Snipe (*Gallinago gallinago*). Bill shape and head pattern aid identification. Sexes are similar.

split supercilium and drooping bill tip

In all birds, legs are relatively short and yellowish, but often obscured in muddy water. Bill is rather long and straight, but with a distinct downward kink at the tip. Adult in spring has mainly brown upperparts and whitish underparts. Pale feather margins on back

vagrants to British estuaries often consort with other small waders, notably Dunlin – identification of distant, active birds can be a challenge

sometimes align to form stripes, and note the split pale supercilium on the otherwise dark crown. Juvenile/1st-winter is similar but with cleaner-looking, more distinct markings on head and back. **VOICE** Call is a high-pitched, trilling *brerit*. **HABITS** Feeds in an active manner, probing deep into soft mud with long bill. **STATUS AND HABITAT** Breeds in N Scandinavia and winters in Africa and Asia. Vagrants here (a handful each year) are most likely to turn up in spring and favour estuaries and mudflats.

TEREK SANDPIPER

Xenus cinereus | TR | LENGTH 22–25cm

upturned bill is unique in a wader of this size

Distinctive little wader with an extremely long, upturned bill. The short yellow legs are set relatively far back, giving it a front-heavy appearance. Sexes are similar.

Adult body plumage is vaguely reminiscent of a miniature winter Greenshank (*Tringa nebularia*): upperparts are overall pale grey, head and neck are streaked, and underparts are otherwise white. In breeding season, note the dark stripe on the scapulars, dark carpal patch and dark shafts to mantle feathers. Juvenile/1st-winter is similar, but upperparts are subtly darker and dark markings are indistinct. **VOICE** Call comprises a series of shrill *pee-pee-pee* whistling notes. **HABITS** An extremely active feeder, dashing around in a frantic manner, running with its body leaning forwards. **STATUS AND HABITAT** Breeds across N Asia and winters on coasts of Africa and Asia. Vagrants here are likely to turn up in spring or autumn, and favour estuaries and mudflats.

126 WADERS

WADERS 127

In general terms, the features of a bird can be divided neatly into two sections: the bare parts (legs and bill); and the feathered parts (wings, body and tail). These elements can be subdivided even further to help describe individual parts of a bird, and it is useful to have a basic understanding of these subdivisions. It helps the reader make easier reference to the species description text in the book and is useful in the process of identification in

axillaries

underwing coverts

tibia

tail

tarsus

feet

primaries

scapular plumes

tail

undertail coverts

flanks

the field. The following annotated photographs show the important
anatomical and topographical features for a range of rare bird species. Where
relevant, they also highlight particular salient features that are crucial for the
identification of rare birds and that aid the separation of similar species.

bill

neck

Black Stork

tertials

breast   secondaries

undertail coverts

primaries

crown

eye   cheek

supercilium

nostril

nape

bill

throat

Baikal Teal

breast

8

American Golden
Plover

crown
eye
lores
bill
throat
supercilium
ear coverts
nape
neck
mantle
breast
belly
wing coverts
tertials
primaries
tibia
tarsus
feet

Terek Sandpiper

eye
eye-ring
eye-stripe
nape
scapulars
primaries
tertials
throat
breast
wing coverts
tibia
undertail
coverts
belly
feet
tarsus

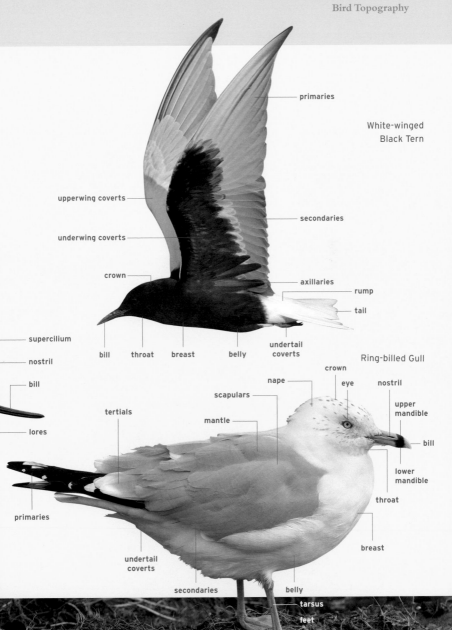

primaries

White-winged
Black Tern

upperwing coverts

underwing coverts

secondaries

crown

axillaries

rump

tail

supercilium

nostril

bill

throat

breast

belly

undertail
coverts

Ring-billed Gull

bill

lores

crown

nape

eye

nostril

scapulars

upper
mandible

mantle

tertials

bill

lower
mandible

primaries

throat

breast

undertail
coverts

secondaries

belly

tarsus

feet

Marsh Warbler

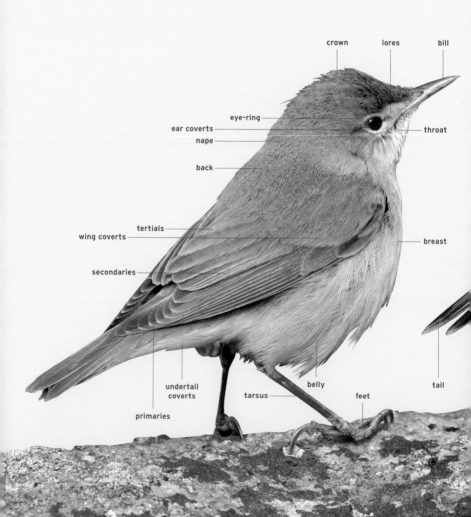

crown   lores   bill

eye-ring

ear coverts

nape

throat

back

tertials

wing coverts

breast

secondaries

undertail
coverts

belly

tail

tarsus

feet

primaries

Icterine Warbler

crown

lores

upper mandible

eye-ring

lower mandible

nape

throat

lesser wing coverts

median wing coverts

greater wing coverts

breast

alula

wing panel

primary wing coverts

secondaries

undertail coverts

belly

primaries

Desert Wheatear

supercilium

crown

nape

ear coverts

bill

back

scapulars

secondaries

uppertail coverts

belly

undertail coverts

tertials

wingbar

greater wing coverts

wing coverts

primaries

tarsus

undertail
coverts

tail

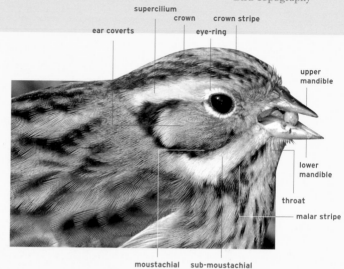

ear coverts

supercilium

crown

crown stripe

eye-ring

upper mandible

lower mandible

throat

malar stripe

moustachial stripe

sub-moustachial stripe

Little Bunting

scapulars

wing coverts

rump

back

breast

tarsus

KNOW YOUR COMMON BIRDS

Acquiring bird identification skills can take a lifetime, and no matter how experienced you are there are always things to learn. When it comes to scarce and rare birds in Britain and Ireland, probably the best advice is to be sure you know your common birds thoroughly. The chances are that most 'mystery' birds you come across will turn out to be members of a 'common' species – perhaps in an unfamiliar plumage, maybe a moulting bird, or an individual seen in poor light.

One of the best tips is to familiarise yourself with the most regularly encountered representatives from a wide range of common birds. To assist you, the companion volume to this title, *Collins BTO Guide to British Birds*, has a section that deals with these 'default' common bird species. The better you know your default birds, the easier the identification of new species becomes.

With practice and by spending time in the field with more experienced birdwatchers, you will soon develop your bird identification skills to the point where you are familiar with most common bird species. Having reached this point you will immediately recognise something that is out of the ordinary, even if you cannot identify it. To assist the process of identification, throughout this book there are pages entitled 'ID Key Features'. These help you concentrate on the most important features when studying a new bird, assuming you have refined your options to the point where you know, for example, you are looking at a pipit and not a lark, or a wader and not a rail.

A Pectoral Sandpiper and a Dunlin, but which is which? Develop your identification skills using *Collins BTO Guide to Common Birds of Britain and Ireland* and then hone your expertise with the species descriptions and 'ID Key Features' pages in this book.

JIZZ

Spend some time with experienced birdwatchers and sooner or later you will hear somebody use the word 'jizz', for example in the context of 'the bird had the jizz of a *Sylvia* warbler' or some similar phrase. It refers to an observer's overall impression of a bird: a distillation of

A combination of tail-flicking behaviour and a rattling call are two good identification features for this Red-breasted Flycatcher.

characters such as size, proportions, shape, bill and leg length, combined with colour, posture and habitat preferences; all made with reference to other known species.

The behaviour of a bird can provide useful clues to identification and is an important element contributing to a bird's 'jizz'; feeding behaviour and flight patterns are particularly important. Take note of any behaviour that strikes you as different from the norm; where this is useful for identification, it is mentioned in the species text.

VOCALISATION

Songs and calls play a key role in the identification of certain species, but learning bird vocalisation has to be one of the greatest challenges that any birdwatcher faces. There are not many short cuts to the learning process and there is no substitute for spending time in the field, preferably with someone who knows the subject. To speed things up, listen to recordings of bird songs and calls as part of your 'homework'. There are also birdsong apps for smartphones that allow the observer to compare instantly a song or call heard in the field with one played through the device.

DIGITAL IMAGING AS AN AID TO IDENTIFICATION

These days most birdwatchers have a camera of one sort or another. Advances in technology mean that amazing detail can be captured even if the subject is rather distant, and as a result photographs of birds can provide valuable information for identification as well as an attractive memento. A digital SLR camera armed with a telephoto lens is obviously ideal for photographing birds. But even a compact camera has a role to play, especially when used to take 'digiscope' shots – for these, the camera is held to the eyepiece of a telescope. With practice, and a steady tripod, the results can be outstanding.

If you are aware of the limitations of the technique, digiscoping can be extremely rewarding and provides a valuable record of observations.

Outside the breeding season, many birds are on the move. In Britain and Ireland alone, around 15 million migrant birds arrive here each spring, and maybe three times that number head south to warmer climes in autumn. In addition, others undertake local dispersal from their breeding territories, or arrive here to escape harsh northern winters or a lack of food. These mass movements are not unique to Britain and Ireland: the same processes are happening right across the northern hemisphere.

For a variety of reasons, during these movements some birds are adversely affected by the weather and become 'lost': carried further than intended by strong winds; 'drifted' off course by persistent airflows; or caught up in a disorientating storm. As a result, unexpected birds sometimes turn up in Britain and Ireland and the following pages discuss the origins of these vagrants to our shores.

Red-eyed Vireo, the most frequently occurring North American landbird on this side of the Atlantic.

ARRIVALS FROM NORTH AMERICA

In autumn, many North American (Nearctic) migrant landbirds attempt to fly directly across the Gulf of Mexico from temperate-latitude breeding grounds to wintering sites in South America. Inevitably, some are caught up in Atlantic storms, low-pressure systems racing across the ocean towards our shores. Undoubtedly most of these bird perish at sea but a few survive to make landfall in Europe; they will have travelled 5,000km and it may have taken just two or three days to get here if it was a fast-moving weather system. More than 700 individual North American landbirds have been found on this side of the Atlantic since 1958 and unsurprisingly most are recorded in October.

North American waders reach our shores in far greater numbers than landbirds, again mostly in autumn but with a few records in spring; their arrival usually coincides with Atlantic storms. Although most Nearctic landbirds that reach our shores probably do not survive the winter, waders fare a lot better: a few overwinter here but most resume their southward journey, albeit on the wrong side of the Atlantic, after a spell of rest and recuperation. The following spring, some of these birds pass through Britain and Ireland as they make their way north once again.

Yellow-browed Warbler.

Radde's Warbler, photographed on
the Isles of Scilly, a western 'hotspot'
for observing the species in Britain.

ARRIVALS FROM ASIA

Situated on the western edge the Eurasian landmass, Britain and Ireland are a natural flyway for
migrant birds from northern Europe heading south. But vagrant birds from further east – as far
away as Siberia and eastern Asia – also turn up on a regular basis. These are birds that should be
wintering in India and Southeast Asia: species like the diminutive Yellow-browed Warbler that
weighs just 6g and breeds no closer than the Ural Mountains, 4,000km away from Britain.

The peak month for arrival here of most Asian vagrants is October, a time when the
prevailing weather normally comes from the west. However, occasionally a high-pressure
anticyclone becomes established over Scandinavia, drawing an easterly flow of air all the way
from Siberia. When these conditions prevail, birdwatchers can expect an influx of interesting
easterly species and predictably, the east coast of Britain receives the lion's share of vagrants
from Asia.

While autumn is the peak season for Far Eastern vagrants to turn up in Britain and
Ireland, a few are seen each spring as well. These may well be birds that have overwintered
successfully in the Western Palearctic and are making their way north at the onset of the
breeding season; whether or not they reach their distant nesting
grounds is unknown.

ARRIVALS FROM THE SOUTH

Every spring, birds that ordinarily breed in southern Europe
and the Mediterranean basin are recorded in Britain and Ireland.
Their occurrence and numbers are linked to classic weather
conditions that assist their journey.

Almost all of the southern species that occur here are
migrants that will have spent the winter in Africa, and
those that occur in spring are heading back to their
breeding grounds. Irrespective of the weather, each year
a few fail to 'switch off' their migration and 'overshoot'
all the way north to Britain. Classic overshooting migrants
include the Hoopoe, Bee-eater and Purple Heron. But in

Bee-eater, a classic
'overshooting' arrival
from the south.

Black-headed Bunting – singing
males have been observed in spring.

some years their northward migration coincides with a
prolonged spell of warm southerly airflow, all the way from
the Sahara; these conditions usually result in more 'southerly'
migrating birds reaching our shores than usual.

Some of these southerly birds may well be pioneers looking
for the opportunity to extend the northern boundary of their
breeding range. A case in point is the Little Egret: once a great
rarity here, it is now a British breeding bird and treated as a
'common' species. Perhaps in indication of global warming and climate
change, Purple Herons and Great White Egrets have also bred in our
region, although they have yet to become established.

In most years, spring also sees the arrival of birds that should be breeding
in southeastern and eastern Europe. High pressure over northern and central Europe and the
resulting warm easterly airflow produce the ideal conditions for birds like Red-footed
Falcon, Bluethroat and Black-headed Bunting to be drifted west of their normal migratory
route and across
the North Sea.

ARRIVALS FROM THE NORTH

Snowy Owl, a
spectacular winter
visitor from the north.

As our summer visitors depart in autumn for a warmer climate further
south, non-breeding visitors begin to arrive, to take advantage of the
relatively balmy weather that a British winter has to offer. In autumn,
hundreds of thousands of thrushes, small passerines and wildfowl
begin to arrive; occasionally, vagrant species are associated with
these mass migrations.

As winter progresses and temperatures plummet in
northern Europe, we sometimes experience cold
weather movements of birds: species that under normal
circumstances do not stray far in winter.
It is during these conditions that vagrants such
as Snowy Owl and Arctic Redpoll are likely
to turn up. In some years a widespread seed
crop failure forces other bird species to
move rather than starve; occasionally
we receive a crossbill invasion from
mainland Europe and sometimes
flocks of Common Crossbills
include Two-barred and
Parrot crossbills as well.

For many of us, contact with seabirds comes during the summer months when they visit our shores to breed. Until recently, little was known about their movements outside the breeding season. Small insights have related mainly to 'common' British birds: for example, an Arctic Tern that was ringed on Anglesey, North Wales, was found subsequently in Australia, 18,056km from its ringing site. But with advances in technology and the development of small tracking devices, the migration routes and wintering areas of other seabirds are gradually being uncovered.

A Great Shearwater photographed off the Isles of Scilly.

Most seabirds are consummate fliers so it is no surprise to discover that they cover huge distances throughout the year. The fact that Cory's and Balearic Shearwaters visit us from Mediterranean latitudes is impressive but most people are amazed to discover that we are also visited by birds that breed on isolated islands in the South Atlantic. Sooty and Great Shearwaters, and Wilson's Storm-petrels, circumnavigate the North Atlantic during their winter (our summer). By July or August they have reached our quadrant of the North Atlantic and are making their way back to their southern ocean breeding grounds. Usually the birds pass offshore and out of the sight of land-based birdwatchers, but during strong onshore winds they are seen occasionally from Atlantic-facing headlands.

Wilson's Storm-petrels pass through British and Irish waters in the summer months but do not willingly venture within sight of land. Nevertheless, land-based seawatchers in the West Country live in hope that an early September storm will produce a sighting.

In autumn, Atlantic storms force other migrating seabirds close to land-based observers: birds moving south from Arctic breeding grounds. Along with more regularly encountered species such as Sabine's Gull, Grey Phalarope, skuas and Leach's Storm-petrels, there is always a chance of some more unusual species being spotted.

RARE BIRDS AND THE BRITISH TRUST FOR ORNITHOLOGY (BTO)

THE BTO'S ROLE

The BTO's primary role as a nature conservation charity relates to bird species that occur regularly in Britain and its remit does not specifically embrace scarce or rare vagrant species in our region. However, BirdTrack – the scheme that helps monitor bird movements into, out of, and around Britain and Ireland – collects data on all species whether they are common, scarce or rare. This data is useful in gauging the extent of an influx of, for example, crossbill and white-winged gull species; their arrival and location can alert observers to the potential for finding even rarer species.

Bird ringing also has an important role to play, in part complementing the data collected by BirdTrack but also in the advancement of identification criteria. Features that help to separate difficult species are often first identified by ringers examining birds in the hand.

ABOVE: Without its colour rings, nobody would be any the wiser that this Glossy Ibis, seen on the Isles of Scilly in the winter of 2011/12, had been ringed in the Doñana National Park, Spain, on 20 May 2011.

BELOW: Home to a long-established bird observatory, Fair Isle is a dramatic island with a reputation for rare bird sightings.

BIRD OBSERVATORIES AND RARE BIRDS

There are 19 accredited bird observatories scattered around the coast of Britain, Ireland and the Isle of Man. They are all strategically located on migration flyways so that observers can monitor and record bird migration events as they happen. The first

bird observatory in Britain was set up in 1933 on the Welsh island of Skokholm and, after a period of closure, it is still operational today.

Long-term datasets of bird observations, some stretching back for many decades, are the foundation that bird observatories stand on. As well as providing information about common migrants, bird observatories have also taught us a lot about the occurrence of rare and scarce migrants, and the weather conditions that are a prelude to their arrival on our shores.

And many 'firsts' for Britain have been found by observatory staff. Fair Isle is top of the league with 26 'firsts' at the time of writing – from Red-rumped Swallow, discovered there in June 1905, to the Chestnut-eared Bunting that was found there in October 2004.

LESSER WHITE-FRONTED GOOSE

Anser erythropus | LC | LENGTH 55–65cm

Superficially similar to a White-fronted Goose (*A. albifrons*) but appreciably smaller. In Britain, invariably seen among flocks of that species. Sexes are similar.

compared to White-fronted Goose, note the smaller, daintier bill and diagnostic yellow orbital ring

Adult has a relatively small bill, a white blaze on forehead that extends above eye, and a diagnostic yellow orbital ring around eye. Body plumage is grey-brown with variable amounts of dark barring on underparts. Immature lacks white on forehead and hence is very similar to immature White-front,

compared to White-fronted Goose, note Lesser White-front's smaller size, and relatively shorter neck and wings

LESSER WHITE-FRONT GOOSE (*TOP LEFT*) IN A FLOCK OF GREENLAND WHITE-FRONTED GEESE

but presence of a dull yellow orbital ring is diagnostic. In all birds, bill is pink and legs are pinkish orange. In flight, pattern of rather uniform upperwings and pale base to tail is similar to that of White-front. **VOICE** Utters barking calls in flight. **HABITS** Feeds mainly by grazing grass leaves and shoots. **STATUS AND HABITAT** Breeds eastwards from N Scandinavia and winters in SE Europe. One or 2 are recorded in most years in our region, usually on traditional wintering grounds of the White-front. Widely kept in captivity, so beware the possibility of escapees.

SNOW GOOSE

Anser caerulescens | SJ | LENGTH 65–75cm

Of the 2 subspecies of Snow Goose, Greater Snow Goose (ssp. *atlanticus*) is the most likely to occur here. There are also 2 colour morphs, referred to as 'white' and 'dark'. Sexes are similar.

bill is proportionately large and bulky with an obvious 'grin patch'

WHITE MORPH

WHITE MORPH

striking black and white wings seen in flight

JUVENILE

grubby plumage, the colour remeniscent of an immature swan

Adult white morph is unmistakable, with mainly white plumage and black primaries, these most striking in flight. Juvenile white morph has whitish plumage except for buff-brown back and dark primaries. Rare adult dark morph has mainly dark grey-brown plumage except for white head and neck, a white rear, and pale wing coverts. Juvenile dark morph is dark buffish brown, except for white rear. All adult birds have a pink bill that shows an obvious 'grin patch', and pink legs; all immatures have a greyish bill and legs. **VOICE** Utters a barking, honking *whook*. **HABITS** Grazes grasses alongside other geese species. **STATUS AND HABITAT** North American species that occurs here annually. Usually found among flocks of Greenland White-fronted (*A. albifrons flavirostris*), Greylag (*A. anser*) or Pink-footed (*A. brachyrhynchus*) geese. Widely kept in captivity; some records relate to free-flying escapes. Also, beware confusion with domesticated white forms of Greylag Goose.

CACKLING GOOSE

Branta hutchinsii | LENGTH 60–70cm

Recently split from Canada Goose and elevated to species status. Three of the four subspecies might occur here. Sexes are similar. Could be confused with small races of Canada Goose (genuine vagrants also occur here).

proportionately short neck, by goose standards

CACKLING GOOSE

plumage is overall much browner than naturalised Canada Geese

has the proportions of a naturalised Canada Goose but looks miniature by comparison

LESSER CANADA GOOSE, FOR COMPARISON

Similar to Canada Goose, but all races are small, compact birds with almost duck-like proportions. Note the short neck and dainty bill, but proportionately longer, more pointed wings in flight; in standing birds, primaries extend beyond tertials and wingtips extend to tip of tail or beyond. All birds have black head and neck, white cheek and white undertail. Body plumage is greyish brown in Richardson's Goose (ssp. *hutchinsii*), 25–50% of which have a white neck-ring; dark reddish brown in Taverner's Goose (ssp. *taverneri*); and dark brown in nominate Cackling Goose (ssp. *minima*), the smallest race. **VOICE** Utters a honking *hronk*. **HABITS** Grazes vegetation. Vagrants mix with other goose species. **STATUS AND HABITAT** North American tundra-nesting species that migrates as far south as Texas for winter. Kept in captivity but presumed genuine vagrants are sometimes seen here among winter flocks of migrant geese. **SIMILAR SPECIES** Cackling Goose is so much smaller than the race of Canada Geese naturalised in Britain (ssp. *canadensis*) that confusion is unlikely. However, the smallest race of Canada (Lesser Canada Goose, *Branta canadensis* ssp. *parvipes*) is a similar size to the largest Cackling Goose, creating potential for confusion there. Relative neck and bill lengths are useful in identification; in standing Lesser Canada, wingtips do not generally extend beyond the tail. Lesser Canada Goose breeds in N Canada and winters as far south as Gulf Coast; as with Cackling, individuals are seen here occasionally among flocks of wintering geese. Some sightings are presumed to relate to genuine vagrants but escapees from captivity cannot be ruled out.

BLACK BRANT

Branta bernicla nigricans | LENGTH 56–61cm

North American subspecies of the familiar Brent
Goose. Separable from its Pale-bellied (ssp. *hrota*)
and Dark-bellied (ssp. *bernicla*) cousins with
care. Sexes are similar.

pale- and dark-bellied
Brent Geese (the commonly
occurring ssp. in Britain)
for comparison

looks strikingly
black and white
in flight

Adult has a black head and neck, with an obvious
large white 'collar', dark grey upperparts and a
white rear. Breast and belly are uniformly dark
grey, contrasting starkly with a noticeable white
flank patch. Juvenile/1st-winter is similar but white collar
is absent until midwinter, and back feathers show pale edges.
VOICE Utters a nasal, honking *kruut*. **HABITS** Vagrants invariably
associate with flocks of Brent Geese. Habits are similar: feeds on
marine eelgrass (*Zostera* sp.) and coastal grassland. **STATUS AND
HABITAT** Occurs naturally mainly on the west coast of North
America, breeding on Arctic coasts and wintering as far south as
Mexico. Kept in captivity here, so escapees cannot be ruled out,
although genuine vagrants undoubtedly occur as well.

white on flanks shows up at a considerable distance; white on
neck is also more obvious than in pale- and dark-bellied Brents

RED-BREASTED GOOSE

Branta ruficollis | EB | LENGTH 55–60cm

A well-marked and unmistakable goose
with a proportionately short bill and
thick neck. Sexes are similar.

Adult has deep red on cheeks, neck
and upper breast, and a complex and
diagnostic pattern of black and white
elsewhere on the body. Juvenile/1st-
winter has a similar pattern of markings but red
elements of the plumage are duller. **HABITS**
Feeds by grazing grass shoots and leaves.
Vagrants here associate with winter flocks
of other goose species; in poor light, they
can be surprisingly hard to pick out
in flocks of Brent Geese (*B. bernicla*).
VOICE Utters a shrill, nasal *kik-yuuk*.
STATUS AND HABITAT Breeds in
Arctic Siberia and winters mainly
on the Black Sea coast of Romania
and Bulgaria. A few are recorded
here each year, these birds typically
arriving with flocks of either White-
fronted (*Anser albifrons*) or Brent geese. Also
widely kept in captivity – some records
undoubtedly relate to escapees.

bill is relatively
small and dainty by
goose standards

relatively
long-winged
in flight

plumage colours
and patterns are
unmistakable
and diagnostic

RUDDY SHELDUCK

Tadorna ferruginea | UD | LENGTH 61–67cm

Distinctive goose-sized duck with similar proportions to
a Shelduck (*T. tadorna*). Sexes are separable with care.

extensive white
and black on wings
is revealed in flight

FEMALE

the beautiful orange-brown
plumage is unique among
wildfowl species likely
to be encountered in
the region

FEMALE

only the male has the black neck-ring

MALE

Adult has an orange-brown body with a clear demarcation from the paler buff head and
upper neck; in summer, male has a narrow black collar separating these 2 body colours.
Juvenile/1st-winter is similar to female. In all plumages, standing birds show black wingtips,
but in flight the wings look black and white. Bill and legs are dark in all birds. **VOICE** Utters
a nasal, gargling, trilling *gyrrrrr* and a sharp *kyerr*. **HABITS** Similar to those of a Shelduck:
usually feeds in open locations, sifting through shallow water and vegetated muddy margins.
STATUS AND HABITAT Occurs naturally from SE Europe eastwards, wintering mainly in
the Indian subcontinent. Wanders outside the breeding season and some records here could
relate to genuinely wild birds. However, also kept in captivity and free-flying escapees
confuse the situation. In Britain, usually favours open wetlands and coasts, notably estuaries
and mudflats.

BAIKAL TEAL

Anas formosa | LENGTH 39–43cm

Compact dabbling duck, the male of which is stunning and unmistakable. Sexes are dissimilar and female is separable from the female Teal (*A. crecca*) with care.

Adult male has a unique head pattern comprising patches of yellow, green and brown defined by black and white lines. Breast is pinkish and spotted, and flanks are bluish, the 2 colours separated by a vertical white line in swimming birds. Rear end is black, bordered at the front by a white line. Back is brown with trailing plume-like feathers marked with black and white. Adult female and juvenile/1st-winter are marbled brown overall, palest and greyish on the head and usually with an obvious pale spot at base of bill (usually more striking than on female Teal and Garganey [*A. querquedula*], with which it can be confused). In flight, both adult male and female have a greenish speculum, bordered at the front by chestnut and with a white trailing margin. **VOICE** Male utters a gulping *kwerp* call. **HABITS** Feeds in a dabbling manner, similar to a Teal. **STATUS AND HABITAT** Breeds in Siberia and winters in Southeast Asia. Widely kept in captivity here – most records probably relate to escapees.

FEMALE

pale spot
at base of
bill is obvious,
even at a distance

MALE

male's striking and colourful
plumage is unique, easily
recognised and diagnostic

similar proportions
to Teal but
marginally larger

GREEN-WINGED TEAL

Anas carolinensis | TA | LENGTH 34–38cm

FEMALE

Tiny dabbling duck. North American counterpart
of the Teal (*A. crecca*), from which only the
male can be distinguished with any degree
of certainty. Sexes are dissimilar.

Adult male has a chestnut-orange head with a green
patch through eye, much less obviously bordered with
yellow than on Teal. Plumage is otherwise mainly
grey and finely marked, with a diagnostic vertical
white stripe on side of breast and black-bordered
yellow rear. Bill is dark grey. Eclipse male resembles
adult female. Adult female has mottled grey-brown plumage; green
speculum is sometimes glimpsed in feeding birds. Bill is grey. On average,
female Green-winged shows a more obvious pale patch at base of bill and
around eye than female Teal, and undertail is usually subtly flushed with
orange-buff. Juvenile is similar to adult female but plumage is warmer buff. In
flight, all birds show a green speculum, defined by white borders. **VOICE** Male
utters a ringing whistle while female utters a soft quack. **HABITS** Similar to Teal, with
which vagrants typically associate: feeds in shallow water, in saltmarshes and on marshy
grassland. **STATUS AND HABITAT** Widespread in North America, breeding in vegetated
wetlands and wintering mainly around coasts. Vagrants here are usually seen
in autumn and winter, typically among coastal flocks of Teal.

MALE

separation of female Teal and
Green-winged is considered
by some to be
impossible in
the field

FEMALE

MALE

vertical white stripe on flanks
is diagnostic in male and allows
easy separation from male Teal

BLUE-WINGED TEAL

Anas discors | TB | LENGTH 37–41cm

Distinctive small duck with a proportionately long bill. Sexes are dissimilar. Male is unmistakable but female recalls a female Teal (*A. crecca*).

blue on innerwing recalls that seen in Shoveler and Garganey

1ST-WINTER

FEMALE

pale patch at base of bill

MALE

white crescent on face is diagnostic

bill is large and long for a duck, and vaguely reminiscent of a Shoveler

Adult male has a bluish head with a diagnostic white crescent. Body is buffish brown, marbled with dark spots. White patch towards rear end contrasts with otherwise black rear. Adult female is marbled brown with a noticeable pale spot at base of bill, a dark eye-stripe and a white surround to eye. Compared to female Teal, female Blue-winged has a longer bill, different wing markings and a pale spot (lacking on most Teal) at base of bill. Juvenile is similar to adult female but lacks strong facial markings. In flight, all birds reveal a blue panel on leading edge of upper innerwing, separated from speculum (green in male, dull in female) by white wedge. **VOICE** Utters a squeaky trill, and a shrill *kwit*. **HABITS** Feeds unobtrusively in well-vegetated wetlands, often remaining partly concealed for much of the time. **STATUS AND HABITAT** Widespread breeder across N North America, wintering predominantly in South America. Transatlantic vagrants turn up here mainly in autumn and winter.

AMERICAN WIGEON

Anas americana | AW | LENGTH 48–56cm

Medium-sized dabbling duck. Sexes are dissimilar. Adult male is distinctive, but separation of other plumages from the Wigeon (*A. penelope*) can be tricky.

Adult male has a bold head pattern comprising a creamy white forehead and crown, a green stripe stretching back from the eye, and a speckled grey face and neck. Body plumage is otherwise pinkish buff except for black and white rear. In flight, has a white patch on upper surface of innerwing. Adult female has a speckled grey head and neck that contrasts with rest of body plumage, which is finely marked and mainly orange-brown apart from white belly. (In female Wigeon, plumage is more uniform reddish brown apart from white belly). Bill and legs in both sexes are grey. Juvenile is similar to adult female. In all birds, axillaries are white (grey in Wigeon). **VOICE** Male utters a distinctive *whee-ooo* whistling call. **HABITS** Vagrants here associate with Wigeon flocks and feed similarly by grazing wetland vegetation. **STATUS AND HABITAT** Widespread in North America, nesting beside tundra pools and wintering on coasts. Vagrants here turn up in autumn and winter.

striking white panels on wings seen in flight, and note white axillaries

MALE

compared to rather uniform female Wigeon, note subtle contrast between intensity of colour of head and neck, compared to rest of body

FEMALE

male's head pattern is diagnostic

MALE

BLACK DUCK

Anas rubripes │ BD │ LENGTH 53–61cm

Robust dabbling duck. Recalls female and eclipse male Mallards (*A. platyrhynchos*), but overall much darker and lacks the reddish breast seen in eclipse males. Sexes are separable.

MALE

striking white axillaries

Adult male has mostly blackish-brown body plumage that contrasts clearly with buffish-brown head and face; crown is dark brown. Bill is yellow and feet are orange. Plumage is similar in eclipse but slightly paler. Adult female and juvenile are similar to male but body plumage is paler overall. Bill is dull greenish grey and legs are orange. Additional features that distinguish adult female from female Mallard include dark (not whitish) tail feathers, purple (not blue) speculum with almost no white edging, and obvious white underwing coverts and axillaries seen in flight (grey on Mallard). **VOICE** Male utters whistles and nasal calls, while female utters quacking calls; both are similar to Mallard. **HABITS** Feeds around the vegetated margins of wetland habitats. **STATUS AND HABITAT** Locally common in E North America, where northern birds move south and to coasts in winter. Vagrants here turn up in autumn and winter, usually favouring coastal wetlands.

FEMALE

compared to female Mallard, note the purple (not blue) speculum and dark (not pale) tail feathers

MALE

uniformly dark plumage

RED-CRESTED POCHARD

Netta rufina | RQ | LENGTH 54–57cm

in flight, shows a striking
amount of white on wings;
male's bright red bill
shows up even
at a distance

Large and distinctive diving duck. Sexes are dissimilar:
gaudy male is unmistakable and female is hard to confuse.

MALE

Adult male has a rounded, bright orange
head. Neck, breast, belly and rear are
black, while flanks are white; latter feature
shows up well in swimming birds. Back is grey-
buff and the long, rather narrow bill is bright red. In
eclipse plumage, male resembles adult female but retains
the red bill. Adult female is mainly grey-buff, darkest on back
and above the eye, and with striking pale cheeks. Bill is mainly dark with a paler
pink tip. Juvenile resembles adult female but the bill is uniformly dark. In flight, all
birds show striking white wingbars. **VOICE** Mostly silent. **HABITS** Vagrants usually
associate loosely with other diving ducks such as Pochard (*Aythya ferina*) and Tufted Duck
(*A. fuligula*). **STATUS AND HABITAT** Its natural range includes much of Europe – some
British records may relate to genuine vagrants. However, the species is also popular in captivity
and most sightings probably relate to escapees. Usually found on large, well-vegetated water
bodies such as flooded gravel pits, lowland lakes
and long-established reservoirs.

FEMALE

head patterns in both male and female make for
straightforward identification of swimming birds

MALE

CANVASBACK

Aythya valisineria | VB | LENGTH 49–56cm

the profile of the
head is a useful aid
to identification, even
of silhouetted birds: a large,
triangular bill whose angle
continues onto the
steep-sloping forehead

Superficially similar to a Pochard (*A. ferina*), but
with distinct structural differences (larger and with
a uniformly dark bill) that allow separation. Sexes
are dissimilar.

FEMALE

MALE

MALE

bill is a subtly different shape from male
Pochard, and uniformly dark, lacking the
grey band seen in that species

Adult male has a rounded reddish-chestnut head, reddish eye, black breast and rear, and
otherwise very pale grey body. Eye is red, and rather long triangular bill is dark grey and
continues slope of forehead (in male Pochard, bill is shorter with a grey band, and forehead
rises steeply to peaked crown). Adult female has a buffish-brown head and neck, and a
pale grey-brown body with a darker rear. Longer length and uniform colour of bill allow
separation from female Pochard; also, Pochard's pale loral patch is absent and pale 'spectacles'
are less obvious. Juvenile is similar to adult female but more uniformly buffish grey. In flight,
all birds show whitish upperwings and pale underwings. **VOICE** Mostly silent. **HABITS**
A diving duck that feeds on submerged plants and aquatic invertebrates. **STATUS AND
HABITAT** Widespread in North America, breeding in freshwater wetlands and wintering
mainly near coasts. Vagrants here turn up in autumn and winter, and favour large lakes and
flooded gravel pits.

REDHEAD

Aythya americana | AZ | LENGTH 44–51cm

Attractive diving duck. Similar to a Pochard (*A. ferina*) but separable by studying the bill and head shape, and in the male, eye colour. Sexes are dissimilar.

bill pattern reminiscent of that seen in male; plumage is overall browner than in female Pochard

FEMALE

In all birds, head has a rounded outline (peaked in Pochard) and bill is tricolored: pale grey along most of its length, with a white sub-terminal band and black tip. Adult male has a reddish-orange head and upper neck, clearly demarcated from black lower neck and breast. Rear is black and body is otherwise grey. In flight, grey upperwing coverts contrast with paler flight feathers. Has a yellowish eye. Adult female and juvenile have mainly buffish-brown plumage with faint, pale 'spectacles' and a whitish throat. In flight, all birds show pale underwings. **VOICE** Mostly silent. **HABITS** A diving duck that feeds on submerged plants and aquatic invertebrates. **STATUS AND HABITAT** Widespread in North America, breeding in freshwater wetlands and wintering mainly near coasts. Vagrants here turn up in autumn and winter, and favour large lakes and flooded gravel pits.

MALE

head shape is useful for identification

MALE

bill is grey along most of its length with a black tip and sub-terminal whitish band (dark with grey median band in male Pochard)

FERRUGINOUS DUCK

Aythya nyroca | FD | LENGTH 38–42cm

all birds look overall reddish brown, the intensity much richer than in other species; the white undertail is a good identification feature, even in distant birds

Attractive and distinctive diving duck. In poor light, distant birds can appear uniformly dark except for the white undertail and male's white eye. Sexes are separable with care.

FEMALE

In flight, all birds show a striking white wingbar on upperwing, white underwings and a white belly. In all birds, crown is peaked and bill is mainly grey, a faint pale band separating this colour from dark tip. Adult male has rich reddish-brown plumage, darkest on the back and becoming almost black on the rump and tail. Has a white rear and white eye; white belly is not visible in swimming birds. Adult female is similar but reddish coloration is duller and eye is dark. Juvenile is similar to adult female but even duller. **VOICE** Mostly silent. **HABITS** Feeds by dabbling around vegetated margins of pools, and by upending and diving. At times incredibly secretive, often spending long periods of time hidden in bankside vegetation. **STATUS AND HABITAT** Widespread from SE Europe eastwards, most birds wintering south of their breeding range. A scarce visitor to Britain (perhaps 20 or 30 each year), most occurring from autumn to early spring. Vagrants here favour lakes and flooded gravel pits with plenty of submerged and emergent vegetation.

striking white wingbar seen in flight

MALE

MALE

beady white eye

RING-NECKED DUCK

Aythya collaris | NG | LENGTH 37–46cm

Distinctive diving duck. Similar to a Tufted Duck (*A. fuligula*) but distinguished from that species by bill markings and head shape. Sexes are dissimilar.

vagrants here often associate with Tufted Ducks

All birds have a peaked crown (rounded and tufted at rear in Tufted Duck) and tricolored bill: dark grey with a white sub-terminal band and black tip (Tufted's bill lacks the pale sub-terminal band). Adult male has a light grey belly and flanks, the leading edge of which is pale and appears as a vertical white 'tooth' in swimming birds. Plumage is otherwise mainly black with a purple sheen to head and neck. Has a white border at base of bill. Adult female has a greyish head with a white loral patch, and white 'spectacles'. Body plumage is brown, palest on belly and flanks. Juvenile is similar to adult female but with a less well-marked bill. In flight, all birds show whitish underwings and pale grey flight feathers, contrasting with darker upperwing coverts. **VOICE** Mostly silent. **HABITS** Similar to Tufted Duck, with which it often consorts. Feeds on submerged seeds, roots and invertebrates. **STATUS AND HABITAT** Scarce winter visitor from North America (20 or so in a good year), found mainly on lakes and flooded gravel pits.

MALES AND FEMALES

in flight, wingbars on upperwings are duller than in Tufted Duck

bill pattern is diagnostic, and white leading edge to grey flanks is also a good identification feature

JUVENILE

FEMALE   white 'spectacles' around eye are obvious

MALE

LESSER SCAUP

Aythya affinis | AY | LENGTH 38–45cm

Compact diving duck. Similar to a Scaup (*A. marila*), but crown shape and wing pattern allow separation. Sexes are dissimilar.

FEMALE

In all birds, crown is peaked behind the eye (rounded in Scaup) and in flight only inner flight feathers are whitish (all flight feathers are white in Scaup). Adult male has a black head and neck; head has purple sheen in good light (green sheen in male Scaup). Belly and flanks are white and back is grey, palest towards front. Rear is black and eye is yellow. Black nail on bill tip is tiny (larger on Scaup). Adult female and juvenile are mainly brown, palest and greyest on back and flanks. White belly is seen only in flight. **VOICE** Mostly silent. **HABITS** Dives frequently, feeding on submerged seeds, roots and invertebrates.

STATUS AND HABITAT

Widespread across North America, most birds wintering south of their breeding range. A scarce visitor to Britain (perhaps 10 in a good year), most turning up from autumn to early spring. Vagrants here favour lakes and flooded gravel pits.

MALE

only inner flight feathers show white, a useful feature for separation from Scaup

MALE

study the shape of the crown to aid identification: peaked behind in Lesser Scaup, rounded in Scaup

HARLEQUIN DUCK

Histrionicus histrionicus | HQ | LENGTH 38–45cm

adult male's plumage pattern and colours are unique and make identification straightforward

Plump-bodied diving duck. Sexes are dissimilar.
Male is stunningly marked and unmistakable.
Female and juvenile plumage recalls that of
female scaups and scoters.

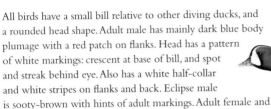

MALE

All birds have a small bill relative to other diving ducks, and
a rounded head shape. Adult male has mainly dark blue body
plumage with a red patch on flanks. Head has a pattern
of white markings: crescent at base of bill, and spot
and streak behind eye. Also has a white half-collar
and white stripes on flanks and back. Eclipse male
is sooty-brown with hints of adult markings. Adult female and
juvenile are brown, palest on belly, with white spots on head and above and

white spots on head

below eye, and a clean round spot on rear edge of ear coverts (it
shares this feature with the male). **VOICE** Mostly silent. **HABITS**
Often solitary and not gregarious. Dives to feed on submerged
invertebrates. **STATUS AND HABITAT** The nearest breeding
population is in Iceland, where the birds nest beside fast-
flowing rivers and winter on coasts.
Vagrants here turn up in autumn and
winter, and are usually seen on sheltered
rocky coasts.

FEMALE

no other duck has plumage
patterns even remotely similar
to a male Harlequin

MALE

KING EIDER

Somateria spectabilis | KE | LENGTH 55–63cm

Distinctive diving sea duck. Sexes are dissimilar.
Adult male is unmistakable but female could be
confused with a female Eider (*S. mollissima*).

in flight, male's wing
markings, and the colours
on the head and neck,
make for easy
identification and
separation from Eider

MALE

Adult male is spectacular, with its outsized-looking blue head and red bill with a large orange basal knob. Areas of colour on the head are defined by black lines. Breast is pinkish orange and body plumage is otherwise mainly black, except for a white patch on side of rear, and horizontal white line on flanks. Raised, sail-like scapulars can be seen at close range. In flight, note the white upperwing and underwing coverts. Adult female and juvenile have marbled, warm brown plumage and a dark grey bill. In flight, note the pale underwing coverts. Compared to female Eider, note King's smaller size, smaller bill and rounded forehead, more prominent pale line running back from eye, and pale eye-surround. **VOICE** Male utters a purring sound. **HABITS** Dives regularly and for extended periods in search of marine invertebrates. Vagrants here typically associate with Eider flocks. **STATUS AND HABITAT** Breeds in the Arctic and winters further south. There are a few records here each year, mostly in autumn and winter, and mainly from coasts of N and E Scotland.

FEMALE

bill shape and size
allow separation from
female Eider, whose
bill is massive by
comparison

MALE

male's plumage colours and pattern are unique and easily recognised, even in distant swimming birds

STELLER'S EIDER

Polysticta stelleri | ES | LENGTH 42–48cm

Small (two-thirds the size of an Eider, *Somateria mollissima*), compact diving sea duck. Sexes are dissimilar. Adult male is unmistakable; identification of female is more of a challenge.

female could perhaps be confused with immature Long-tailed Duck (*Clangula hyemalis*) but uniformly dark plumage aids identification

All birds have a distinctly squarish-looking head, a bill that is broad along its entire length, and mainly white underwings. Adult male is mainly black above and pale orange-buff below, with a black rear and collar, and a black spot on side of breast. Pale greenish-grey head is marked with a black eye-surround and throat, and a greenish tuft at rear of crown. Bill is grey and, in flight, upper surface of innerwing is white except for blue speculum. Eclipse male resembles female except for pale belly and flanks. Adult female and juvenile are brown. Bill is grey-buff and, in flight, bluish speculum is bordered with white. Adult female has longer tertials than juvenile. **VOICE** Mostly silent. **HABITS** Favours sea coasts; vagrants here usually associate with Eider flocks. **STATUS AND HABITAT** Breeds in the high Arctic and winters mainly on Arctic coasts. Vagrants here are usually found in winter, mostly in N Scotland.

FEMALE

white-edged tertials are long and decurved

no other duck has the head pattern of a male Steller's Eider

MALE

black spot on side of breast is easy to see in standing bird, but sometimes hard to discern when bird is swimming

BUFFLEHEAD

Bucephala albeola | VH | LENGTH 32–39cm

although superficially Smew-like in terms of size, shape and behaviour, male's head pattern is unique and diagnostic

Distinctive small diving duck with a dainty bill. Sexes are dissimilar. Male is unmistakable and female is relatively easy to identify.

FEMALE

MALE

oval white cheek patch is a good identification feature and shows up at a distance

FEMALE

In flight, all birds show white inner flight feathers and take off almost vertically from water when alarmed. Adult male has a relatively large rounded head that looks black and white in poor light; black elements of head plumage have a purple sheen in good light. Body plumage is otherwise white except for black back. Eclipse and 1st-winter males recall adult female. Adult female and juvenile have a mainly dark brown back and head, with a striking white oval patch on cheek. Underparts are grey-buff and white on wing can often be glimpsed in swimming birds. **VOICE** Mostly silent. **HABITS** Dives regularly and feeds on submerged invertebrates. **STATUS AND HABITAT** Widespread in North America. Widely kept in captivity, hence escapees cannot be ruled out. However, many records (mainly in autumn and winter) are thought to relate to genuine vagrants; usually discovered here on lakes and flooded gravel pits.

BLACK SCOTER

Melanitta americana | DX | LENGTH 44–54cm

Rather uniformly dark diving duck. The North American counterpart of the Common Scoter (*M. nigra*), but subtly thicker-necked than that species. Its relatively long tail is sometimes elevated when swimming. Sexes are dissimilar.

MALE

In flight, all birds look mainly dark, although in good light subtly paler flight feathers are sometimes noted. Adult male has uniformly black plumage. Bill has a striking bulbous orange/yellow knob at base (note that in male Common Scoter bill knob is dark at base, and only culmen is orange-yellow). Plumage of similar 1st-winter male is browner and bill colour is dull. Adult female and juvenile are very similar to their Common Scoter counterparts, with mainly dark brown plumage but well-defined pale buff cheeks and throat. Some females have yellow on their bill. **VOICE** Mostly silent. **HABITS** Vagrants here usually associate with Common Scoter flocks. **STATUS AND HABITAT** Widespread in North America, wintering on the North Atlantic seaboard. Vagrants here turn up in autumn and winter, mainly on Scottish coasts.

1ST-WINTER MALE

MALE

extent of orange at base of bill allows separation from male Common Scoter

SURF SCOTER

Melanitta perspicillata | FS | LENGTH 45–46cm

Robust sea duck with a large bill. Sexes are dissimilar. Male is distinctive. Female could be confused with females of other scoter species: head markings, bill size and dark wings are useful pointers.

markings on female's head invite confusion with female Velvet Scoter but note Surf Scoter's smaller body size, greater extent of white at base of bill, and different bill size and proportions

FEMALE

In flight, all birds show uniformly dark wings. Adult male has mainly black plumage, but note the white patches on the nape and forecrown. Bill is orange-yellow with a white basal patch centred with a black spot; at close range note the whitish eye. In 1st-winter male, plumage is brownish but bill has a hint of adult's pattern. Adult female and juvenile have mainly dark grey-brown plumage with a white patch at base of bill and another behind eye; some individuals have white on nape. Crown often appears darker and contrasts with rest of head. **VOICE** Mostly silent.

HABITS Dives frequently and for long periods, feeding on marine invertebrates. Vagrants here usually associate with Common Scoter (*M. nigra*) flocks. **STATUS AND HABITAT** Widespread in North America, wintering on coasts. Vagrants here favour relatively shallow inshore seas and usually appear in autumn and winter.

MALE

unique head markings show up well, even in distant flying birds

MALE

head pattern is unique and diagnostic

BARROW'S GOLDENEYE

Bucephala islandica | VG | LENGTH 43–53cm

Compact diving duck. Similar to a Goldeneye
(*B. clangula*), but note the Barrow's steeper
forehead and smaller bill. Sexes are dissimilar.

head and bill shape
offer the best clues
to separating female
Barrow's Goldeneye and
Goldeneye: Barrow's
forehead is steeper and
bill is smaller than its
common counterpart

FEMALE

Adult male has a large
rounded head with
a purple sheen and
steep forehead; white
crescent-shaped facial
patch is diagnostic
(oval in Goldeneye).
Greater extent of black on back is also a useful identification feature, and note the ladder of
white markings; black extends forward as 'spur' in swimming birds. Rear is black, neck and
underparts are white, and eye is yellow. In flight, white on inner upperwing is less extensive
than in Goldeneye. In 1st-winter male plumage resembles that of adult female but face has a
hint of male's crescent. Adult female has a dark brown head separated from grey-brown body
plumage by pale neck. Bill is mainly pinkish orange in winter (colour confined to tip in
female Goldeneye) and dark in summer; eye is yellow. Juvenile is similar to adult female but
bill and eye are dark. **VOICE** Mostly silent.
HABITS Dives frequently and feeds
on submerged invertebrates. Vagrants
here often associate with Goldeneye.
STATUS AND HABITAT Nearest breeding
population is in Iceland. Vagrants here
usually favour large lakes and lochs, and
turn up in autumn and winter.

MALE

MALE

HOODED MERGANSER

Lophodytes cucullatus | HO | LENGTH 42–50cm

compared to a 'redhead' Smew, female Hooded Merganser has a more orange and more shaggy crest, and the cheeks and throat are grey-brown, not white

Small, bizarrely shaped diving duck with a slender bill and large head. Sexes are dissimilar. Male is unmistakable; size, proportions and colour of female are useful identification features.

FEMALE

Adult male has a large erectile crest; when fanned, a white patch on the otherwise dark head is revealed. Bill is dark and eye is yellow. Back is mainly dark and breast is white, marked with 2 black lines on sides that separate breast from orange-brown flanks. Eclipse male is similar to adult female but with duller colours; it retains its yellow eye. Adult female and juvenile have an orange-buff head with a long, shaggy crest. Plumage is otherwise mainly grey-brown, darkest on back, whitish on belly. Eye is dark. **VOICE** Mostly silent. **HABITS** Dives frequently in search of small fish and invertebrates. **STATUS AND HABITAT** Widespread in North America. Widely kept in captivity here and many records undoubtedly relate to escapees. However, genuine vagrants are also thought to occur, mainly in autumn and winter; they favour lakes and flooded gravel pits.

MALE

limited extent of white on wings in flight

markings on head in particular make identification of male a straightforward matter

MALE

GOLDEN PHEASANT

Chrysolophus pictus | GF |

LENGTH, INCLUDING TAIL, 90–100cm (♂), 60–80cm (♀)

Large gamebird. Sexes are dissimilar. Male is gaudy and unmistakable; female is similar to a female Pheasant (*Phasianus colchicus*) but easily separable.

compared to female Pheasant, female Golden Pheasant is more compact, overall darker, and its plumage is adorned with neat barring

Adult male has mainly red body plumage, a golden-yellow crown and barred 'cape', a yellow rump, and blue on wings and back; tail is buffish with intricate dark markings and has a pale, unbarred tip. Adult female is buffish brown with distinct dark barring all over (including belly), and overall much darker than female Pheasant; note the contrast between pale brown face and darker crown and nape. Tail is long and barred. Juvenile/1st-winter recalls a small, short-tailed female. **VOICE** Territorial male utters a shrill, disyllabic, strangled *ker-cheek*, sometimes repeating the 2nd syllable 3 or 4 times. Also utters a soft *hwit* call and a Curlew-like call. **HABITS** Secretive and hard to observe in the wild, such that views are typically brief. Least retiring in Mar–Apr, when males are establishing territories. **STATUS AND HABITAT** Native to China. Released here in the 18th century and now established in a few locations; around 50–250 pairs are thought to live wild, favouring dense, dark woodland. Also widely kept in captivity.

MALE

FEMALE

despite its colourful plumage, male can be hard to spot amongst shaded, dense woodland vegetation

LADY AMHERST'S PHEASANT

Chrysolophus amherstiae | LM |

LENGTH, INCLUDING TAIL, 100–120cm (♂), 60–80cm (♀)

compared to female Golden Pheasant, female Lady Amherst's plumage is colder reddish brown rather than buffish brown; it has noticeably paler underparts

Large gamebird. Sexes are dissimilar. Male is showy and unmistakable; female is similar to a female Golden Pheasant but separable on close inspection.

Adult male has body plumage that is overall mainly whitish below and black above; some dark feathers have a blue sheen. Black-edged white feathers form a cape; has red on rear of crown, and red and yellow on rump. Tail is long and grey with intricate black markings. Adult female is reddish brown (more rufous than female Golden) with greyish cheeks and a paler, unbarred belly (barred in female Golden). Tail is long and barred. Juvenile/1st-winter resembles a small, short-tailed female. **VOICE** Male utters a shrieking song, typically at night. **HABITS** A shy bird that is hard to observe well. **STATUS AND HABITAT** Native to China. Introduced to Bedfordshire and formerly fairly well established there, with a few colonies elsewhere; current population may have declined to just a handful of pairs. Favours conifer plantations where a dense canopy effectively excludes ground-layer vegetation.

MALE

tail is incredibly long with striking, unique markings

FEMALE

PACIFIC DIVER

Gavia pacifica | LENGTH 60–70cm

Buoyant waterbird. Similar to the larger Black-throated Diver (*G. arctica*) but with subtly different plumage, a smaller bill and a more rounded head. Sexes are similar.

compared to similar Black-throated Diver, Pacific's neck markings in winter, and smaller bill aid separation

Adult in summer has a grey nape and head (paler than in Black-throated); throat is black and sides of neck are marked with black and white lines. Black back has a chequerboard of white spots while underparts are white. Adult in winter (plumage most likely to be seen here) has whitish underparts and mainly grey-brown upperparts, darker on back than on neck (upperparts are overall paler than in Black-throated). Demarcation between brown and white on neck is well defined. Most birds show a narrow, dark 'chin strap'. Note that the patch of white feathering usually visible at water level towards the rear of swimming Black-throateds is absent in Pacific. Juvenile/1st-winter is similar to winter adult but pale feather margins make back appear 'scaly'. **VOICE** Vagrants here are silent. **HABITS** Dives frequently in search of fish. **STATUS AND HABITAT** Very locally common in North America, wintering on coasts. Vagrants here turn up in autumn and winter and favour mainly coasts, or occasionally lakes and flooded gravel pits.

rounded outline to head

SUMMER

dark 'chin strap' can usually be discerned

WINTER

WHITE-BILLED DIVER

Gavia adamsii | WV | LENGTH 77–80cm

in plumage terms, White-billed is similar to Great Northern but the shape of its pale, massive bill allows easy separation

Large waterbird. Similar to a Great Northern Diver (*G. immer*) but separable by noting the bill shape and colour; the bill is also often held pointing upwards. Sexes are similar.

Summer adult has a black neck (sheen visible in good light) with 2 rows of white stripes. Upperparts are blackish, with a chequerboard of white spots on mantle (larger and fewer than in Great Northern). Underparts are white. Bill is yellow and dagger-like with a straight culmen (curved in Great Northern). Winter adult has dark grey upperparts and whitish underparts, including throat and front of neck; note dark half-collar on neck. Bill is pale yellowish, including outer half of culmen (culmen is dark in Great Northern). Juvenile/1st-winter is similar to winter adult but brownish-grey upperparts appear scaly due to pale feather margins, and underparts are grubby white. In flight, all birds hold head and neck outstretched while feet and legs trail behind. **VOICE** Vagrants here are silent. **HABITS** Swims buoyantly, relatively low in the water. Dives frequently and submerges in a 'gliding' manner. **STATUS AND HABITAT** An Arctic breeder that usually winters in northern seas. Its status here is mainly that of a winter vagrant to northern and western coasts (usually 6 or so a year); some individuals, seen in breeding plumage, linger in summer.

SUMMER

occasionally, birds in breeding plumage spend the summer months in northern British waters

WINTER

RARE PETRELS, STORM-PETRELS AND SHEARWATERS

Petrels and storm-petrels are small, fast-flying birds whose fluttering flight is hard to follow at the best of times, especially when seen from a moving boat. Shearwaters are medium-sized, fast-flying birds whose gliding flight is seemingly effortless on stiffly held wings. The annotations on the photo below highlight key features to aid identification. For comparison, European Storm-petrel is the default common storm-petrel species in British waters and Manx Shearwater is the default common shearwater.

WILSON'S STORM-PETREL

Study the pattern on the upperwing.

Study the rump – Swinhoe's has a dark rump; Wilson's has a square white rump patch; Madeiran has a narrow white rump band.

Is the tail forked or square-ended?
Of the rare species, only Swinhoe's has a noticeably forked tail.

Study the leg length – in Wilson's the legs project beyond the tail in flight.

Are the underwings plain or marked in some way?
The rare storm-petrels covered in this book have uniformly dark underwings whereas those of the region's commonest species – European Storm-petrel – show a pale band.

Try to gauge the bird's size relative to known species nearby – Cory's, Great and Sooty are relatively large birds; Balearic is closer to Manx in size; Macaronesian is smaller than Manx.

GREAT SHEARWATER

Look at the rump – Great has an obvious white patch; in Cory's the dark tail contrasts with paler uppertail coverts; other species are uniform in appearance.

Look at the head – Great has an obvious dark cap and white collar; other species lack a distinct cap; Macaronesian has a pale face and isolated eye.

Study bill colour – yellow in Cory's; dark in other species.

Underwing markings and colours are useful with shearwater identification. Sooty has whitish coverts that contrast with the otherwise dark plumage; Great has distinct black markings on the otherwise mainly white underwings; other shearwater species are more uniform in appearance.

Note the overall colour of the bird – underparts are noticeably paler than upperparts in Cory's and Great; Sooty is uniform except for silvery underwing coverts; Balearic is rather dusky overall with subtly paler underwings coverts.

BLACK-BROWED ALBATROSS

Thalassarche melanophris | AA | WINGSPAN 200–235cm

Massive seabird. Unmistakable when seen well, but potential for confusion exists with a Great Black-backed Gull (*Larus marinus*) and immature Gannet (*Morus bassanus*), particularly in 2nd calendar year. Sexes are similar.

uniformly dark upperwings and back

Adult has long, narrow wings that are uniformly dark above; underwing is white with a broad black margin. Body plumage is white except for black tail. Bill is massive and yellow, and note the short black eye-stripe. Swimming birds appear white except for black back, wings and tail. Immature is similar but bill is dull pink and dark-tipped. On any flying albatross the underwing pattern (extent of white and black) is important for identification. **VOICE** Vagrants here are silent. **HABITS** Usually seen in flight, which is effortless and gliding, in the manner of a Fulmar (*Fulmarus glacialis*). Swimming birds are buoyant and sit high on the water. **STATUS AND HABITAT** Breeds on sub-Antarctic islands and wanders the South Atlantic for much of its life. Vagrants occasionally stray into the North Atlantic and are seen at sea off British and Irish coasts. Individuals have also summered in Scottish Gannet colonies.

glides on outstretched wings with hardly a wingbeat

massive yellow bill

FEA'S PETREL

Pterodroma feae | WINGSPAN 86–94cm

Consummate seabird, invariably seen in flight, which is masterful in rough weather and faster than that of most other tubenoses; high, arcing glides are a good identification pointer. Sexes are similar.

glides masterfully; outstretched wings slightly bowed when banking

Adult and immature have shearwater-like proportions but body is bulkier and bill is larger and more thickset. In flight and from above, mantle, nape and crown are grey, and wings have dark flight feathers and show a faint, dark 'W' in good light; rump and tail are pale grey. Note the dark bill and eye-surround. From below, wings usually appear all dark except for white 'armpits', which merge with white underside to body. **VOICE** Vagrants here are silent. **HABITS** Usually seen in flight, which is effortless and gliding. **STATUS AND HABITAT** A great rarity and the Holy Grail for many seabird enthusiasts. Breeds on Madeira and the Cape Verdes, and feeding range includes much of North Atlantic.

MACARONESIAN SHEARWATER

Puffinus baroli | WINGSPAN 58–67cm

Recalls a small Manx Shearwater (*P. puffinus*), with proportionately shorter, broader wings and a pale eye-surround. Invariably seen in flight. Sexes are similar.

Adult and immature in flight are mainly dark above and pale below. In good light, blackish upperwing is relieved by a pale panel on inner trailing edge (inner flight feathers). Underparts are white except for dark margin to wings. Note the white 'cheeks' and eye-surround, and clearly defined dark eye; in Manx Shearwater, 'cheeks' and eye-surround are dark. **VOICE** Silent at sea. **HABITS** Compared to Manx Shearwater, glides are less extended and usually interspersed with bouts of rapid wingbeats. Head is often held up above the body in flight. **STATUS AND HABITAT** Formerly known as Little Shearwater. Breeds on Macaronesian islands and feeding birds sometimes wander into British waters in summer (perhaps 1 record per year).

size, facial pattern and flight pattern allow separation from Manx Shearwater

SOOTY SHEARWATER

Puffinus griseus | OT | WINGSPAN 95–105cm

Medium-sized, dark-looking shearwater with relatively long wings. Invariably seen in flight over the sea. Sexes are similar.

Adult and immature can appear all dark at a distance. Angle and intensity of light affects appearance of plumage colours, but at close range, and in good light, note the sooty-brown plumage and silvery-white underwing coverts; these form a striking bar, palest and broadest towards the wingtip. Bill is rather long and narrowest in the middle. **VOICE** Silent at sea. **HABITS** A consummate flyer that banks and glides effortlessly, low over the sea, on long, stiffly held wings. **STATUS AND HABITAT** Breeds in the southern hemisphere (in our winter). Undertakes a clockwise circum-Atlantic migration outside the breeding season, passing through our seas in late summer and early autumn. Seen from ferries, pelagic trips and headlands, especially off west and southwest coasts of Britain and Ireland, during periods of strong onshore winds. Several hundred birds might be recorded in the region in a good year.

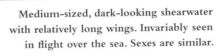

silvery-white underwing coverts are usually striking

often associates with feeding groups of Manx Shearwaters, as well as seabirds that gather to feast on by-catch from trawlers

sooty-black plumage

BALEARIC SHEARWATER

Puffinus mauretanicus | YQ | WINGSPAN 80–90cm

Critically endangered seabird. Superficially similar to a Manx Shearwater (*P. puffinus*), with which it often associates while in British waters. The 2 species are separable with care. Sexes are similar.

Adult and immature have brown upperparts and grubby white underparts, lacking the clean contrast between the two as seen in Manx. Undertail coverts are grey-brown (white in Manx), underwings show a comparatively limited amount of white and dark 'armpits', and throat is grey-buff. In flight, feet project noticeably beyond tail. **VOICE** Silent at sea. **HABITS** Flies on stiffly held wings, banking and gliding low over the water. **STATUS AND HABITAT** In our region, seen only at sea. Breeds in the W Mediterranean; migrates to the Bay of Biscay and coasts from N Britain to S Britain to moult – typically observed here in late summer and autumn. Even on a good day, however, several hours' seawatching is unlikely to yield more than a handful of sightings.

feet project noticeably beyond tail in flight

unlikely though it may sound, many Balearic Shearwaters visit British waters to moult, during late summer and autumn

CORY'S SHEARWATER

Calonectris borealis | CQ | WINGSPAN 115–125cm

Large and impressive seabird. Only ever seen
at sea, and views are typically distant
and brief. Sexes are similar.

flight is seemingly effortless, on stiffly
held wings, and reminiscent
of a miniature albatross

bill is yellow and
relatively large

underwings, and
body underparts
are mostly white

Adult and immature have mainly buffish-
brown upperparts with darker wingtips and a
dark tip to tail (sometimes with a limited amount
of white at base of tail). Underparts are white, the
wings with dark margins. Bill is yellow with a dark
sub-terminal band. Shows a diagnostic dirty grey cowl
on nape, neck sides and breast that is surprisingly easy to see
at distance. **VOICE** Silent at sea. **HABITS** Flight is effortless;
it usually banks and glides on wings that are held stiffly and
slightly bowed. Infrequent wingbeats are relaxed and relatively
slow. **STATUS AND HABITAT** Breeds on Macaronesian islands and
islands in the W Mediterranean. Wanders into British waters in summer
and early autumn, numbers observed varying from year to year. Most
records are from SW Britain, and birds are seen from coastal seawatches,
ferry crossings and pelagic trips.

GREAT SHEARWATER

Puffinus gravis | GQ | WINGSPAN 105–120cm

Similar to the slightly larger Cory's Shearwater
but separable with care on plumage details,
and because it generally flies on
stiffer wings. Sexes are similar.

compared to Cory's, head
usually appears dark-capped,
this separated from the
mantle by a pale collar

dark belly smudge

dark bill

underwings are strongly
marked with a black
and white pattern

Adult and immature have brown upperwing
coverts and mantle, contrasting with darker wingtips.
Note the dark tail and contrasting white uppertail
coverts. Dark cap is separated from the
mantle by a white collar, behind
which it also shows an obvious
dark shoulder patch.
Underparts are mainly
white, but note that the
wings have dark margins, and a dark diagonal bar
and 'armpits'. When seen well, there is a dark 'oil
smudge' on the central lower belly. **VOICE** Silent
at sea. **HABITS** Often attracted to fishing vessels,
and to chum. Compared to Cory's, wings are
usually held stiffer and flatter, and wingbeats
are more rapid. **STATUS AND HABITAT**
Breeds in the South Atlantic (in our winter)
and undertakes a circum-Atlantic non-
breeding migration. Passes through British
waters in summer and autumn. Mostly
offshore (out of sight of land) and seen
from ferry crossings and pelagic trips, but
occasionally also during coastal seawatches
in SW Britain.

WILSON'S STORM-PETREL

Oceanites oceanicus | WINGSPAN 38–42cm

A tiny seabird. Superficially similar to
other storm-petrels but separable using
structural and plumage differences, and
recognising its distinctive flight pattern.
Size is between the European (*Hydrobates
pelagicus*) and Leach's (*Oceanodroma leucorhoa*)
storm-petrels. Sexes are similar.

pale upperwing panel

square-ended tail

feet project beyond
tail in flight

Adult and immature at a distance look all dark with a striking white rump. At close range,
dark elements of plumage are grey-brown. Legs are dark and feet have yellow webs. When
compared to other commoner storm-petrels, note the broad wings, square-ended tail, relatively
long legs (when outstretched, feet project beyond tail) and pale upperwing panel. In European,
feet do not project beyond square-ended tail, upperwings have, at best, an indistinct pale
panel, and underwings show a striking white band (absent in Wilson's). Leach's has an
obvious pale upperwing panel, but tail is distinctly forked and feet do not project. **VOICE**
Silent at sea. **HABITS** Often glides for extended periods on outstretched flat wings, but
also flutters low over the water, pattering the surface with its dangling feet. **STATUS AND
HABITAT** Breeds in the southern hemisphere (in our winter). Outside its breeding season
visits the North Atlantic, including seas off SW Britain and Ireland. Very rarely seen from
land but encountered regularly on summer pelagic trips from the Isles of Scilly.

BAND-RUMPED STORM-PETREL COMPLEX

Oceanodroma complex | WINGSPAN 43–46cm

Formerly referred to as Madeiran Storm-petrel (*O. castro*), members of this species complex are superficially similar to both European (*Hydrobates pelagicus*) and Leach's (*Oceanodroma leucorhoa*) storm-petrels. Much larger than European but approaching Leach's in size. Separable using structural and plumage differences, and by assessing flight pattern. Sexes are similar. For further information on classification, see p. 288.

pale wing panel

broad white rump

compared to European Storm-petrel, underwings are dark and lack that species' white band

Adult and immature at a distance look all dark with a striking white rump. At close range and in good light, note the following: faint buffish wing panel (less obvious than in Leach's, more striking than in European); dark underwings (Leach's shares this feature but European has a white band); slightly notched tail (deeply forked in Leach's, square-ended in European); and broad white rump (rump is elongated and faintly notched in Leach's, relatively small and square in European). **VOICE** Silent at sea. **HABITS** Flight pattern often seems to be constantly changing, twisting, turning and gliding in rapid succession. Leach's flight pattern is also variable but involves more powerful wingbeats and more prolonged glides; that of European is appreciably more fluttering and 'bat-like'. **STATUS AND HABITAT** Breeds on some Macaronesian islands (including Madeira and the Canaries). Very rarely wanders into British and Irish waters, mainly in the southwest, and mostly in summer and early autumn.

SWINHOE'S STORM-PETREL

Oceanodroma monorhis | WINGSPAN 45–48cm

Enigmatic storm-petrel. Structurally very
similar to Leach's (*O. leucorhoa*) but lacks
that species' white rump. Sexes are similar.

dark rump
(white in
superficially
similar Leach's
Storm-petrel)

Adult and immature look all dark at a distance. At close range,
plumage appears mainly sooty grey except for the pale panel on
upperwing coverts (similar to that of Leach's), and the blackish
flight feathers, the primaries with subtly pale shafts. Tail is forked
but this feature is not always easy to discern in the field, and rump
is dark (same colour as back and tail). **VOICE** Silent at sea. **HABITS**
Flight pattern recalls that of Leach's but perhaps more purposeful,
with fewer twists and turns and more direct flight. **STATUS AND
HABITAT** Primarily thought of as an East Asian and Pacific breeding
species; rare in our region but regular records in the North Atlantic hint at
the possibility of populations elsewhere, albeit tiny ones. British records relate mainly
to birds mist-netted after dark. The chances of seeing one at sea in daylight are slim.

RED-BILLED TROPICBIRD

Phaethon aethereus | WINGSPAN 100–115cm

Elegant seabird that is unmistakable when seen
well. Body and wing proportions recall that of
Caspian Tern, but note the extremely long
tail projections. Sexes are similar.

tail streamer is unique among
seabirds seen in British waters

Adult has mainly white plumage with black outer
primaries and fine dark barring on back and
upper innerwing. Bill is dagger-like and bright
red, and note the black eye-stripe. Central tail

red bill, black 'mask' and
otherwise mostly white plumage
make for easy identification

projections are very long. Immature is similar but tail streamers are absent and tail itself has
a black terminal band; bill is dull yellow with a dark tip. **VOICE** Silent at sea. **HABITS** A
mainly pelagic seabird that plunge-dives after fish and squid. Flight is buoyant and recalls that
of a Sandwich Tern (*Sterna sandvicensis*), on 'rowing' wingbeats. **STATUS AND HABITAT**
A tropical species that breeds mainly in the Caribbean and South Atlantic, but also on the
Cape Verdes. Has been recorded here during autumn seawatches in the west and southwest.

AMERICAN BITTERN

Botaurus lentiginosus | AM | LENGTH 60–70cm

head pattern allows separation from Bittern: American Bittern has brown, not black, crown and pale supercilium, a feature absent in its British cousin

Bulky wetland bird whose cryptic plumage blends in with dead wetland vegetation. Very similar to a Bittern (*B. stellaris*) but separable with care by noting plumage details. Sexes are similar.

Adult has intricately patterned brown plumage. Back and upperwing are marbled and finely marked (more uniform than Bittern), while neck and breast have lines of chestnut feathers on a paler background. Has a white throat and black malar stripe. Note the brown crown and pale supercilium (in Bittern, crown is dark and supercilium is absent). Dagger-like bill is yellow and legs are greenish. Juvenile/1st-winter is similar but facial markings are less striking. In flight, wing pattern is diagnostic. Primaries and secondaries are unbarred and dark, contrasting with pale upperwing coverts (heavily barred in Bittern and with no contrast). Secondaries have a paler trailing edge (dark in Bittern). **VOICE** Vagrants here are silent. **HABITS** Remains motionless or moves stealthily, making it hard to spot. Flies with deep, powerful wingbeats, head and neck held hunched.

beautifully patterned brown and buff plumage

STATUS AND HABITAT

Widespread in North America, where northern and interior birds move south in autumn. Vagrants here turn up in autumn and winter, favouring freshwater wetlands.

GREEN HERON

Butorides virescens | HR | LENGTH 46cm

Small, compact heron with a long dagger-like
bill. Plumage is well marked but blends in
with wetland vegetation. Sexes are similar.

immature is brownish
overall with pale margins
to wing feathers; plumage
is much more streaked
than in adult

IMMATURE

Adult has a black crown, rufous-
maroon face and neck, and white
running from throat through the
breast to the whitish belly. Upperparts
are otherwise greenish grey, the wing
feathers having pale margins. Juvenile
is mainly brown, tinged rufous on the
face; underparts have rufous streaks
on sides, with a paler throat, neck and
breast. **VOICE** Utters a sharp *skeeok* call in flight. **HABITS** Sometimes perches on branches
overhanging water. Moves stealthily and will remain motionless for minutes on end waiting
for fish and amphibians to pass within stabbing range of its bill. **STATUS AND HABITAT**
Widespread in North America, where northern birds move south outside the breeding
season. Vagrants here turn up in autumn and early winter, and favour coastal wetlands.

greenish sheen
to upperwings

sometimes clambers up
branches near water and
other wetland vegetation

LITTLE BITTERN

Ixobrychus minutus | LL | LENGTH 35–38cm

**A tiny heron (barely the size of a Teal,
Anas crecca) and the smallest of its kind to
be encountered here. Sexes are dissimilar.**

in both sexes, pale panels on wings are striking in flight and contrast with the dark flight feathers

FEMALE

Adult male has a greyish face, a black cap, back and flight
feathers, and orange-buff underparts. In flight, an obvious
wing panel that grades from orange-buff to greyish white
is revealed. Adult female is similar but plumage
is overall browner, back is streaked, and
patterns and markings are subdued. Juvenile
is similar to adult female but plumage is even
more brown and streaked, and its appearance recalls a
Bittern (*Botaurus stellaris*) in miniature. **VOICE** Call is a sharp
kwekek, usually uttered in flight. Song is a
monotonous, gruff croak, uttered mostly at
night. **HABITS** Generally keeps to the
cover of wetland vegetation.
Occasionally feeds on margins
or clambers up stems, but
usually seen in brief, low-level flight. **STATUS
AND HABITAT** Associated with wetland
habitats, particularly reedbeds. A summer visitor
to S Europe that winters in Africa. Has bred in
Britain in the past but most sightings here relate
to solitary birds that appear in spring; there might
be 4 records in a good year.

FEMALE

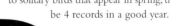

MALE

male has much darker upperparts than female, with unstreaked underparts

NIGHT HERON

Nycticorax nycticorax | NT | LENGTH 60–65cm

Stocky, large-headed heron with a hunchbacked appearance at rest. Flies on broad, rounded wings, with neck hunched up. Sexes are similar.

in all plumages, note the proportionately large head and eye, and rather steep forehead

Adult has a black bill, crown and back, with grey wings and a pale face and underparts. Eyes are large and red, legs are yellowish, and head is adorned with white plumes. In flight, grey upperwings contrast with black back. Juvenile has mainly brown plumage, heavily marked with white spots; bill is dull yellow. Acquires adult plumage over subsequent 2 years. **VOICE** Utters a barking *quaak* call in flight. **HABITS** Typically roosts during the day (in waterside bushes) and feeds actively only at night. **STATUS AND HABITAT** Breeds in S Europe and winters in Africa. Vagrants (on average, around 10 each year) turn up mainly in spring and autumn, favouring freshwater wetland habitats.

JUVENILE

mainly black, grey and whitish plumage

orange-yellow eye

obvious pale spots on upperparts

JUVENILE

SQUACCO HERON

Ardeola ralloides | QH | LENGTH 45–47cm

Compact, stocky heron. Its mainly buffish-brown plumage is transformed in flight by the pure white wings. Sexes are similar

in flight, the pure white wings contrast with its buffish-brown body plumage

legs can look yellow or pinkish, depending on the light and the age of the bird

Adult is overall pale buffish brown with streaking on crown and trailing plumes on nape; underparts are buff and white. Legs are yellowish and dagger-like bill is bluish yellow with a dark tip. Immature and non-breeding adult look similar, although head and neck are more heavily streaked and head plumes are absent. Wings are broad, rounded and white. **VOICE** Utters a quacking *kwaak*. **HABITS** Often stands still for extended periods, waiting for prey to pass within range. **STATUS AND HABITAT** Breeds in S Europe and winters in Africa, and is always associated with well-vegetated wetlands. A few vagrants are recorded here each year, mostly in spring.

dagger-like blue-based bill

white wings are largely concealed in standing birds

CATTLE EGRET

Bubulcus ibis | EC | LENGTH 48–52cm

Stocky, pure white heron. Favours drier habitats than many of its relatives and often associated with grazing animals. Sexes are similar.

bill is yellow at all times, but buffish wash to crown and nape is seen only in spring

BREEDING

BREEDING

dark legs and feet

NON-BREEDING

bulging throat apperance

Adult has pure white plumage, although sullied when compared to striking white Little Egret (*Egretta garzetta*). Compared to similar-sized Little Egret, Cattle is more bulky. Bill is yellow (not dark) and much shorter, and legs are also shorter and greenish brown (not black with yellow 'feet'). In addition, note Cattle's 'bulging throat' appearance and rather steep forehead. In breeding plumage (seldom seen here), adults acquire a buffish tinge to crown and back. Juvenile/1st-winter is similar to non-breeding adult but legs and bill are dark at first. In flight, all birds have broad, rounded wings and neck is held hunched up. **VOICE** Utters a soft, croaking call in flight. **HABITS** An active bird that feeds mainly on insects and earthworms in grassland habitats, often following cattle and sheep and catching prey disturbed by the animals' passage. **STATUS AND HABITAT** Until recently, confined mainly to SW Europe, with a few vagrant records here each year, but its range appears to be expanding northwards. A large influx into Britain in the winter of 2007/08 led to the first pair breeding here successfully.

SNOWY EGRET

Egretta thula | NY | LENGTH 55–65cm

in plumage terms, Snowy looks identical to Little Egret and its behaviour is indistinguishable too

Elegant, pure white heron that is very similar to Little Egret (*E. garzetta*). Can be distinguished by studying the coloration on the legs and face. Sexes are similar.

uniformly yellow feet, compare Little Egret

yellow lores help distinguish Snowy from Little Egret when foot colour cannot be seen

Not seen here in breeding plumage. Non-breeding adult has white plumage, a dagger-like bill and a long neck. Feet are uniformly yellow (soles of toes are dark in Little Egret) and back of visible part of legs (the tarsus) is extensively yellow (legs are uniformly dark in Little Egret). Lores are yellow (bluish green in Little Egret). Juvenile/1st-winter is similar to adult but with marginally duller colours. **VOICE** Mostly silent. **HABITS** Feeds in the manner of a Little Egret: wades in the water, stabbing at fish and shrimps; occasionally chases prey more actively. **STATUS AND HABITAT** Widespread in North America and usually winters south of its breeding range. Vagrants here are likely to turn up in autumn and winter, and favour coastal wetlands and marshes.

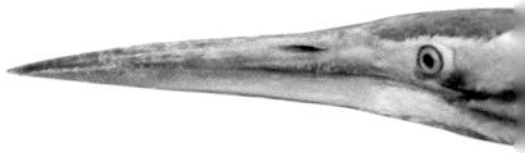

GREAT WHITE EGRET

Ardea alba | HW | LENGTH 85–100cm

Large, long-legged wetland bird, with the stature of a Grey Heron (*A. cinerea*) and nearly twice the size of a Little Egret (*Egretta garzetta*). Sexes are similar.

extremely long, uniformly dark legs

massive, yellow bill

Non-breeding adult and immature have pure white plumage. Legs are uniformly dark (Little Egret has dark legs but yellow feet), and dagger-like bill is yellow (dark in Little Egret) and extremely large and powerful-looking. For a brief period in the breeding season, adult's bill becomes dark, upper legs (tibiae) take on a yellowish-orange flush, and long, trailing plumes appear on back. In flight, all birds have long, broad wings and legs that project further behind the body than in Little Egret. **VOICE** Mostly silent. **HABITS** Wades in a stately manner and stands motionless for extended periods, often with its neck hunched. Also perches in trees. Flight is buoyant, on slower, deeper wingbeats than Little Egret, recalling a Grey Heron. **STATUS AND HABITAT** Breeds locally in mainland Europe and seen here mainly as a winter vagrant (around 30 birds in a typical year). However, records appear to be on the increase and the species bred here in 2012. Favours large lakes and extensive wetlands.

PURPLE HERON

Ardea purpurea | UR | LENGTH 80–90cm

Elegant and slender wetland bird. Superficially similar to Grey Heron (*A. cinerea*) but separable by studying its colours and noting its slender, rakish proportions. Sexes are similar.

very slender proportions to head and neck when compared to Grey Heron, with orange-buff elements to plumage, not seen in that species

JUVENILE

overall brown plumage with pale margins to back feathers

Adult's body plumage looks overall greyish purple. Head and neck are orange-buff and a black stripe runs down side of neck on both sides. Also has long head plumes and long, streaked breast feathers. In standing birds, 'thighs' and 'shoulders' are orange-chestnut. In flight, wings look broad and rounded; upperwing is purplish brown with darker flight feathers, while underwing is grey with a maroon leading edge. Juvenile is similar but plumage is more uniformly brown; back feathers have pale margins. In flight, all birds hold the neck in a snake-like curve; the hind toe is often cocked upwards (usually held flat in Grey Heron). **VOICE** Utters a harsh *kruuk* call. **HABITS** Generally rather shy and secretive, keeping to the cover of dense wetland vegetation. **STATUS AND HABITAT** Locally common breeder in mainland Europe, wintering in Africa. Its status here is essentially that of a spring and early summer vagrant, with perhaps 20 recorded in a good year. However, it bred successfully in S England in 2010.

BLACK STORK

Ciconia nigra | OS | LENGTH 90–105cm

Large, long-legged and long-necked bird.
Proportions are similar to a White Stork, but
black and white elements of White's plumage
are reversed in Black. Sexes are similar.

in flight, head, neck
breast and wing coverts
are black allowing
separation from White
Stork

Adult has mainly black plumage that shows an oily green and violet sheen in good light. White
elements of plumage are confined to breast, belly and inner underwing coverts, and are most
obvious in flight. Dagger-like bill, eye-surround and legs are red. Immature is similar to adult
but black elements of plumage are greenish brown, and bill, eye-surround and legs are olive-
yellow. **VOICE** Vagrants here are silent. **HABITS** Walks in a stately manner and feeds on
amphibians, fish and large insects. Soars on broad wings, with the head and neck outstretched
and legs trailing. **STATUS AND HABITAT** Breeds in mainland Europe and winters in Africa.
Vagrants here (perhaps 3 in a good year) are seen mainly in spring,
having drifted away from their usual migration route. Also
kept in captivity, so some records may relate to escapees.

bright red bill and
eye-surround

oily-looking sheen on black
elements of plumage

WHITE STORK

Ciconia ciconia | OR | LENGTH 100–115cm

Large, long-legged and long-necked black and white bird. Unmistakable both on the ground and in flight. Sexes are similar.

consummate aeronaut, capable of soaring on thermals to a great height

Adult has mainly grubby white plumage except for the black flight feathers. Bill is long, dagger-like and red, and the long legs are pinkish red. Immature is similar to adult but leg and bill colours are duller. **VOICE** Vagrants here are silent. **HABITS** Walks in a stately manner and feeds on amphibians, fish and large insects. Soars effortlessly on broad wings, with the head and neck outstretched and legs trailing. **STATUS AND HABITAT** Breeds in mainland Europe and winters in Africa. Vagrants here (perhaps 20 in a good year) are seen mainly in spring, having drifted away from their usual migration route. Also kept in captivity, so some records may relate to escapees.

white plumage can look rather grubby on close inspection

bright red bill and legs

GLOSSY IBIS

Plegadis falcinellus | IB | LENGTH 55–65cm

Elegant wetland bird with the proportions of a heron
but the bill shape of a Curlew (*Numenius arquata*).
In flight, all birds hold their neck extended and
legs trailing. Sexes are similar.

IMMATURE

Adult can appear black in silhouette,
but in good light it looks deep
maroon with a metallic sheen on
wings and back. In summer, has a
narrow white line framing eye,
running from base of bill. Bill is
pinkish brown and legs are dull red.
In winter, legs are dull reddish
yellow and plumage also appears
duller overall, with pale streaks on
head and neck. Immature is similar to winter adult but plumage
colours are even duller. **VOICE** Mostly silent. **HABITS** Walks
and wades in a stately manner, and feeds by probing for aquatic
invertebrates. **STATUS AND HABITAT**
Breeds in S Europe and most birds
winter in Africa. In our region
2 or 3 vagrants are recorded
in most years, but in
some years small
influxes
occur.

long, curved
bill makes
identification
straightforward
in all plumages

in flight, neck and
rather bulbous-looking
head are held extended

IMMATURE

PIED-BILLED GREBE

Podilymbus podiceps | PJ | LENGTH 31–38cm

bill is larger and more robust than in Little Grebe

Stocky, plump-bodied grebe with a pale 'powderpuff' of fluffy feathers at its rear end, and a large, thick bill. Sexes are similar.

WINTER

SUMMER

compared to Little Grebe, note the thickset, uniformly dark neck

dark band on bill is most obvious in spring and summer, but a subtle suggestion of this pattern is often visible in winter too

Adult in summer has grey-brown plumage, palest on flanks and neck. Throat is black and bill is pale grey with a striking black band. In winter, adult plumage is more orange-buff, particularly on neck. Throat is pale and bill is uniformly yellowish grey. Immature is similar to winter adult. Compared to a Little Grebe (*Tachybaptus ruficollis*), note Pied-billed's larger size and its proportionately more chunky bill; from behind, neck is uniformly dark (in Little, a dark central line is offset by pale sides to neck). **VOICE** Vagrants here are silent. **HABITS** Dives regularly for small fish and aquatic invertebrates. **STATUS AND HABITAT** Widespread and common in North America, where northern birds move south in winter. Vagrants here usually turn up in autumn and winter, often staying for extended periods and acquiring the summer bill pattern.

BIRDS OF PREY

Birds of prey are usually observed in flight, so views can be distant and against the light. Be aware that size can be difficult to judge accurately and the silhouette effect can play tricks on the perception of colour and markings. Here are some key features to aid identification. For comparison, Kestrel is the default common falcon species in Britain, while Red Kite, Buzzard and Marsh Harrier are the default common medium-sized raptors.

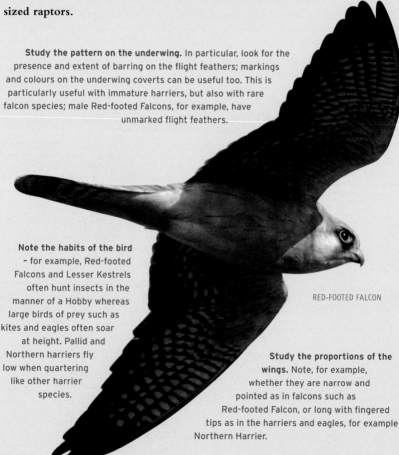

Study the pattern on the underwing. In particular, look for the presence and extent of barring on the flight feathers; markings and colours on the underwing coverts can be useful too. This is particularly useful with immature harriers, but also with rare falcon species; male Red-footed Falcons, for example, have unmarked flight feathers.

Note the habits of the bird – for example, Red-footed Falcons and Lesser Kestrels often hunt insects in the manner of a Hobby whereas large birds of prey such as kites and eagles often soar at height. Pallid and Northern harriers fly low when quartering like other harrier species.

RED-FOOTED FALCON

Study the proportions of the wings. Note, for example, whether they are narrow and pointed as in falcons such as Red-footed Falcon, or long with fingered tips as in the harriers and eagles, for example Northern Harrier.

Are the wings held above centre, level or bowed? This can be a very useful pointer to identification. Most harriers, for example, glide or soar with their wings held above centre; Black Kites often soar on level wings but hold them bowed in tight manoeuvres.

Does the upperwing have a pattern? This can be useful for separation from common species. Red Kite has a much stronger rufous upperwing pattern than Black Kite for instance.

Pay attention to the colour of the rump – harriers have white rumps (with the exception of Marsh); this feature is absent in other raptor groups.

BLACK KITE

What shape is the tail? Black Kite is the only rare raptor to have a forked tail (although this is much less obvious than in Red Kite).

Size is a good tool to help in identification but hard to judge, especially at distance. However, birds of prey are often mobbed by other species, for example crows, which helps assess size more accurately.

BLACK KITE

Milvus migrans | KB | WINGSPAN 145–165cm

**Medium-sized raptor that could be confused
with a female Marsh Harrier (*Circus aeruginosus*)
or immature Red Kite (*M. milvus*).**

Adult has mainly brown plumage, palest on the head. In flight, note the shallow-forked tail; this can appear straight-ended when broadly fanned. Has a pale panel on the outer flight feathers of otherwise rather dark wings. At very close range, note the yellow base to the bill, yellow legs and pale eye. Immature is similar but feathers on upperwing coverts have pale margins, and eye is dark with a dark 'mask'. **VOICE** Utters a whistling, whinnying call, similar to that of Red Kite but more shrill. **HABITS** Soars for extended periods and flexes its tail to assist manoeuvring. Scavenges at carcasses but also feeds on invertebrates. **STATUS AND HABITAT** Widespread breeder in mainland Europe that winters in Africa. Has bred in Britain but its status here is really that of a vagrant, usually turning up in spring and autumn; perhaps 10 or so might be recorded in a good year, generally favouring wetlands and open, lightly wooded countryside.

broad wings and
obvious 'fingers'

eastern birds tend to be rather
uniformly brown, lacking any
'warmth' in the colour

tail can look
square-ended
when fully fanned

NORTHERN HARRIER

Circus cyaneus hudsonius | WINGSPAN 100–115cm

Long-winged, long-tailed raptor and the North American race of the Hen Harrier. Sexes are dissimilar in plumage terms and males are smaller than females.

IMMATURE

underparts are flushed orange; head and neck are dark and unstreaked

MALE

streaking and spotting on underparts

FEMALE

Adult male has a blue-grey head and upperparts; white rump is obvious only in flight. Underparts are pale with reddish streaks. In flight, dark trailing edge to white underwings and black wingtips are most striking when seen from below. Note the faintly barred, black-tipped tail. (Male Hen Harrier is similar but lacks red streaking on underparts; tail is barred in birds in their 2nd calendar year but unbarred in adult). Adult female is brown with darker barring on upperwings and tail, and a narrow white rump. Underparts are pale with dark barring on wings and tail, and streaking on breast. Immature recalls adult female; seen from below and in flight, its dark head contrasts with pale underparts (tinged reddish orange on body) and wing coverts, which have little or no streaking (immature Hen Harrier only rarely flushed orange, but invariably shows considerable streaking). A distinctive broad, dark neck band, or 'boa', that almost meets on the foreneck is a good identification feature when present. **VOICE** Mostly silent. **HABITS** In typical flight, glides low over the ground. **STATUS AND HABITAT** Widespread in North America. Vagrants here turn up in autumn and winter, and favour open country.

PALLID HARRIER

Circus macrourus | WINGSPAN 97–118cm

Elegant long-tailed, long-winged raptor. Shares plumage characters with both Hen (*C. cyaneus*) and Montagu's (*C. pygargus*) harriers, but has the proportions of the latter. Sexes are dissimilar.

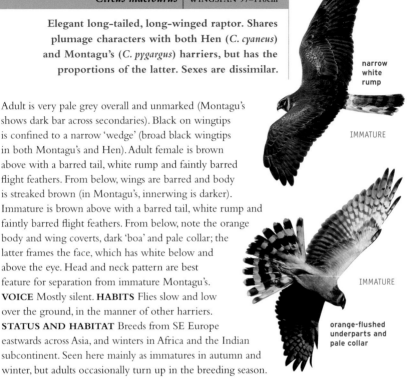

narrow white rump

IMMATURE

Adult is very pale grey overall and unmarked (Montagu's shows dark bar across secondaries). Black on wingtips is confined to a narrow 'wedge' (broad black wingtips in both Montagu's and Hen). Adult female is brown above with a barred tail, white rump and faintly barred flight feathers. From below, wings are barred and body is streaked brown (in Montagu's, innerwing is darker). Immature is brown above with a barred tail, white rump and faintly barred flight feathers. From below, note the orange body and wing coverts, dark 'boa' and pale collar; the latter frames the face, which has white below and above the eye. Head and neck pattern are best feature for separation from immature Montagu's. **VOICE** Mostly silent. **HABITS** Flies slow and low over the ground, in the manner of other harriers. **STATUS AND HABITAT** Breeds from SE Europe eastwards across Asia, and winters in Africa and the Indian subcontinent. Seen here mainly as immatures in autumn and winter, but adults occasionally turn up in the breeding season.

IMMATURE

orange-flushed underparts and pale collar

MALE

'ghostly' white appearance except for black 'wedge' on primaries (black is much more extensive in both male Montagu's and Hen harriers)

LESSER KESTREL

Falco naumanni | WINGSPAN 65–72cm

pale claws, a diagnostic
feature, are not always
easy to see

Superficially similar to Kestrel (*F. tinnunculus*),
but with proportionately shorter wings and tail.
Attention to plumage details is needed for
certain identification. Sexes are dissimilar.

FEMALE

FEMALE

Adult male has a white throat and unmarked blue-grey head (streaked in
Kestrel, and with pale cheek). In flight and from above, unmarked back and
wing coverts are separated from dark flight feathers by a bluish panel (in Kestrel,
mantle is spotted and blue panel is absent). From below, underwings are paler
than those of Kestrel and with fewer markings except for dark trailing edge
and 'dipped-in-ink' wingtips; body is flushed pinkish orange and lightly
spotted. Adult female and juvenile are similar to their Kestrel counterparts;
from above and in flight, back and wing coverts are orange-brown and
barred, flight feathers are dark, rump is blue-grey and tail is brown
and barred. From below, appears paler overall than Kestrel, with
lightly barred wings and a streaked body. All birds have pale
claws (black in Kestrel). **VOICE** Utters a partridge-like *tche-
tche-tchee*, quite unlike that of Kestrel. However, vagrants here
are usually silent. **HABITS** Glides, circles and occasionally
hovers like a Kestrel. **STATUS AND HABITAT** Breeds in
S Europe and winters in Africa.
Vagrants here usually turn up in
spring and favour open country.

MALE

blue border to unmarked
orange-brown wing
coverts and back

MALE

RED-FOOTED FALCON

Falco vespertinus | FV | WINGSPAN 65–75cm

An elegant falcon. Sexes are dissimilar. Male and female are unmistakable but juvenile could be confused with a juvenile Hobby (*F. subbuteo*).

MALE

FEMALE

dark 'mask'

MALE

FEMALE

IMMATURE

barred tail, compare juvenile Hobby

Adult male is dark grey overall with silvery primaries obvious from above in flight. Note the red vent and thighs; also has red feet and red skin around the eye. Immature male is similar but with paler underparts and a pale face and throat. Adult female has an orange-buff crown and underparts, a barred grey back, white cheeks and throat, and a dark 'mask' around the eye. Juvenile has a whitish face and dark 'mask' around the eye, and a dark-streaked brown crown. Feathers on back and upperwing coverts are dark with brown margins, and tail is barred and brown (juvenile Hobby's tail is unbarred). Underparts are pale with dark streaks. **VOICE** Vagrants here are mostly silent. **HABITS** Often hovers like a Kestrel (*F. tinnunculus*), and sits on telegraph wires and fenceposts. **STATUS AND HABITAT** Breeds from E Europe eastwards, and winters in Africa. Spring migration has an easterly bias and hence most records here (10–20 in a good year) are at this time of year. Vagrants favour open country, including heaths and wetlands.

GYR FALCON

Falco rusticolus | YF | WINGSPAN 110–134cm

Impressive falcon the size of a Buzzard (*Buteo buteo*). White morph is unmistakable, other morphs could be confused with Peregrine (*F. peregrinus*). Sexes have similar plumages; female is larger than male.

GREY MORPH

wings are broad and body is bulky

Compared to Peregrine, note the Gyr Falcon's much larger size, more bulky body and broader, less pointed wings. Adult white morph has a mainly white head and underparts; upperparts, including uppertail, are white with variable amounts of dark barring, and black-tipped primaries. Adult grey morph has a grey head and upperparts; underparts are pale with dark barring. Adult dark morph has a dark brown head and upperparts, with overall paler but heavily streaked underparts. Immatures are similar to their adult morph counterparts but overall more grubby. **VOICE** Mostly silent. **HABITS** Often perches on rocky outcrops and cliffs. **STATUS AND HABITAT** Widespread Arctic breeder that moves south in winter. Vagrants here usually turn up in winter or early spring, generally favouring rugged coastlines.

WHITE MORPH

GREY MORPH

ELEONORA'S FALCON

Falco eleonorae | WINGSPAN 87–104cm

Elegant, aerobatic falcon. Recalls an outsized Hobby (*F. subbuteo*) but note the proportionately longer wings and tail. Occurs in 2 colour morphs; sexes are similar.

PALE MORPH

Adult dark morph is dark sooty brown overall with darker underwing coverts. Adult pale morph has dark grey-brown upperparts. Head pattern comprises a dark 'mask', and white throat and cheeks. Underside of body is otherwise orange-buff with dark streaking. Underwings are overall dark grey with blackish underwing coverts, and tail is barred. Immature has a grey-buff head with a dark 'mask'. Upperparts are otherwise grey-brown with pale feather margins on back and mantle; underwings are strongly barred, mostly dark grey but buffish on coverts; body is buffish and heavily streaked. Legs, feet, cere and eye-surround are yellow in all birds. The underwing coverts are always the darkest part of the bird in all ages. **VOICE** Vagrants here are mostly silent. **HABITS** A superb flyer that catches small birds in flight. Soars and 'stoops' with ease; wingbeats are deep and rapid in direct flight. **STATUS AND HABITAT** A Mediterranean breeder (Sep–Oct) that winters in Madagascar. Vagrants here are likely to occur in late summer and autumn.

dark underwing coverts

DARK MORPH

PALE MORPH

DARK MORPH

long-winged, long-tailed appearance
is unique among falcons

SHORT-TOED EAGLE

Circaetus gallicus | WINGSPAN 165–175cm

Large, broad-winged and overall rather pale eagle when seen from below. Head is proportionately rather large. Sexes are similar.

IMMATURE

head often darkest part of bird when seen from below

Adult has a brown head and upperparts, the wing coverts subtly paler and more rufous, and the tail with dark barring. Seen from below in flight, the dark head contrasts with the otherwise overall whitish plumage; also shows dark wingtips and carpal bar, faintly grey barring on underwing and dark spotting on breast. Immature is similar but upperparts are paler with pale margin to upperwing coverts; pale underparts are less heavily marked than in adult. All birds have yellow eyes, legs and feet. **VOICE** Vagrants here are mostly silent. **HABITS** Soars on flattish wings and sometimes 'hangs' motionless in headwinds and on updraughts, occasionally appearing to hover. Feeds primarily on reptiles. **STATUS AND HABITAT** A Mediterranean breeder that winters in Africa. Vagrants here are likely to turn up in autumn, and favour open country and coastal districts.

BAILLON'S CRAKE

Porzana pusilla | VC | LENGTH 16–18cm

Tiny, dumpy wetland bird that vaguely recalls a miniature short-billed Water Rail (*Rallus aquaticus*). Its favoured habitat and unobtrusive habits make it a challenge to see well. Sexes are similar.

consider yourself lucky if you get good views of Baillon's Crake – they favour the cover of dense wetland vegetation. Calling males in spring offer the best opportunities for getting clear views

short primary projection

Adult has chestnut-brown upperparts heavily marked with white and black on back. Underparts and face are mainly blue-grey but flanks, as well as undertail, are barred black and white (in Little Crake, flanks are unbarred and back has a few white markings). Bill is uniformly bluish green (all Little Crakes have a reddish base to bill). Juvenile/1st-winter is paler overall, the bluish elements of plumage particularly pale but heavily barred except on face. Legs are dull yellowish in all birds. **VOICE** Territorial males have a 'croaking' song that is remarkably similar to the call of a Marsh Frog (*Pelophylax ridibundus*). **HABITS** Usually keeps to the cover of dense wetland vegetation, venturing into the open only briefly. Fortunately, some birds in spring are vocal. **STATUS AND HABITAT** Breeds locally in mainland Europe and winters in Africa. Vagrants here are likely to turn up in spring and autumn, and favour well-vegetated freshwater marshes.

LITTLE CRAKE

Porzana parva | JC | LENGTH 17–19cm

Tiny wetland bird. Similar to Baillon's Crake (particularly male) but with subtly different plumage and a relatively longer tail and primary projection. Sexes are dissimilar.

MALE

bill is yellow with a red base in all birds

long primary projection

almost unmarked flanks

FEMALE

Adult male has brown upperparts, heavily marked with black on back (Baillon's also shows extensive white). Underparts and face are mainly blue-grey. Flanks are virtually unmarked (barred black and white in Baillon's). Bill is yellow with a reddish base (uniformly bluish green in Baillon's). Female is paler overall, particularly on underparts which are overall pale buffish; throat is white. Juvenile/1st-winter recalls adult female but underparts are whitish with barring on flanks, and it has 2 pale 'tiger stripes' on mantle and a distinctive pale face. **VOICE** Male's song (sung at night) is a repeated, yapping *kwip* that gradually accelerates and lowers in pitch. **HABITS** Usually keeps to dense cover but occasionally feeds in the open on muddy wetland margins. **STATUS AND HABITAT** Widespread breeder in E Europe eastwards, wintering in Africa. Vagrants here are perhaps most likely to turn in early spring, favouring well-vegetated freshwater wetlands.

SORA

Porzana carolina | JR | LENGTH 18–21cm

Dumpy waterbird that is very similar to a Spotted Crake
(*P. porzana*). Attention to plumage details is needed to
ensure correct identification. Sexes are similar.

face is darkish in all birds
and lacks the white spots
seen in Spotted Crake

1ST-WINTER

For separation from Spotted Crake, note
the absence of white spots on the face,
throat and breast, and the lack of white
transverse bars on the tertials. Crown
is unstreaked, with a dark central stripe
(uniformly streaked in Spotted Crake), and
bill is yellow (red-based in Spotted). Adult
has a blue-grey face, neck and breast with
a black patch between base of bill and
eye, running down centre of throat. Belly
is pale but flanks are barred brown, black
and white. Upperparts are brown, spangled
with white on back; undertail is creamy white. Juvenile/1st-winter recalls adult but blue-
grey elements of plumage are buff, and bill is darker. Legs are yellowish green in all birds.
VOICE Vagrants here are silent. **HABITS** Typically skulks along marsh margins and walks
with a bobbing action. **STATUS AND HABITAT** Widespread breeder in North America
that winters in Central America and N South America. Vagrants here are likely to turn up in
autumn and favour coastal freshwater wetlands.

PURPLE GALLINULE

Porphyrio martinicus | LENGTH 29–33cm

Plump-bodied wetland bird. Rather like a Moorhen (*Gallinula chloropus*) but with longer, stouter legs and plumage differences. Sexes are similar.

Adult has a mostly deep bluish-purple head, neck and underparts (dark in Moorhen), and a green back and wing coverts (dull brown in Moorhen). Has pale undertail coverts but lacks the white line on the flanks seen in Moorhen. Legs are yellow, eye is red, and bill is red with a yellow tip and a pale blue frontal shield (frontal shield is red in Moorhen). Juvenile/1st-winter is mostly warm orange-buff on head and neck, with a bluish tinge to underparts; undertail coverts are pale, and back and wing coverts are greyish green. Bill and legs are dull yellow. Note that juvenile/1st-winter Moorhen is overall buffish brown with a pale line along flanks. **VOICE** Vagrants here are mostly silent. **HABITS** Long toes allow it to walk on floating vegetation. Swims well but also clambers through vegetation. **STATUS AND HABITAT** Locally common breeder in North America that winters in Central America and N South America. Vagrants here are likely to turn up in autumn and favour freshwater wetlands.

although immature birds lack the vivid blue of adults, they are nevertheless colourful birds

1ST-WINTER

striking yellow legs and feet seen in all birds

AMERICAN COOT

Fulica americana | AO | LENGTH 31–37cm

Dumpy, mainly dark waterbird. Superficially very similar to a Coot (*F. atra*) but separable on plumage and structural details. Sexes are similar.

dark band on bill provides the easiest means of separating this species from Coot, whose bill is pure white

Adult has essentially all-dark plumage (marginally paler than in Coot), darkest on head and neck; note the white on the outer-tail feathers. Bill and frontal shield are mainly white except for dark sub-terminal band on bill and small red patch on forehead. Also lacks black tick of feathering at base of frontal shield seen in Coot. Beady eye is red, and legs are greenish yellow with long, lobed toes that facilitate swimming. In flight, has a white trailing edge to otherwise dark, rounded wings. Juvenile is dark greyish brown with a dull pink bill at first, but acquires adult-like plumage by 1st-winter; bill is pure white until early autumn and red on forehead is absent. **VOICE** Utters a loud *kwoot* call. **HABITS** Feeds by upending or by making shallow dives, but also grazes waterside vegetation. **STATUS AND HABITAT** Widespread breeder in North America, where northern birds move south and to coasts in winter. Vagrants here are likely to turn up in autumn and winter, and should be looked for among Coot flocks on fresh waters.

white on outer-tail feathers can be seen most easily in flight

SANDHILL CRANE

Grus canadensis | LENGTH 80–90cm

Large, long-legged bird. Similar to a Crane (*G. grus*) but smaller and with subtly different plumage. Sexes are similar.

Adult has overall blue-grey plumage, palest on face and with variable rufous feathering on back and upperwings. Neck is uniformly coloured (strikingly black and white in adult Crane). Has a red crown; legs and dagger-like bill are dark. Immature has variably blue-grey and rufous plumage; usually rufous predominates on head, neck and back, and coloration is more intense than in immature Crane. Bill is dull pink, and red on crown is absent. **VOICE** Vagrants here are usually silent. **HABITS** Has a stately posture and gait, like a Crane. **STATUS AND HABITAT** Very locally common breeder in North America that winters in southern states. Vagrants here are likely to turn up in autumn and favour open habitats.

rufous elements of plumage are far more intense and striking than in immature Crane

IMMATURE

LITTLE BUSTARD

Tetrax tetrax | LENGTH 40–45cm

Stocky bird that recalls a long-legged, long-necked grouse or perhaps a short-tailed female pheasant. Wing pattern is diagnostic in flying birds. Sexes are dissimilar.

in terms of shape, recalls a large duck or small goose in flight but extent of white in wings is diagnostic

In flight, all birds are unmistakable owing to extensive white on upperwings, which contrasts with black primaries and primary covert margins, and brown innerwing coverts; underwings are white with black tips and trailing margins to primaries. Adult breeding male has grey, black and white on head and neck, with otherwise marbled sandy-brown upperparts and white underparts. Adult female, non-breeding adult male and immature have a marbled sandy-brown head, neck and upperparts, and a paler belly. **VOICE** Vagrants are silent. **HABITS** Generally wary, keeping to the cover of vegetation. Typical views are brief or partial, or of flying birds. **STATUS AND HABITAT** Locally common resident and partial migrant in Iberia and S France. Vagrants here are likely to turn up in late autumn or winter, and usually favour arable crops and grassland.

GREAT BUSTARD

Otis tarda | US | LENGTH 75–105cm

Huge, long-legged, long-necked bird. Sexes are dissimilar, the male appreciably larger and thicker-necked than the female, and with subtly different plumage.

MALE

FEMALE

Adult male has a blue-grey head and neck, grading to a chestnut 'collar' and upper breast; shows clear demarcation from otherwise white underparts. Back, uppertail and innerwing are mostly chestnut brown with fine, dark markings (tail is white-tipped); white panel on wing coverts shows as white lower margin to wings in standing birds. In flight, upperwings show extensive black and white. Adult female is similar but slimmer overall, with a grey-brown neck and less extensive white on wings. Immature male recalls adult female but has more white on wings and hint of chestnut collar. **VOICE** Vagrants are mostly silent. **HABITS** Wary and hard to observe at close range; takes flight at the slightest sign of danger. **STATUS AND HABITAT** A bird of wide-open country. Mostly sedentary in Iberia and E Europe; birds from further east wander outside breeding season, especially when winter weather is bad. Formerly bred here but extinct by 1840s; now reintroduced.

MALE

BLACK-WINGED STILT

Himantopus himantopus | IT | LENGTH 33–36cm

Elegant and unmistakable wader with incredibly
long legs and a needle-like bill. Extent of black on
head and neck is subtly variable. Males and
females are generally separable.

females generally
have whiter heads
than males; some males
have an intense black
crown and mask

Adult male has a mainly white head, neck and underparts, with variable amounts of black on
crown and nape, and behind eye. Back and wings are jet black. In flight, wings are uniformly
black and contrast with white 'wedge' on back and white tail. Adult female and immatures are
usually subtly dark sooty brown (not jet black) on back, and markings on head and neck are
grubby grey (not black). Immature is similar to adult female, but many wing and back
feathers have brown margins, wings have a white trailing edge, and white elements of head
and neck plumage are grubby. In all birds, bill is dark and legs are red. **VOICE** Vagrants are
mostly silent, but birds occasionally utter a shrill, tern-like *kyerk,
kyerk…* **HABITS** Wades in open water and
catches invertebrates with its fine bill.

STATUS AND HABITAT
Favours open water-
bodies (including saline
lagoons). Breeds in S
Europe and winters
mainly in Africa.
Vagrants here are
likely to turn
up in spring.

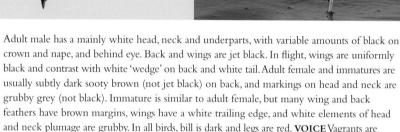

long, red legs and black and white plumage
are diagnostic features for the species

CREAM-COLOURED COURSER

Cursorius cursor | LENGTH 24–27cm

often adopts an upright stance but typically tilts forward to feed

Atypical and unmistakable wader. Superficially plover-like but with a proportionately large head and downcurved bill. Sexes are similar.

1ST-WINTER

contrasting black outerwing is striking in flight

Adult has overall sandy-brown upperparts and white underparts. Diagnostic head pattern comprises a blue-grey rear crown and black eye-stripe behind eye, the two separated by broad white supercilia that meet on the nape. Seen in flight from above, black outerwing contrasts with otherwise sandy upperparts; seen from below, underwings are all black. Juvenile/1st-winter has a subtly 'colder', greyer-looking head, neck and upperparts, the feathers on the back with dark markings; head pattern recalls that of adult but crown and face are streaked. All birds have pale legs; adult's bill is dark, while that of juvenile/1st-winter is pale and dark-tipped. **VOICE** Vagrants here are silent. **HABITS** Runs at speed with a horizontal stance, then pauses and stands still, adopting a rather upright posture. **STATUS AND HABITAT** Resident and partial migrant from North Africa and Middle East. Vagrants here have turned up mainly in autumn, but also in spring. A desert bird by nature, vagrants invariably favour open habitats with short vegetation.

COLLARED PRATINCOLE

Glareola pratincola | KM | LENGTH 24–28cm

Atypical wader that is unmistakable as a pratincole. Has long wings and a forked tail; supremely aerobatic on the wing. Sexes are similar.

reddish underwing coverts are a feature shared with Oriental Pratincole

white trailing edge to innerwing

on the ground, stands and runs like a plover

Adult has mainly dark sandy-brown upperparts and a pale belly. Has a dark sandy-brown head and neck with a creamy-yellow throat, defined by a black border. Bill is slightly hook-tipped, red at the base and with a black tip; legs are dark. Seen in flight from above, blackish primaries contrast with sandy-brown innerwing, and note the white trailing edge to innerwing (beware, this feature is sometimes reduced through wear by summer). White rump contrasts with black tail. Seen in flight from below, has maroon wing coverts (hard to discern in harsh light). Juvenile/1st-winter is similar to adult but back feathers have pale margins, bill is uniformly dark, and pattern on throat is subdued. On perched birds the tail extends beyond the primary tips (beware broken tail feathers though). **VOICE** Vagrants are mostly silent. **HABITS** Sometimes feeds on the ground but typically catches insects on the wing; flight pattern recalls a tern or an outsized Swallow (*Hirundo rustica*). **STATUS AND HABITAT** Breeds in S Europe and winters in Africa. Vagrants are likely to turn up in spring or early summer; 3 or 4 might be recorded in a good year. Favours margins of coastal freshwater and brackish pools.

ORIENTAL PRATINCOLE

Glareola maldivarum | GM | LENGTH 23–27cm

Marginally smaller than Collared and Black-winged pratincoles, but with plumage characters in common with both. Sexes are similar.

lacks white trailing edge to innerwing seen in Collared

on the wing, flies and feeds like an outsized Swallow

relatively short tail, when compared to Collared Pratincole

Adult has mainly sandy-brown upperparts and a pale lower belly. Has a sandy-brown head and neck, with a creamy-yellow throat defined by a black border; breast is sandy brown, grading to warm buff on upper belly. Bill has a black tip with red at base (similar to Collared); legs are dark. Seen in flight from above, dark primaries are darker than sandy-brown innerwing; white trailing edge to innerwing is absent (as with Black-winged). White rump contrasts with black tail, but tail itself is shorter than in Collared and Black-winged. Seen in flight from below, underwings have reddish underwing coverts (as with Collared). In standing birds, primaries project well beyond tail (as in Black-winged, but tail is even shorter). Juvenile/1st-winter is similar to adult but back feathers have pale margins, bill is uniformly dark, and pattern on throat is subdued. **VOICE** Vagrants are mostly silent. **HABITS** Sometimes feeds on the ground but typically catches insects on the wing. **STATUS AND HABITAT** Breeds in South Asia and winters from Southeast Asia to N Australia. Vagrants here are likely to turn up in spring and favour open coastal wetlands.

BLACK-WINGED PRATINCOLE

Glareola nordmanni | KW | LENGTH 24–28cm

Atypical wader that is very similar to a Collared Pratincole. Separable using subtle plumage and structural differences. Sexes are similar

dark underwings allow separation from Collared and Oriental pratincoles

innerwing lacks the white trailing edge seen in flying Collared Pratincole

has much less red on bill than in Collared and Oriental pratincoles

Adult has mainly grey-brown upperparts (darker than in Collared) and a pale belly. Has a grey-brown head and neck, with dark lores and a creamy-yellow throat that is defined by a black border. Bill is slightly hook-tipped, with a black tip and less red at base than in Collared; legs are dark. Seen in flight from above, blackish primaries are subtly darker than grey-brown innerwing, and note the absence of a white trailing edge to innerwing seen in Collared; white rump contrasts with black tail. Seen in flight from below, underwings are uniformly dark (Collared has maroon underwing coverts). In standing birds, primaries project beyond tail (in Collared, tail projects beyond primaries). Juvenile/1st-winter is similar to adult but back feathers have pale margins, bill is uniformly dark, and pattern on throat is subdued. **VOICE** Vagrants are mostly silent. **HABITS** Sometimes feeds on the ground but typically catches insects on the wing. **STATUS AND HABITAT** Breeds in E Europe and winters in Africa. Vagrants here (on average, 1 per year) are likely to turn up in spring or early summer. Favours margins of coastal freshwater and brackish pools.

primaries project beyond tail in standing birds

SEMIPALMATED PLOVER

Charadrius semipalmatus | TV | LENGTH 16–17cm

Small, dumpy wader. North American counterpart of the Ringed Plover (*C. hiaticula*), which it closely resembles. Sexes are subtly dissimilar only as adults.

WINTER

in all individuals, bill is noticeably stubbier than in Ringed Plover

1ST-WINTER

Compared to Ringed Plover, smaller size, head pattern, short and very stubby bill, and call are best characters for identification. Slimmer build and webbing between outer toes are hard to discern. Adult male has mainly sandy-brown upperparts and white underparts with a black breast band and collar. Black patch through eye and on forecrown defines squarish white patch in front of eye; supercilium behind eye is very narrow (much larger in Ringed). Legs are orange-yellow and bill is orange with a dark tip. In other adult plumages and seasons, black elements of plumage on head are mainly brown, especially on forecrown; bill is mainly dark but with dull orange at base of lower mandible. 1st-winter is similar to winter adult but breast band is small and often incomplete. Legs are often bright yellow. A good field character is white 'wedge' at base of mandible, above gape. **VOICE** Utters a soft *tchu-eep* call (vaguely like that of a Spotted Redshank, *Tringa erythropus*). **HABITS** Runs at speed and then stands still for a few seconds before picking a food item from the ground. **STATUS AND HABITAT** Widespread breeder across Arctic North America that winters on coasts further south. Vagrants here are likely to turn up in autumn, where they are found on shores with Ringed Plovers.

KILLDEER

Charadrius vociferus | KL | LENGTH 24–26cm

Boldly marked, long-legged, long-tailed
plover. Its 2 black breast bands are striking
and diagnostic. Sexes are similar.

double breast band is a
good identification feature
in all individuals

1ST-WINTER

Long wings and tail give
all standing birds an
elongated appearance. In
flight, striking features are
the long wings with a bold
white wingbar, and the long,
wedge-shaped tail with an orange
rump. Adult has mainly brown
upperparts and white underparts.
Has 2 black breast bands (upper
one continues as a narrow collar)
and striking black and white
markings on face. Bill is slender
and dark, and legs are pale.
Tail darkens towards tip,
but note the terminal
white margin.
1st-winter is similar to
adult but black elements
of plumage are dark brown.
VOICE Utters a shrill, piping
kiu-dee or *tee-dee-dee*. **HABITS**
Runs at speed for short distances,
then pauses to pick invertebrate
prey from the ground. **STATUS
AND HABITAT** Widespread North
American breeder that moves south in
autumn and winter. Vagrants here
(on average, 1 per year) are likely
to turn up in autumn and early
winter, and favour open areas
of short grassland.

long-winged
and long-tailed
appearance

KENTISH PLOVER

Charadrius alexandrinus | KP | LENGTH 15–17cm

Dumpy little plover that is invariably found on the coast. Overall much paler than species with which it might be confused. Sexes are dissimilar.

MALE

Summer adult male has mainly pale sandy-brown upperparts and white underparts. Sandy crown is marked with black at front and rufous at back; also has black through the eye and a black patch on side of breast. Legs and bill are black. Summer adult female, immature and winter adult are similar but black elements of plumage are pale sandy-brown (concolourous with the rest of the upperparts); legs are dull brown. All birds show a striking wingbar in flight. **VOICE** Utters a soft *bruip* call. **HABITS** Feeds like other small plover species: runs quickly, then pauses to pick food items from the ground. **STATUS AND HABITAT** Breeds in S Europe and winters from the Mediterranean region southwards. Scarce passage migrant here, mainly in spring and autumn, with around 30–35 records in most years. Usually found on sandy estuaries, although visitors seldom stay for long.

FEMALE

appears pale faced at any distance

MALE

LESSER SAND PLOVER

Charadrius mongolus | DQ | LENGTH 17–19cm

Summer adults could be confused only with summer Greater Sand and Caspian plovers. Non-breeding birds could be confused with those species or winter Kentish. Sexes are dissimilar.

compared to Greater Sand Plover, bill is more 'in proportion' to head

WINTER

SUMMER

In all birds, bill is much stouter than in Kentish or Caspian, but smaller than in Greater Sand. Legs are longer than in Kentish but shorter than in Caspian. Adult male has a speckled black forehead, black 'mask' and white throat, these framed by orange-red that extends as a breast band. Note that in the eastern race forecrown is white with a dark central line. Crown and upperparts are otherwise sandy brown, and underparts are otherwise white. Bill and legs are dark. Shows a white wingbar in flight. Adult female is similar but black elements and colours in plumage are usually duller and paler. Winter adults have white underparts; sandy-brown upperparts extend as a patch on side of breast. **VOICE** Utters a soft *trrrk* call. **HABITS** Like other plovers, runs at speed for short distances, then pauses to pick invertebrate prey from the sand. **STATUS AND HABITAT** Breeds in Central Asia and winters on coasts of Southeast Asia and East Africa. Vagrants here are likely to turn up in late summer and autumn, favouring coasts.

GREATER SAND PLOVER

Charadrius leschenaultii | DP | LENGTH 19–22cm

Large-billed plover. Summer adults could only really be confused with summer Lesser Sand and Caspian plovers. Non-breeding birds could be confused with those species or winter Kentish. Sexes are dissimilar.

bill is large and chunky

WINTER

FEMALE, SUMMER

In all birds, bill looks disproportionately large. Legs are relatively long too, and paler than in Lesser Sand. Adult male has a white forehead, black 'mask' and white throat, the two framed by orange-red that extends as a breast band. Crown and upperparts are otherwise sandy brown, and underparts are otherwise white. Bill is dark. Shows a white wingbar in flight. Adult female is similar but black elements and colours in plumage are paler and duller. Winter adults have white underparts; sandy-brown upperparts extend as a patch on side of breast. **VOICE** Utters a trilling *trrrr* call. **HABITS** Like other plovers, runs at speed for short distances, then pauses to pick invertebrate prey from sand. **STATUS AND HABITAT** Breeds in Central Asia and winters on coasts of Southeast Asia and East Africa. Vagrants here could turn up at any time, on coasts.

MALE, SUMMER

rather long-legged appearance

CASPIAN PLOVER

Charadrius asiaticus | LENGTH 19–21cm

Long-legged, plump-bodied plover. Sexes are dissimilar. Summer adult male could be confused with a female Dotterel (*C. morinellus*). In other plumages, potential exists for confusion with other similar-sized plovers.

long, pale legs
and long, thin bill

All birds have very long, pale legs and a thin, dark bill. Summer adult male has a white face, dark brown crown, and a dark stripe behind the eye that connects with the otherwise sandy-brown upperparts. Breast is maroon with a black border on lower margin; underparts are otherwise white. In summer adult female and winter birds, reddish breast band is replaced by sandy brown, the feathers having pale fringes. 1st-winter resembles a winter adult but back feathers have pale fringes; also recalls an immature Dotterel but lacks that species' pale breast band. In flight, all birds have a pale wingbar, prominent only at the base of the primaries. **VOICE** Utters a soft *chrrrp* call. **HABITS** Runs at speed for short distances, then pauses to pick invertebrate prey from the sand. **STATUS AND HABITAT** Breeds in Central Asia and winters in Africa. Vagrants here are most likely to turn up in spring and favour open areas with short vegetation.

FEMALE, SUMMER

MALE, SUMMER

combination of white face
and reddish chest make
male unmistakable

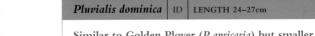

AMERICAN GOLDEN PLOVER

Pluvialis dominica | ID | LENGTH 24–27cm

Similar to Golden Plover (*P. apricaria*) but smaller and longer-legged. Subtle plumage differences also exist, and aid separation from rarer Pacific Golden. Most vagrants here are immatures. Sexes are dissimilar as adults.

1ST-WINTER

short tertials, long primary projection

longer-legged than Golden Plover

1ST-WINTER

dusky underwing (white in Golden Plover)

SUMMER

In all birds, note the dusky grey-brown underwings (Pacific Golden shares this feature but Golden Plover has white axillaries or 'armpits'). In standing birds, primaries project well beyond tail, and 4 or 5 primaries extend beyond tertials. Tips of tertials fall well short of the tail tip. Summer adult male has striking black underparts, merging into golden-spangled dark upperparts with a broad white band running from forehead down side of neck (in Golden and Pacific Golden in same plumage, white extends down flanks). Summer adult female is similar but dark elements of plumage are mottled. Winter adult looks grey overall, with faint spangling on back, a dark crown and a pale supercilium. 1st-winter is similar to winter adult (greyer than 1st-winter Golden, and with a much more prominent pale supercilium and dark cap). **VOICE** Utters a mournful, disyllabic *chlu-ee*. **HABITS** Feeds like a Golden Plover: stands still, then runs quickly before pausing to pick food items from the ground. **STATUS AND HABITAT** Breeds in N North America and typically flies non-stop to NW South America, then to the south of the continent. Vagrants usually turn up in autumn, generally favouring short coastal grassland.

PACIFIC GOLDEN PLOVER

Pluvialis fulva | IF | LENGTH 21–25cm

Another relative of Golden Plover (*P. apricaria*). Longer-legged and further separated from that species (and American Golden) by subtle plumage differences. Sexes are dissimilar during breeding season.

WINTER

dusky underwing is a feature in common with American Golden Plover

In all birds, note the dusky grey-brown underwings (American Golden shares this feature but Golden Plover has white axillaries or 'armpits'). In standing birds, projection of primaries beyond tail is shorter than in American Golden; tertials are relatively long, with only 2–3 projecting primaries. Tertial tips are equal to tail tip, or slightly longer. Summer adult male has black underparts separated from golden-spangled upperparts by a broad white band running from forehead, down sides of neck and along flanks. On average, upperpart spangling includes more white than in Golden. Adult summer female is similar to male but dark elements of plumage are mottled. Winter adult looks grey overall with gold spangling on back, and yellow flush to face and breast. Juvenile/1st-winter is similar to winter adult (and 1st-winter Golden); features to concentrate on are leg length, underwing colour, length of exposed tertials and call. **VOICE** Utters a sharp *chlu-it*, reminiscent of the call of a Spotted Redshank (*Tringa erythropus*). **HABITS** Feeds like an American Golden Plover: stands still, then runs quickly before pausing to pick food items from the ground. **STATUS AND HABITAT** Breeds in NW North America and NE Siberia, and winters further south on the West Coast. Vagrants here might turn up in autumn, usually favouring short coastal grassland.

WINTER

long tertials, short primary projection

SUMMER

broad white band continues along flanks

SOCIABLE PLOVER

Vanellus gregarius | IP | LENGTH 27–30cm

Plump-bodied plover with extremely distinctive plumage patterns, especially when seen in flight. Sexes are similar.

striking black and white pattern on wings seen in flight

1ST-WINTER

Summer adult has mostly grey-brown plumage with a dark crown and eye-stripe, and a white supercilium and white below eye. Has a dark belly that is rich chestnut at rear margin; rear of underparts, and undertail, are white. Almost unmistakable when seen in flight from above: upperwing pattern (reminiscent of a juvenile Sabine's Gull, *Xema sabini*) comprises triangles of black on wingtips, white on centre of wings, and grey-brown across innerwing and back. Tail is white with a black tip. Winter adult is similar to summer adult except markings are duller and paler, and belly is white, not black. Juvenile/1st-winter is similar to winter adult but browner overall, with pale fringes to back feathers. **VOICE** Vagrants are mostly silent. **HABITS** Vagrants here often associate with winter Lapwing (*V. vanellus*) flocks. **STATUS AND HABITAT** Breeds in Central Asia and winters further south. Vagrants here (on average, 1 per year) are most likely to turn up in late autumn and winter.

1ST-WINTER

long white undertail coverts

WHITE-TAILED PLOVER

Vanellus leucurus | LENGTH 26–29cm

Elegant plover with long, bright yellow legs and a distinctive upperwing pattern in flight. Sexes are similar.

pale-faced appearance is common to all birds; overall plumage is brightest in spring adults

Adult has mostly grey-brown upperparts with an almost unmarked paler head. Neck and breast are brown and contrast with otherwise white underparts; black and white colours of wing feathers are visible along lower margin of wing in resting birds. Seen in flight from above, upperwing pattern (reminiscent of juvenile Sabine's Gull, *Xema sabini*, or adult Sociable Plover) comprises triangles of black on wingtips, separated by a broad white band from grey-brown across innerwing and back. Tail is pure white. Bill is long, thin and dark, and legs are very long and yellow, and extend well beyond the tail tip in flight. Juvenile/1st-winter is similar to adult but paler overall, the back feathers with dark centres and pale margins. **VOICE** Vagrants are mostly silent. **HABITS** Often feeds in the cover of vegetation and is easily overlooked at times. **STATUS AND HABITAT** Breeds in Central Asia, and winters in India and East Africa. Vagrants here are likely to turn up in spring and autumn, and favour well-vegetated freshwater wetlands.

1ST-WINTER

long yellow legs

STILT SANDPIPER

Calidris himantopus | MI | LENGTH 18–23cm

Elegant wader with long yellowish legs. Long bill has a downcurved tip. In flight, note the long, trailing legs and white rump and uppertail. Sexes are similar.

white rump

Summer adult has a dark-streaked face and neck, with chestnut on crown and ear coverts, and a broad, pale supercilium. Underparts are strongly marked with dark bars; feathers on back have dark centres and scalloped rufous or white margins. Non-breeding adult has mainly grey upperparts and white underparts with streaks on flanks; note the pale supercilium. Juvenile/1st-winter is similar to winter adult but feathers on back have cleaner-looking pale or chestnut margins. **VOICE** Vagrants here are generally silent. **HABITS** Usually feeds in deep water, probing mud in a deliberate manner. **STATUS AND HABITAT** Breeds in N North America and winters in Central and South America. Vagrants here are most likely to occur in summer and early autumn, and favour coastal pools.

MOULTING ADULT

very long legs

1ST-WINTER

SEMIPALMATED SANDPIPER

Calidris pusilla | PZ | LENGTH 13–15cm

Small, dark-legged wader that could be confused with a
Little Stint (*C. minuta*) or Western Sandpiper. Webbing
between the toes is noticeable only at very close range.
Sexes are similar.

bill length varies considerably
between individuals

In all birds, the short, dark bill appears 'blob-tipped'
(tapering in Little Stint and Western, and also
longer and downcurved in the latter); primaries
do not project beyond tail as they do in Little
Stint. Summer adult has streaked brown
upperparts, neck and chest, and otherwise white
underparts. Many back feathers are dark-centred with rufous margins, forming a noticeable
dark area from shoulder to tertials; rufous on crown is never as striking as in Western.
Non-breeding adult has grey-brown upperparts and white underparts. Juvenile/1st-winter
has overall brown upperparts and white underparts, with rufous feathering and indistinct
white 'V's on back (very noticeable in Little Stint). Long, bold supercilium meets and
bulges at front of head; also has a rather dark crown and ear coverts, and a scaly-looking
back (due to pale feather margins). **VOICE** Utters a clipped *tchrrp* call. **HABITS** Feeds
actively like other small *Calidris*
waders, but less frenetic than
Little Stint. **STATUS AND
HABITAT** Widespread breeder
across Arctic North America,
wintering in South America.
Vagrants here (on average, 2 per
year) are likely to be 1st-winter
in autumn; they usually favour
coastal lagoons and saltmarshes.

1ST-WINTER

WESTERN SANDPIPER

Calidris mauri | ER | LENGTH 14–17cm

1ST-WINTER

Small North American wader that is similar
to a Semipalmated Sandpiper and Little Stint
(*C. minuta*). Like the former, its toes
are half-webbed. Sexes are similar.

1ST-WINTER

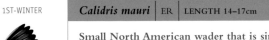

All birds have relatively long, dark legs and a tapering dark bill; bill length is variable and some birds recall a small Dunlin (*C. alpina*). Summer adult has bright rufous on crown and ear coverts, and on dark-centred back feathers. Underparts are white with streaking on neck and chest, and arrowhead streaks on breast and flanks. Non-breeding adult has grey-brown upperparts and white underparts. Juvenile/1st-winter recalls summer adult but lacks streaking on breast and flanks, and has just a hint of rufous on crown and ear coverts. Mantle has rufous feathering and indistinct white 'V's; by contrast, rest of back is grey. **VOICE** Utters a shrill *jeet* call. **HABITS** Feeds actively like other small *Calidris* waders. **STATUS AND HABITAT** Breeds in Arctic North America and winters in southern states and South America. The rarest North American wader recorded here; vagrants are likely to turn up in autumn and winter, and favour estuaries and mudflats.

longer-legged than
Semipalmated Sandpiper

rufous on face
and back

1ST-WINTER

RED-NECKED STINT

Calidris ruficollis | LENGTH 13–16cm

**Tiny wader with a short, straight bill. Immature is similar
to immature Little Stint (*C. minuta*); summer adult recalls
summer Sanderling (*C. alba*), which is much larger, with
rufous on breast as well as neck. Sexes are similar.**

Longer-bodied than Little Stint. Summer adult has reddish-orange
face and neck, streaked crown, and rufous on mantle that contrasts
with grey wing coverts. Underparts are white with streaking on
breast. Non-breeding adult has grey upperparts and white
underparts. Juvenile/1st-winter has streaked crown and
ear coverts, pale supercilium and rufous on sides of breast.
Mantle has rufous feathering and indistinct white 'V's; upperparts
are otherwise greyish and underparts are white. Separated from
juvenile/1st-winter Little Stint by grey-centred tertials (black-
centred in Little). **VOICE** Utters a shrill *chrrt* call. **HABITS** Feeds
like other small *Calidris* waders. **STATUS AND HABITAT** Breeds in NE Siberia and winters
in Southeast Asia and Australia. Vagrants are likely to turn up in autumn, and favour mudflats.

SUMMER

LONG-TOED STINT

Calidris subminuta | LENGTH 14–15cm

**Tiny, yellow-legged wader. Potential exists for confusion
with Least Sandpiper and, in certain plumages,
Temminck's Stint (*C. temminckii*).
Sexes are similar.**

Has longer legs (tarsi in particular), longer
toes and darker forecrown than Least
Sandpiper. Has shorter tail, longer legs and
shorter bill than Temminck's. Summer adult
has grey-brown upperparts with streaked
crown and rufous margins to mantle feathers.
White underparts are streaked on neck and
upper breast. Non-breeding adult has grey upperparts and white underparts. Juvenile/1st-
winter has streaked rufous crown and darkish cheek patch on otherwise pale face. Back is
brown with pale feather margins; mantle has rufous feathers and striking white 'V's. White
underparts are streaked on neck and upper breast. **VOICE** Utters a soft, trilling *chrrrp* call.
HABITS Sometimes adopts a rather upright posture. **STATUS AND HABITAT** Main range
is Asia. Vagrants here are likely to turn up in autumn.

LEAST SANDPIPER

Calidris minutilla | EP | LENGTH 13–14.5cm

Tiny wader and the smallest of its kind. Potential exists for confusion with Temminck's (*C. temminckii*) and Long-toed stints (all three are small, with yellow legs). Sexes are similar.

Slightly downcurved bill is a feature shared with Temminck's; short tail, short primary projection and compact body shape are shared with Long-toed. Summer adult has a streaked brown head and neck with a clear demarcation from white underparts; note the pale supercilium. Upperparts are brownish overall, many feathers with dark centres and buff or white margins. Winter adult is more uniformly grey-brown on upperparts and chest, with a clear demarcation from white underparts. Juvenile/1st-winter recalls summer adult but upperparts are warmer brown, feather margins are cleanly defined, and pale margins to mantle feathers align to create striking 'V's. All birds show a faint white wingbar and white sides to tail in flight. **VOICE** Utters a thin *kreet* call. **HABITS** Feeds actively around muddy margins of pools. **STATUS AND HABITAT** Breeds in Arctic North America and winters from southern USA southwards to South America. Vagrants here are likely to turn up in autumn and winter, and favour coastal pools and mudflats.

downcurved bill

1ST-WINTER

1ST-WINTER

SUMMER

yellow legs

WHITE-RUMPED SANDPIPER

Calidris fuscicollis | WU | LENGTH 16–18cm

Plump-bodied wader with an elongated-looking rear
end due to its long wings. The diagnostic white rump is
obvious only in flight. Sexes are similar.

1ST-WINTER

1ST-WINTER

In all birds primaries project well beyond tail at rest, a feature shared by
Baird's Sandpiper. Downcurved bill is mainly dark but lower mandible
has an orange base. Summer adult has rufous on back; bold streaking on
crown, neck and chest; distinct long, pale supercilium (largely lacking in Baird's); and
streaking on breast and flanks. Underparts are otherwise white. Winter adult is greyish above
and white below. Juvenile/1st-winter has dark-centred rufous back feathers with pale
margins, some of which align to create a white 'V'. Reddish-brown crown and ear coverts
contrast with otherwise pale face and long, pale supercilium. Has faint streaks on flanks.
VOICE Utters a thin *tseet* call. **HABITS** Feeds in a fairly deliberate manner. **STATUS AND
HABITAT** Breeds in N North American tundra and winters in South America. Vagrants
here are likely to turn up in autumn; they favour mudflats and
margins of coastal freshwater pools near coasts.

long wings create an
elongated appearance
to rear end

subtle orange
base to lower
mandible

BAIRD'S SANDPIPER

Calidris bairdii | BP | LENGTH 14–17cm

Short-legged wader whose long-bodied appearance allows for confusion with a White-rumped Sandpiper. Sexes are similar.

dark rump, compare White-rumped Sandpiper

1ST-WINTER

1ST-WINTER

long wings

In all birds, wings extend well beyond tail at rest. Compared to White-rumped Sandpiper, note the brown (not white) rump and uniformly dark, straight bill (no orange base to lower mandible). Summer adult has grey-brown upperparts with dark centres to some back feathers. Neck and chest are streaked but underparts are otherwise white. Winter adult has greyish upperparts and white underparts. Juvenile/1st-winter has a scaly-looking back (feathers have dark centres and pale margins) and a buffish wash to face, neck and chest; has a clear demarcation between streaked brown chest and otherwise white underparts. Indistinct pale supercilium is most obvious in front of eye. **VOICE** Utters a trilling *prrrp* call. **HABITS** Feeds in a deliberate manner. **STATUS AND HABITAT** Breeds in Arctic North America and winters in South America. Vagrants here are likely to be immatures and turn up in autumn, favouring short coastal grassland and beaches.

PECTORAL SANDPIPER

Calidris melanotos | PP | LENGTH 19–23cm

**Well-marked wader. All birds have yellowish legs, a clear
pectoral demarcation between the streaked neck and
breast, and white underparts. Sexes are similar, although
male is larger than female.**

1ST-WINTER

All birds have a gently downcurved, mainly dark bill
with a dull orange base. Summer adult has overall brown
upperparts, the back feathers having dark centres and buff margins.
Crown is rufous and contrasts with white supercilium. Non-breeding
adult is similar but markings are less intense and colourful. Juvenile/1st–
winter is similar to summer adult but with brighter upperparts; back feathers
have buff, rufous or white margins, these creating lines on the mantle and
scapular feathers. **VOICE** Utters a trilling *krrrk* call. **HABITS** Feeds in a deliberate
manner, at a slower pace than smaller *Calidris* waders. **STATUS AND HABITAT**
Breeds across Arctic North America and winters in South
America. Vagrants here (50 or so each year) are most likely
to turn up in late summer and autumn, but spring birds
have also been recorded. Freshwater pools are
usually favoured.

1ST-WINTER

JUVENILE

SHARP-TAILED SANDPIPER

Calidris acuminata | VV | LENGTH 16–18cm

Extremely well-marked wader and in many ways the Asian counterpart of the Pectoral Sandpiper. Compared to that species, the breast pattern and markings, and the call, are useful for identification. Sexes are similar.

vagrants to Britain and Ireland are likely to turn up on coastal pools

1ST-WINTER

Bill is dark with a dull yellow base. Summer adult has brown upperparts, back feathers with dark centres and buff margins. Rufous crown contrasts with white supercilium. Neck and breast are flushed orange-buff and marked with dark chevrons that continue along flanks to undertail coverts (unmarked in Pectoral Sandpiper). Non-breeding adult is less well-marked. Juvenile/1st-winter recalls summer adult but has brighter upperparts; back feathers have buff, rufous or white margins, aligning to form lines. Breast and neck are flushed orange; streaking is confined to sides (no obvious pectoral band); belly is white. **VOICE** Utters a soft *kweep* call. **HABITS** Feeds in a deliberate manner. **STATUS AND HABITAT** An Asian species. Vagrants are likely to turn up in autumn on coastal pools.

GREAT KNOT

Calidris tenuirostris | KO | LENGTH 24–27cm

compared to Knot, proportions of head and bill provide the best pointers for identification

Relatively large, plump-bodied wader with a disproportionately small head and a relatively large, long bill. Sexes are similar.

Adult (plumage most likely to be seen here) has grey-brown upperparts, feathers with clean, pale margins, tinged orange-brown on back and 'shoulders'. Head and neck are streaked, markings grading into dark arrowhead spots on lower breast and along flanks; underparts are otherwise white. Winter adult has mostly grey upperparts and immature's pattern of spotting on lower breast and flanks. Summer adult (unlikely to be seen here) has underpart markings like a juvenile/1st-winter, but upperparts reminiscent of a summer Turnstone (*Arenaria interpres*). All birds have a dark bill and dull yellow legs; in flight, note the indistinct white rump. **VOICE** Utters a soft *prrrt* call. **HABITS** Generally wary and hard to observe. **STATUS AND HABITAT** An Asian species. Vagrants here are likely to turn up in autumn and favour mudflats.

BUFF-BREASTED SANDPIPER

Tryngites subruficollis | BQ | LENGTH 18–20cm

Endearing wader whose plumage is buffish overall. Its dark eye is emphasised by a dark cap and otherwise pale buffish face. Sexes are similar.

birds have been known to turn up in spring, on return passage north – occasionally they will even display

1ST-WINTER

1ST-WINTER

All birds have a rather short, dark bill and relatively long yellow legs. In flight, note the whitish underwings (dark primary coverts appear as a contrasting dark crescent). Adult has a streaked crown, nape and back, and dark centres to otherwise buff feathers on wings. Seen in flight, uppertail and rump are dark. Underparts are buffish and mainly unmarked. Juvenile/1st-winter (most likely plumage to be seen here) is similar but pale buff margins to the uniformly dark-centred back feathers create a scaly look. **VOICE** Vagrants here are mostly silent. **HABITS** Usually indifferent to human observers, allowing close views to be obtained. **STATUS AND HABITAT** Breeds in Arctic North America and winters in S South America. Vagrants here usually turn up in late summer and early autumn, and favour areas of short grassland.

UPLAND SANDPIPER

Bartramia longicauda | UP | LENGTH 28–32cm

Unusual wader with a long neck, a short, straight bill and a long-bodied appearance (due to its long wings and very long, barred tail). Sexes are similar.

In all birds, legs are yellow and dark eye appears relatively large against otherwise rather pale face. Adult has grey-brown upperparts, the back feathers having dark centres. Underparts are mainly pale but with streaking on neck and chevron-shaped markings on breast and flanks. Juvenile/1st-winter is similar to adult but plumage is subtly flushed buffish brown. In flight, wingtips of all birds are noticeably darker than rest of wings, and long tail is obvious. **VOICE** Call is a bubbling *quilip-ip-ip*. **HABITS** Feeds in a deliberate manner and often adopts an upright posture when standing. **STATUS AND HABITAT** Breeds on remaining North American prairie grassland and winters mainly on the Argentinean Pampas. Vagrants here are likely to turn up in autumn and favour areas of short grassland.

in flight, long wings and tail look striking

1ST-WINTER

standing birds look long-necked

RARE *CALIDRIS* WADERS AND RELATIVES

Members of the genus *Calidris* and their relatives are rather small waders. In addition to commonly occurring species, rarer species from North America and Asia turn up regularly, often in autumn in juvenile/1st-winter plumage. If you find a mystery wader, pay attention to the features highlighted on these pages. This will help you eliminate Dunlin (the default common *Calidris* species) and other species such as Little Stint and Curlew Sandpiper, which is half the battle when it comes to identifying small waders in Britain.

Study the markings and patterns on the back – prominent white 'V' markings are a feature in juveniles of some small North American waders – White-rumped and Western sandpipers for example – as well as their common European counterpart, Little Stint; the feature is absent or at best indistinct in Baird's and Semipalmated sandpipers.

Look carefully at the bill shape – many unusual waders have straight or gently downcurved bills, but there are exceptions. For example, Broad-billed has a distinct downward kink at the tip; Semipalmated is often described as 'blob-tipped'; and Least has a strongly downcurved bill.

Study the wing length and primary projection, especially relative to the tail length – some North American species have very long wings, for example American Golden Plover.

PECTORAL SANDPIPER

Look for a clear pectoral band – a good identification feature in Pectoral and Baird's, for example.

What colour are the legs? If they are yellow then the wader is likely to be an unusual species, for example Least Sandpiper or Long-toed Stint.

Head pattern can give a good clue to identity. For example, a forked pale supercilium is a key feature for Broad-billed.

Check the flanks. In autumn, all juvenile/1st-winter Dunlin have streaked flanks; unusual waders at this time of year will have 'clean-looking' flanks. Note that in spring, adult Broad-billeds have arrowhead streaks on their flanks.

BROAD-BILLED SANDPIPER

Look for colour at the base of the bill – a few unusual species have this feature.

WILSON'S SNIPE

Gallinago delicata | LENGTH 23–28cm

Plump-bodied, long-billed wader. The North American counterpart of Snipe (*G. gallinago*) and very similar to that species; only recently elevated to species status. Sexes are similar.

overall, all birds look much greyer and less rufous than Snipe

All birds have overall brown upperparts and white underparts with dark barring. Compared to Snipe, features to look for include: overall 'colder' grey appearance (parts of plumage are almost black and white); unmarked white centre of belly (as in Snipe) but dark barring on flanks extending uniformly to axilliaries and underwing coverts (underwings of Snipe appear banded); broader pale fore-supercilium, creating a different facial appearance; almost black scapulars (brown in Snipe); strongly barred outer-tail feathers (more lightly barred in Snipe). All birds have yellowish-green legs. **VOICE** Utters a sneezing *ske-erch* call in alarm. **HABITS** Probes soft mud and waterlogged ground with its bill, in the manner of a Snipe. Flight is zigzagging and fast. **STATUS AND HABITAT** Widespread breeder across N North America, most birds wintering further south. Vagrants here are likely to turn up in autumn and early winter, and favour freshwater and brackish wetlands.

GREAT SNIPE

Gallinago media | DS | LENGTH 26–30cm

Long-billed wader. Superficially very similar to a Snipe but separable with care. Sexes are similar.

All birds are overall brown and beautifully patterned above with dark and white stripes on the head; underparts are pale and heavily barred. Compared to a Snipe, features to look for include: the relatively short bill; 3 striking white wingbars (not obviously in Snipe); and much more extensively barred underparts. In addition, when taking off, the outer-tail feathers are revealed as being largely white (orange-brown and barred in Snipe). All birds have yellowish-green legs. **VOICE** Vagrants here are usually silent. However, spring vagrants have been known to display, accompanied by a *chipp-a, chipp-a...* song. **HABITS** Vagrants here usually favour drier habitats than Snipe; nettle-covered wetland margins are ideal. **STATUS AND HABITAT** Breeds in E Europe and winters in Africa. Most records here (4 or 5 in a good year) occur in autumn and in the Northern Isles.

SHORT-BILLED DOWITCHER

Limnodromus griseus | LENGTH 25–29cm

Stout-bodied shorebird with a long, straight grey bill. Very similar to Long-billed – specific identification is often not possible with poor views. Sexes are similar.

WINTER

All birds have yellowish-green legs and a pale supercilium; in flight, note the dark upperwing with a white trailing edge, and the white rump and lower back. Summer adult has most feathers on back beautifully patterned with dark centres and orange margins, although some appear uniform grey. Underparts are flushed orange on neck and breast, grading to white on belly and towards vent; intensity and extent of colour, and of dark barring, varies. Winter adult has grey upperparts, neck and breast, and otherwise white underparts. Juvenile/1st-winter has back feathers with dark centres and orange margins; diagnostically, tertials have dark internal bars and stripes on otherwise paler background. Neck and breast are flushed orange-buff, and face often appears contrastingly pale; underparts are otherwise whitish. In all birds, terminal quarter of bill is noticeably downcurved. **VOICE** Utters a rattling *tu-dlu* call, vaguely reminiscent of a Turnstone (*Arenaria interpres*). **HABITS** Feeds by probing mud in a deliberate sewing machine-like manner. **STATUS AND HABITAT** Widespread breeder across N North America; winters in South America. Vagrants here are likely to turn up in autumn; more likely to favour shores (rather than freshwater pools) than Long-billed.

1ST-WINTER

SUMMER

LONG-BILLED DOWITCHER

Limnodromus scolopaceus | LD | LENGTH 27–30cm

Very similar to a Short-billed Dowitcher. Bill length is
not a foolproof identification feature; subtle differences
in plumage and call are more useful.
Sexes are similar in plumage terms.

**looks rather Snipe-like
in flight**

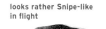

WINTER

WINTER

WINTER

Summer adult has beautifully marked upperparts, the back feathers with dark centres and
orange or white margins. Cap is dark and underparts are flushed orange, more extensively so
than in Short-billed, and with more extensive dark barring on neck and breast. Winter adult has
grey upperparts, neck and breast, grading less abruptly into otherwise white underparts than in
Short-billed. Juvenile/1st-winter is similar to juvenile/1st-
winter Short-billed, but note the uniformly dark-
centred tertials, which lack the internal barring seen
in juvenile/1st-winter Short-billed. **VOICE** Utters
a shrill *kyeep* call. **HABITS** Feeds by probing mud
in a deliberate sewing machine-like manner.
STATUS AND HABITAT Widespread breeder
across N North America; winters in Central and
South America. Vagrants here are most likely
to turn up in autumn. Some individuals
stay for extended periods,
occasionally into spring.

**bill length varies
between individuals
but on average it
is longer than in
Short-billed
Dowitcher**

SUMMER

HUDSONIAN GODWIT

Limosa haemastica | HU | LENGTH 37–42cm

WINTER

Elegant wader with structural and plumage features
in common with both Bar-tailed (*L. lapponica*)
and Black-tailed (*L. limosa*) godwits.
Sexes are separable in summer.

1ST-WINTER

very long-legged

Compared to other godwits, bill is
more noticeably upcurved towards the tip. In
flight, plumage recalls a Black-tailed, with a pale
bar on upperwing (bright only at base of primaries)
and a pale rump with contrasting black tail; from
below, note the black underwing coverts (white in
Black-tailed). Summer adult has feathers on back
and wings intricately patterned with black centres
and scalloped white and chestnut margins. Head
and neck are streaked grey-brown and underparts
are barred and flushed chestnut. Female is duller and less colourful than male.
Winter adult has uniform grey-brown upperparts and paler grey-buff
underparts. Juvenile/1st-winter is similar to winter adult but feathers on
back and wing coverts have pale margins. In all birds, bill is pink with
a dark tip and legs are black. **VOICE** Vagrants here are mostly silent.
HABITS Likely to associate with godwit flocks in Britain.
STATUS AND HABITAT Local breeder in Arctic
North America; winters in South America. Vagrants
here are likely to turn up in autumn, and
favour estuaries and mudflats.

WINTER

HUDSONIAN WHIMBREL

Numenius hudsonicus | LENGTH 37–42cm

warm buff underparts give a clue to the identity of Hudsonian Whimbrel, but the brown (not white) rump and centre to the back are diagnostic

North American counterpart of the Whimbrel (*N. phaeopus*), which it closely resembles. Careful attention must be paid to subtle plumage differences to ensure correct identification. Sexes are similar.

Adult has a long, downcurved bill, bluish legs, patterned brown upperparts and pale brown underparts, streaked from head to breast. Compared to Whimbrel, Hudsonian is marginally smaller and overall paler, with more uniformly marked, warmer buff underparts. Head pattern is more striking (dark elements are dark brown, pale elements are creamy buff). Rump and back are uniformly brown (Whimbrel has a pale wedge from rump onto back), and tail is uniformly barred brown (in Whimbrel, tail is pale-tipped). Juvenile/1st-winter is similar to adult but feathers on back and wings have more distinct pale spots. **VOICE** Call is a series of 7 whistling notes. **HABITS** Feeds using its bill to probe in mud and under seaweed and boulders. **STATUS AND HABITAT** Breeds in Arctic North America and winters mainly in South America. Vagrants here are likely to turn up in autumn and favour coastal habitats.

BROAD-BILLED SANDPIPER

Limicola falcinellus │ OA │ LENGTH 15–17cm

Slightly smaller than, but superficially similar to, a Dunlin (*Calidris alpina*) but with some plumage features reminiscent of a Snipe (*Gallinago gallinago*). Bill shape and head pattern aid identification. Sexes are similar.

split supercilium and drooping bill tip

In all birds, legs are relatively short and yellowish, but often obscured in muddy water. Bill is rather long and straight, but with a distinct downward kink at the tip. Adult in spring has mainly brown upperparts and whitish underparts. Pale feather margins on back

vagrants to British estuaries often consort with other small waders, notably Dunlin – identification of distant, active birds can be a challenge

sometimes align to form stripes, and note the split pale supercilium on the otherwise dark crown. Juvenile/1st-winter is similar but with cleaner-looking, more distinct markings on head and back. **VOICE** Call is a high-pitched, trilling *brrrtt*. **HABITS** Feeds in an active manner, probing deep into soft mud with its long bill. **STATUS AND HABITAT** Breeds in N Scandinavia and winters in Africa and Asia. Vagrants here (a handful each year) are most likely to turn up in spring and favour estuaries and mudflats.

TEREK SANDPIPER

Xenus cinereus | TR | LENGTH 22–25cm

upturned bill is unique in a wader of this size

Distinctive little wader with an extremely long, upturned bill. The short yellow legs are set relatively far back, giving it a front-heavy appearance. Sexes are similar.

Adult body plumage is vaguely reminiscent of a miniature winter Greenshank (*Tringa nebularia*): upperparts are overall pale grey, head and neck are streaked, and underparts are otherwise white. In breeding season, note the dark stripe on the scapulars, dark carpal patch and dark shafts to mantle feathers. Juvenile/1st-winter is similar, but upperparts are subtly darker and dark markings are indistinct. **VOICE** Call comprises a series of shrill *pee-pee-pee* whistling notes. **HABITS** An extremely active feeder, dashing around in a frantic manner, running with its body leaning forwards. **STATUS AND HABITAT** Breeds across N Asia and winters on coasts of Africa and Asia. Vagrants here are likely to turn up in spring or autumn, and favour estuaries and mudflats.

SPOTTED SANDPIPER

Actitis macularius | PQ | LENGTH 18–20cm

North American counterpart of the Common
Sandpiper (*A. hypoleucos*), which it closely resembles
(except in breeding plumage). Typically seen here in
1st-winter plumage. Sexes are similar.

1ST-WINTER

1ST-WINTER

In all birds, tail projection is much
shorter than in Common Sandpiper;
bill is pale pink and dark-tipped, and legs
are yellow (pinkish in Common Sandpiper).
Juvenile, 1st-winter and winter adult have
grey-brown upperparts. Head is mainly
grey-buff with a pale supercilium and
throat. Chest is grey-brown and note the
clear demarcation from the otherwise white
underparts. Best identification features for a
juvenile/1st-winter are the plain tertials and
greater wing coverts (strongly barred in

unmarked tertials and
greater wing coverts
(barred in Common
Sandpiper)

Common Sandpiper). Summer adult (rarely seen here) has rich brown upperparts and whitish
underparts marked boldly with dark spots. **VOICE** Call is a sharp *weet* or *peet-weet-weet*…
HABITS Bobs its body up and down as it walks, like a Common Sandpiper. Flies low
over water on bowed wings and with shallow, rapid wingbeats.
STATUS AND HABITAT Widespread breeder across North
America that winters mainly in Central and South America.
Vagrants here are likely to turn up in autumn, and some stay
through winter. They usually favour estuaries
and mudflats.

adults in 'spotted' breeding
plumage occasionally turn
up here in spring

SUMMER

SOLITARY SANDPIPER

Tringa solitaria | I. | LENGTH 18–21cm

**primaries extend further
beyond tertials and
tail than in similar
Green Sandpiper**

Compact, medium-sized wader and the North
American counterpart of the Green Sandpiper (*T.
ochropus*). Most likely to be seen in 1st-winter plumage.
Sexes are similar.

1ST-WINTER

In all birds, wings are dark above
and below. A useful identification
feature is the tail pattern: dark
centre, white margins, and barred
towards tip (Green Sandpiper has
a white rump and upper tail, with
barring towards tip). 1st-winter
has dark brown upperparts, the
back feathers with pale marginal
spots. Head and neck are streaked
brown, and note the white eye-
surround. Underparts are white,
with faint barring on flanks. Legs are dull yellow; relatively long bill is slightly downcurved
(straight in Green Sandpiper) and dull pink with a dark tip. Adult is similar but more heavily
streaked on the head and neck. **VOICE** Utters a shrill *teweet-wheet* when flushed. **HABITS**
Bobs its body up and down as it walks. Flight is rapid and often rises steeply if flushed.
STATUS AND HABITAT Breeds in N North America and winters in South America.
Vagrants here are likely to turn up in autumn.

bobbing gait when it walks

RARE *TRINGA* WADERS AND RELATIVES

These small to medium-sized waders are elegant birds that generally live up to the name 'wader', feeding in or near water. A study of plumage and structural features will aid identification, and a bird's behaviour can be helpful in this respect too. The annotations on these wader photos will help the process. For comparison, Redshank is the default common *Tringa* wader in Britain.

Study the upperwing markings on wing-stretching or flying birds. Some rare species have a trailing pale margin or wingbar (Terek and Spotted sandpipers, for example); absence of these features (as in Marsh Sandpiper and both yellowleg species) can also aid identification.

Note the shape and build of the bill – for example, Terek has a diagnostic upturned bill; that of Marsh is long and needle-like; and dowitchers have long bills that are of even width along the length.

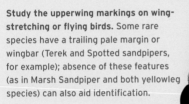

MARSH SANDPIPER

Look at the upperside rear end in flight – some unusual species have a white rump (for example, Lesser Yellowlegs); others have a white rump and lower back (for example, Greater Yellowlegs). In some the back and rump are uniform in colour; this feature allows separation of Solitary Sandpiper from the similar, regularly encountered Green Sandpiper (which is white-rumped).

Study the feeding manner of the bird in question – dowitchers often adopt a regular 'sewing machine' action; other species are much more active and dashing.

Note the relative length of the bill – for example, dowitchers have extremely long bills; in others it is more in proportion to the size of the head.

SHORT-BILLED
DOWITCHER

Note the relative length of the legs – some rare wader species have particularly long legs, and both yellowleg species and Marsh Sandpiper are good examples.

Leg colour can be a clue to identity – for example, both yellowlegs species have bright yellow legs, as do dowitchers and several unusual sandpiper species.

MARSH SANDPIPER

Tringa stagnatilis | MD | LENGTH 22–25cm

Elegant wader. Recalls a miniature Greenshank (*T. nebularia*) but its yellowish legs are longer in relative terms, and its bill is thin, needle-like and straight (not upcurved). Sexes are similar.

white 'wedge' running up centre of back is obvious in flight

SUMMER

Summer adult has mainly grey-brown upperparts, spangled with blackish spots; underparts are white and streaked on neck, breast and flanks. Non-breeding adult has mainly grey upperparts and clean white underparts. Juvenile/1st-winter recalls a summer adult but back appears rather scaly due to pale feather margins. In flight, all birds show uniformly dark wings, a pale tail and a white rump extending as a wedge up back. Potential exists for confusion with immature Wilson's Phalarope (*see* opposite entry). **VOICE** Utters a sharp *kyu-kyu* call. **HABITS** Often feeds in relatively deep water and probes in a relatively slow, deliberate manner. **STATUS AND HABITAT** Breeds in Central Asia and winters in Africa and S Asia. Vagrants here are most likely to occur in spring and favour freshwater pools.

needle-like bill

WINTER

long yellow legs

SUMMER

WILSON'S PHALAROPE

Phalaropus tricolor | WF | LENGTH 22–24cm

Elegant wader with a needle-like bill. Potential exists for confusion between 1st-winter (when wading, not swimming) and small *Tringa* waders, notably Marsh Sandpiper. Adults are unmistakable; sexes are dissimilar.

All birds have yellowish legs with lobed feet used for swimming. Summer adult female (the more colourful sex) is stunning, with a black and maroon stripe on side of neck and a yellowish-orange throat and chest. Back is grey and maroon, and underparts are white. Summer adult male is similar, but darker overall and less colourful. Non-breeding adult has pale grey upperparts and whitish underparts. Juvenile/1st-winter recalls a winter adult but upperparts are brownish, the back feathers with pale margins. **VOICE** Vagrants here are mostly silent. **HABITS** Swims well but also wades in shallows around wetland margins. **STATUS AND HABITAT** Breeds across central North America and winters in South America. Vagrants here are most likely to turn up in autumn (a few spring birds have also been noted) and favour coastal pools.

feeds around muddy margins more regularly than other phalarope species, inviting confusion with unrelated waders

1ST-WINTER

FEMALE, SUMMER

GREATER YELLOWLEGS

Tringa melanoleuca | LZ | LENGTH 29–33cm

Elegant wader. Recalls a Greenshank (*T. nebularia*), but plumage differences, extremely long orange-yellow legs and long bill aid identification. Sexes are similar.

appreciably larger than Lesser Yellowlegs and with more robust, almost Greenshank-like, bill

white rump extends up back in a wedge

1ST-WINTER

Confusion is possible with Lesser Yellowlegs, but Greater is a larger and altogether more robust bird (*see also* opposite entry). In flight, all birds have mainly dark upperparts with a contrasting white rump extending up the back in a white wedge, and pale-barred tail. Summer adult has intricately patterned brown, black and white feather markings on back and upperwings. Head, neck and breast are streaked with brown, and underparts are mainly white but with brown spots and barring on flanks. Bill is usually all dark. Winter adult looks overall paler with grey-brown feathers on back, and upperwings marked with marginal white spots and scallops. Bill is pale-based. Juvenile/1st-winter is similar to winter adult but feathers on back have buffish marginal spots and breast has obvious dark streaking. Bill is pale-based. **VOICE** Flight call is a shrill *tiu-tiu-tiu.* **HABITS** Often feeds in deep water but equally at home on open mudflats. Often chases wildly after prey. **STATUS AND HABITAT** Breeds in N North America and winters from southern states to South America. Vagrants here are most likely to appear from autumn to spring, and favour coastal lagoons.

1ST-WINTER

LESSER YELLOWLEGS

Tringa flavipes | LY | LENGTH 23–25cm

Elegant wader. Recalls a Wood Sandpiper (*T. glareola*) but with much longer, yellow legs and a marginally longer, needle-like bill. Sexes are similar.

bright yellow legs can be picked out easily, even in distant birds

white confined to rump

1ST-WINTER

Compared to Greater Yellowlegs, bill length only just exceeds head length (Greater's bill is much longer than head length) and bill is all dark (Greater's is pale-based in juvenile/1st-winter and winter adults). In flight, dark upperparts contrast with white rump and pale-barred tail. Summer adult has back feathers beautifully patterned with brown, black and white. Head and neck are heavily streaked brown and underparts are mainly whitish. Winter adult looks much paler overall with a grey-brown head and neck, and pale marginal spots and scallops on back feathers. Underparts are white. Juvenile/1st-winter is similar to winter adult but with more streaking on neck and breast, and buffish marginal spots and scallops on back feathers. **VOICE** Flight call is a sharp *tew-tew*. **HABITS** Feeds in a more precise manner than Greater Yellowlegs (which runs about wildly), rather like a Wood Sandpiper. **STATUS AND HABITAT** Breeds across N North America and winters mainly in South America. Vagrants here are most likely to turn up in autumn and early winter, and favour coastal pools.

SLENDER-BILLED GULL

Chroicocephalus genei | EI | LENGTH 37–42cm

Elegant gull that shares features with the Black-headed
Gull (*C. ridibundus*). Unusual head and bill shape
and overall pale appearance are useful pointers
in identification. Sexes are similar.

wing pattern recalls that
of Black-headed Gull

1ST-SUMMER

pink flush to underparts
is not always obvious

English name is misleading because bill is not especially slender. Rather, combination of
appreciably long bill and elongated forehead are distinctly different from Black-headed. All
birds have a relatively long neck. Adult has a white head, neck and underparts with a pale
eye (dark in Black-headed). Resting birds show pale grey upperparts and black wingtips
(lacking any white spots). In flight, note that the outerwing has a white wedge on leading
edge and a black trailing margin. In summer, breast is flushed pink; bill is black for a brief
period but otherwise red, as are legs. Similar 1st-winter has a dark-tipped pink bill and pink
legs, dark smudges on head, and subtle brown pattern on upperwing coverts and secondaries.
VOICE Vagrants here are silent. **HABITS** Vagrants here usually associate with Black-headed
Gulls. **STATUS AND HABITAT** Resident around the Mediterranean. Vagrants here are
likely to turn up in spring and favour coastal lagoons.

BONAPARTE'S GULL

Chroicocephalus philadelphia | ON | LENGTH 31–34cm

Reminiscent of a small Black-headed Gull
(*C. ridibundus*) but with relatively long wings.
Subtle plumage differences allow identification.
Sexes are similar.

in non-breeding plumage,
most likely to be confused
with Black-headed Gull

WINTER

1ST-WINTER

1ST-WINTER

black bill in all ages
distinguishes this species
from Black-headed Gull

WINTER

In flight, all adults show a white leading
edge and dark trailing margin to primaries.
Apart from these elements, underwing is
uniformly pale grey (inner primaries are
dark in Black-headed). Summer adult has
a pale grey back and upperwings, white
underparts and neck, and a blackish hood.
Bill is dark and legs are red. Winter adult
is similar but dark hood is lost and dark
ear coverts contrast with otherwise white
head. In 1st-winter plumage, recalls winter adult but with dark trailing edge
to entire wing (not just primaries), a less striking pale leading edge (some
dark feathering), and dark bar on inner upperwing; legs are pale pink.
Primary coverts have dark edges (pale in Black-headed). **VOICE**
Call is nasal and higher-pitched than other gulls. **HABITS**
Flight is buoyant and, at times, tern-like.
STATUS AND HABITAT Widespread
breeder in North America that winters
on coasts. Vagrants here
are likely to turn up in
autumn and winter,
and associate with
Black-headed Gull flocks.

SUMMER

RARE GULLS

A range of unusual gull species turn up in Britain from time to time, generally mixing with their commoner cousins. Some species are distinctive and easy to identify; others are confusingly similar to regularly encountered gulls in our region. Use the annotations on these Ring-billed Gull images to determine the important features to scrutinise. For comparison, Herring Gull and Black-headed Gull are the default common gull species in Britain.

Note the colour of the eye - both that of the iris and orbital ring.

How long are the wings? Some gull species are much longer-winged than others, especially when compared to their common counterparts (see text). Slender-billed, Audouin's and Laughing gulls are all rather long-winged species.

Pay attention to the colour of the bill and the location and colour of any markings. This feature is useful when separating Ring-billed Gull from its widespread cousin the Common Gull.

RING-BILLED GULL

Leg colour can be a useful tool in identification.

Many unusual gull species have wingtips (primaries) with black and white markings. The extent of the white markings, and the number of primaries that possess them, is useful in identification. This is particularly useful when trying to identify, for example, adult Caspian and American Herring gulls, and rule out the far commoner Herring Gull.

Try to determine the age of the bird you are looking at. Adults of most species have clean white bodies. Non-adult birds usually have variable amounts of brown on the upperwings, or dark bands.

RING-BILLED GULL

ROSS'S GULL

Rhodostethia rosea | QG | LENGTH 30–32cm

Small but relatively long-winged gull. All birds have a dainty dark bill and short reddish legs. Most records of Ross's Gull and its Arctic companion Ivory Gull are from northern coasts. Sexes are similar.

Adult has a wedge-shaped white tail, a very pale back and upperwings, and smoky grey underwings; a broad white trailing edge can be seen in flight, both from above and below. Plumage is otherwise white but, in spring it acquires a black neck-ring and a pink flush to underparts. In winter, has a dark smudge around eye; hint of neck-ring can sometimes be discerned. In 1st-winter bird upperwing pattern recalls a 1st-winter Little Gull (*Hydrocoloeus minutus*), with a black 'W' line on upperwings; note the white trailing edge to wings and relatively long, wedge-shaped tail with black tip. **VOICE** Vagrants here are silent. **HABITS** Picks food from the water surface in flight; sometimes feeds at the water's edge in the manner of a Black-headed Gull (*Chroicocephalus ridibundus*). **STATUS AND HABITAT** Breeds in the high Arctic and usually winters in northern seas. Vagrants are likely to turn up in winter (a couple each year) favouring coasts and harbours; vagrants are sometimes long-stayers if feeding is good.

WINTER

wedge-
shaped
tail

WINTER

striking
upperwing
pattern

1ST-WINTER

dainty
bill

WINTER

IVORY GULL

Pagophila eburnea | IV | LENGTH 41–48cm

A dainty and elegant Arctic gull whose distinctive plumage makes it almost unmistakable. Sexes are similar.

Adult has pure white plumage and relatively short, black legs. Rounded head, dark eye and dainty bill create an almost dove-like appearance. At close range, note the bill's bluish base and yellow tip. In similar 1st-winter face is grubby-looking and upperwings are adorned with neat black spots. **VOICE** Vagrants here are silent. **HABITS** A carrion-feeder (at Polar Bear, *Ursus maritimus*, kills) by nature, vagrants here sometimes lingering if they discover a beached seal or cetacean corpse. **STATUS AND HABITAT** Breeds in the high Arctic and usually winters in northern seas. Vagrants here (mostly 1st-winter birds) typically turn up in midwinter and records (a couple in a good year) predictably have a northerly bias.

1ST-WINTER

1ST-WINTER

grubby-looking face

1ST-WINTER

AUDOUIN'S GULL

Larus audouini | LENGTH 44–52cm

Attractive long-winged gull. Midway in size between Common (*L. canus*) and Herring (*L. argentatus*) gulls, with features that are distinctive enough to ensure identification is straightforward. Sexes are similar.

1ST-WINTER

colourful bill markings

long bill, sloping forehead and small head aid identification in all ages

Adult has a white head, neck and underparts, a grey back, and black primaries with white 'windows' at tips. Legs are a dull, dark greenish colour, eye is dark, and bill is red with a dark sub-terminal band and yellow tip. In flight, mainly grey upperwing shows a white trailing edge and black wingtips, the primary tips with white 'windows'. In 1st-winter, pale grey head and nape are streaked; underparts are otherwise white. Grey upperparts show dark centres to feathers on back and upperwing coverts, and dark flight feathers. Underwing pattern is much stronger than in any other similar-sized gull and shows a contrasting white panel in the mid-wing. Bill is dull pink and dark-tipped. Has 4 age groups. **VOICE** Vagrants here are silent. **HABITS** An opportunistic feeder, like other similar-sized gulls. **STATUS AND HABITAT** A rather rare Mediterranean species. Vagrants here are likely to turn up in spring and favour coastal lagoons.

RING-BILLED GULL

Larus delawarensis | IN | LENGTH 41–49cm

In size terms, midway between Herring (*L. argentatus*) and Common (*L. canus*) gulls, and with plumage and structural features in common with both. Sexes are similar.

WINTER

striking bill pattern

1ST-WINTER

1ST-WINTER

WINTER

Summer adult has a pale grey back and upperwing except for white-spotted black wingtips and pale trailing edge. Plumage, including tail, is otherwise white. Bill is yellow with an obvious dark sub-terminal band, and eyes and legs are yellow. Winter adult is similar but head and neck are streaked brown and leg and bill colours are duller. In 1st-winter head and neck are streaked, wing coverts have brown centres, and primaries and trailing margin to innerwing are dark; bill is pink and dark-tipped, and tail has a dark terminal band. In 2nd-winter plumage, resembles winter adult but retains a faint, narrow, dark band on tail; iris is pale. In younger plumages, always appears much dirtier than Common Gull. **VOICE** Vagrants here are mainly silent. **HABITS** Vagrants usually associate with other large gulls, notably Herring and Common gulls. **STATUS AND HABITAT** North America's most widespread and common gull; winters mainly on coasts. Vagrants here are likely to turn up in autumn and winter, and mix with other coastal gull flocks.

CASPIAN GULL

Larus cachinnans | YC | LENGTH 55–60cm

Very similar to Yellow-legged Gull (*L. michahellis*) and only recently elevated to separate species status. Sexes are similar.

compared to Herring Gull, head is rather long and tapering towards the bill

1ST-WINTER

1ST-WINTER

SUMMER

SUMMER

Compared to Yellow-legged (*L. michahellis*) and Herring gulls (*L. argentatus*), on average looks longer-legged and longer-winged, with a relatively smaller, pear-shaped head that tapers into a rather long, slender bill. In plumage terms, adult can be confused with adult Yellow-legged; immatures can be confused with similar-aged Yellow-legged and Herring. Summer adult has a paler grey back and upperwings than Yellow-legged, with more white in wingtips and white 'tongues' at tips of outer primaries. Winter adult is similar, sometimes with limited dark streaking on head. Juvenile and 1st-winter birds have a silvery-grey back and wing coverts, with some dark markings (paler overall than similar species). **VOICE** Similar to a Herring Gull. **HABITS** Often adopts a more upright stance than other similar-sized gulls, with the neck more extended. **STATUS AND HABITAT** Main range is from the Danube Delta and Caspian Sea eastwards. Wanders outside the breeding season; vagrants here are likely to turn up in autumn and winter, and associate with other large gulls.

AMERICAN HERRING GULL

Larus smithsonianus | LENGTH 52–58cm

North American counterpart of the Herring Gull
(*L. argentatus*) and only recently elevated to separate
species status; easily confused with that species. Sexes
are similar.

WINTER

very
grubby-looking
head and
neck

WINTER

1ST-WINTER

1ST-WINTER

SUMMER

Adult is very similar to
adult Herring and many
individuals are inseparable.
Some winter adults have
darker and more extensive
streaking on head and
nape than the average
Herring, and black tertial
spots. Plumage of
1st-winter is darker overall
than its Herring counterpart, with unmarked brown
underparts (pale and streaked in Herring); tail is darker and
rump is darker and more heavily barred than in Herring. In
2nd-winter, back is grey and has grey areas on upperwing;
tail is dark-tipped but otherwise white. In
3rd-winter, plumage resembles winter adult but
has more black on wingtips
and a dark tail band. Both
2nd- and 3rd-winter birds are
hard to distinguish from their
Herring Gull counterparts. **VOICE**
Utters a distinctive *kyaoo* and an anxious *ga-ka-ka*. **HABITS** Vagrants
here are likely to associate with Herring Gull flocks. **STATUS
AND HABITAT** Widespread in North America.
Vagrants here are likely to turn up in
autumn and winter, and favour coastal
locations where gulls congregate.

LAUGHING GULL

Larus (Leucophaeus) atricilla | LF | LENGTH 36–41cm

Medium-sized gull with long wings that extend well beyond the tail at rest. Alert birds look long-necked, and bill is rather long and slightly downcurved. Sexes are similar.

1ST-WINTER

WINTER

1ST-WINTER

WINTER

Summer adult has a dark grey back and upperwings except for a white trailing edge and dark tips to wings. Underwings show contrast between mainly dark flight feathers and white wing coverts. Underparts and neck are white, and note the dark hood and white 'eyelids'. Bill and legs are dark red. Winter adult is similar but dark hood is lost except for dark streaking on nape; bill and legs are dark. In 1st-winter, back is grey, inner upperwing coverts are grey and brown, and outerwing and flight feathers are dark. Plumage is otherwise mainly grubby white, with a dark tail band and a streaked grey breast and neck. Bill and legs are dark. **VOICE** Vagrants here are mainly silent. **HABITS** An opportunistic feeder that often mixes with gull species at good feeding locations. **STATUS AND HABITAT** Widespread in North America. Vagrants here are most likely to turn up in autumn and winter; long-stayers usually favour docks and harbours.

SUMMER

FRANKLIN'S GULL

Larus (Leucophaeus) pipixcan | FG | LENGTH 32–36cm

Recalls a Laughing Gull but much smaller and
daintier, and with a shorter bill and legs. Adult's
white–black–white wingtip pattern is useful
for identification. Sexes are similar.

1ST-WINTER

SUMMER

1ST-WINTER

Summer adult has a black hood with white 'eyelids',
grey upperparts and pink-flushed white underparts.
Winter adult is similar but dark hood is replaced by dark
markings (notably on the nape); retains more extensive
dark markings on head than winter Laughing Gull. In 1st-winter, back is grey, inner
upperwing coverts are grey and brown, outerwing and flight feathers are dark, and trailing
edge to upperwing is white. Dark tail band is narrower than in similar-aged Laughing.
VOICE Vagrants here are mostly silent. **HABITS**
Vagrants here are likely to associate with gull
flocks, notably those of Black-headeds
(*Chroicocephalus genei*). **STATUS AND HABITAT**
Local breeder in North America that winters
in South America. Vagrants here are
likely to turn up in autumn
and winter, and favour
coastal habitats.

compared to appreciably
larger Laughing Gull,
bill is much smaller
and more dainty

SUMMER

SOOTY TERN

Onychoprion fuscatus | LENGTH 42–45cm

Relatively large and distinctive sea tern that could only really be confused with a Bridled Tern. Sexes are similar.

compared to Bridled Tern, white on forehead only just reaches the eye, and does not run above it

Adult has long, broad-based, pointed wings, and a long, deeply forked tail. Upperparts are mostly blackish and underparts are white; in flight, white underwings contrast with blackish wingtips and dark trailing margin. Head pattern comprises a white forehead, a black cap and nape, and a black stripe running through eye, narrowing to base of bill. Juvenile/1st-winter is shorter-tailed than adult, and mostly dark sooty brown above with pale spots on back and innerwing. Head, neck and breast are dark, and underparts – including underwing – are otherwise grubby white, with a dark trailing margin and tips to wings. All birds have short black legs. **VOICE** Vagrants are mostly silent. **HABITS** Flight is powerful and direct, and less buoyant than that of a Bridled Tern. **STATUS AND HABITAT** A tropical oceanic seabird whose nearest breeding colonies are in the Caribbean. Wanders outside the breeding season. Vagrants here are most likely to turn up in summer and autumn, although individuals have summered at tern colonies.

BRIDLED TERN

Onychoprion anaethetus | LENGTH 37–42cm

note that the pale
feathering, separating
black nape from dark
back, is not always
immediately obvious

Black and white sea tern that is similar to a Sooty
Tern. Subtle plumage differences allow separation,
notably the pattern on the head.
Sexes are similar.

Marginally smaller than a Sooty
Tern and with narrower wings. Adult
has long, pointed wings, and a long, deeply
forked tail. Upperparts are mostly dark
greyish brown (paler than Sooty), but
dark elements of head pattern are
distinctly blackish; underparts are
white. In flight, white underwings contrast with blackish
wingtips and dark trailing margin. Head pattern comprises a
black cap and nape, and a narrow white forehead that extends back
as a white stripe above and behind eye; black stripe through eye does not
narrow to base of bill (cf. Sooty). Juvenile/1st-winter is shorter-tailed than
adult; plumage recalls that of adult but paler overall and with a scaly-looking back.
All birds have short black legs. **VOICE** Vagrants are mostly silent. **HABITS** Flight is buoyant,
recalling a Sandwich Tern (*Sterna sandvicensis*). **STATUS AND HABITAT** A tropical oceanic
seabird whose nearest breeding colonies are in the Caribbean. Wanders outside the breeding
season. Vagrants here are most likely to turn up in summer and autumn.

GULL-BILLED TERN

Gelochelidon nilotica | TG | LENGTH 35–40cm

Bulky tern. Similar to a Sandwich Tern (*Sterna sandvicensis*) but with broader wings, a thicker, all-dark bill and a stockier body. Sexes are similar.

bill is indeed bulky and gull-like, especially when compared to Sandwich Tern

SUMMER

Summer adult (typical plumage for vagrants here) has pale grey upperparts, a black crown and nape, and white underparts. In flight, wings appear almost uniformly white except for dark edges to underside of primaries. Bill and legs are black. Non-breeding adult is similar, but head is white except for mask-like dark streaking from behind eye to nape. Juvenile/1st-winter is similar to winter adult, but back, upperwings and crown have faint brown feathering. Legs and bill are dark reddish. **VOICE** Vagrants here are mostly silent. **HABITS** Flight is direct and more reminiscent of a small gull than a tern. Feeds by hawking insects, not plunge-diving, and often hunts over land. **STATUS AND HABITAT** Breeds from the Mediterranean region eastwards and winters in Africa and Southeast Asia. Vagrants here are most likely to turn up in spring and autumn, and favour coastal regions.

WINTER

non-breeding birds look very white, except for dark 'mask' and bill

SUMMER

CASPIAN TERN

Hydroprogne caspia │ CJ │ LENGTH 48–55cm

flight is powerful and gull-like; huge colourful bill is obvious in all plumages

Huge and unmistakable tern, the size of a Herring Gull (*Larus argentatus*). In all birds, the massive blood-red bill is diagnostic. Sexes are similar.

Summer adult has a black crown, a white face, neck and underparts, and a grey back and upperwings. Outer primaries are blackish when seen from below in flight. Legs are dark. Non-breeding adult is similar but dark crown is incomplete and particularly pale, and is streaked on forecrown. Juvenile/1st-winter recalls a non-breeding adult but outer half of upperwing is dark, with dark bands on inner half; tail is dark-tipped. Legs are dull red. Blood-red bill often shows a dark tip. **VOICE** Vagrants here are mostly silent. **HABITS** Flight is gull-like with slow, powerful wingbeats. **STATUS AND HABITAT** Breeds from the Baltic region eastwards and winters off Africa. Vagrants here (5 or 6 annually) are likely to turn up at migration times, particularly in spring. They usually favour freshwater sites (lakes, flooded gravel pits and coastal marshes) and seldom stay longer than a few hours before moving on.

SUMMER

a huge tern, with the stature of a medium-sized gull

SUMMER

WHISKERED TERN

Chlidonias hybrida | WD | LENGTH 24–27cm

Elegant wetland bird that recalls a
miniature Common Tern (*Sterna hirundo*),
with a proportionately shorter, much
less forked tail. Sexes are similar.

spends much of the time
on the wing, hunting
flying insects and picking
prey from water surface

Summer adult (typical adult plumage of vagrants seen here) has a black crown and nape, and
a contrasting white throat and cheeks; plumage is otherwise smoky grey, darkest on breast and
belly. Bill and legs are dark red. Non-breeding adult is mainly white with pale grey upperwings
and blackish streaking on hindcrown. Juvenile/1st-winter is similar to non-breeding adult
but shows a dark-spotted orange-brown mantle; upperwing, including flight feathers, is
unmarked silvery grey. **VOICE** Vagrants here are mostly silent. **HABITS** Flight is
buoyant. Hawks for insects over freshwater lakes, reservoirs and flooded gravel
pits. **STATUS AND HABITAT**
Breeds locally in S Europe and
winters mainly in Africa. Vagrants
here (5 or 6 in a good year) are likely
to turn up in spring and autumn; they
favour freshwater wetlands, including lakes
and reservoirs.

JUVENILE/1ST-WINTER

SUMMER

SUMMER

SUMMER

reminiscent of a tiny,
compact Common Tern;
note obvious white cheeks

AMERICAN BLACK TERN

Chlidonias niger surinamensis | LENGTH 24cm

North American race of the Black Tern, and assigned separate subspecies status. Sexes are similar.

compared to 1st-winter Black Tern, note the rather uniform upperwings and back, and grey flanks

1ST-WINTER

1ST-WINTER

Summer adult is hard to distinguish from the Black Tern but has overall darker black body plumage; also has a white undertail and forked tail. Non-breeding adult has mostly dark grey upperparts and white underparts; black on head extends to mantle (restricted to cap and nape in Black), and leading edge to wing is white in some birds. Juvenile/1st-winter birds have uniformly grey upperparts (juvenile/1st-winter Black shows contrast between darker, scaly brown back and paler grey upperwings). Underwings are grey, colour extending onto flanks (flanks and underwing coverts are white in Black Tern); dark 'wedge' at front of flanks is more extensive than in Black Tern. Head pattern comprises a grey cap and black ear coverts (cap and ear coverts are uniformly black in Black Tern). **VOICE** Vagrants here are silent. **HABITS** Flight is buoyant, like that of a Black Tern. **STATUS AND HABITAT** Locally common in North America. So far, only immatures have been recognised here; vagrants are likely to turn up in autumn and favour coastal pools and reservoirs.

SUMMER

WHITE-WINGED BLACK TERN

Chlidonias leucopterus | WJ | LENGTH 20–24cm

Striking tern that, in breeding plumage, could be confused only with a Black Tern (*C. niger*). Sexes are similar.

Breeding adult has a black head, neck and body, pale grey upperwings that are palest on leading edge, and underwings with black coverts and pale grey flight feathers. Rump, undertail and tail are pure white, while bill is dark and legs are red. Adults begin to moult black elements of the plumage by July, and non-breeding adult is grey above and white below; note the whitish collar and rump, streaking on hindcrown, and dark spot on ear coverts. Juvenile and 1st-winter are similar to winter adult but note the blackish mantle, hood and nape, and contrasting white rump and sides to neck and breast. **VOICE** Vagrants here are silent. **HABITS** Flight is buoyant; hawks insects and picks food items from the water surface. **STATUS AND HABITAT** Breeds from E Europe eastwards and winters in Africa. Vagrants to our region (a dozen or so in a good year) usually turn up in spring and autumn, and favour freshwater pools and marshes.

JUVENILE

SUMMER

wing pattern makes adult unmistakable

SUMMER

SUMMER

LESSER CRESTED TERN

Sterna bengalensis | TF | LENGTH 33–40cm

Elegant seabird. Has similar proportions to a Sandwich Tern (*S. sandvicensis*) but is slightly smaller. Sexes are similar.

uniformly orange-yellow bill allows separation from superficially similar Sandwich Tern

WINTER

grey rump

1ST-WINTER

Summer adult has a grey back, upperwings and rump; cap is dark and crested, but plumage is otherwise white. Legs are black and relatively short; bill is long, slender and orange. In flight, upperparts show a contrast between grey back and innerwing, paler inner primaries and darker outer primaries. Winter adult (plumage seen from late summer onwards) is similar but forehead is white. Juvenile and 1st-winter are similar to winter adult but back is barred and inner flight feathers are dark-centred; in flight, upperwing shows a contrast between seemingly pale but barred innerwing, and darker outerwing with pale inner primaries. **VOICE** Vagrants here silent. **HABITS** Vagrants in our region are likely to associate with Sandwich Terns. **STATUS AND HABITAT** Breeds locally on coasts of North Africa. Vagrants here are likely to turn up in spring and autumn, but the species has formed a mixed pair (with a Sandwich Tern) during the breeding season.

FORSTER'S TERN

Sterna forsteri | FO | LENGTH 33–36cm

Similar proportions to a Common Tern (*S. hirundo*) but
with longer tail streamers and legs, and a different
upperwing pattern. Sexes are similar.

Forster's is the least
unlikely *Sterna* tern to
turn up here in winter

WINTER

looks very
pale except
for black
'highwayman's
mask'

JUVENILE

SUMMER

Typically seen here in non-breeding plumage.
Non-breeding adult looks very pale overall (pale grey back and
upperwings, and white underparts) except for a dark 'mask' behind
eye and dark trailing margin to primaries. Legs are orange-red and bill
is dark. Summer adult is similar except that cap is dark and bill is red and
dark-tipped. In juvenile/1st-winter, plumage is similar to that of non-breeding adult except
for dark centres to inner flight feathers, dark primary tips and shorter tail streamers.
Compared to 1st-winter Sandwich Tern (*S. sandvicensis*), it is smaller and has a pale (not
dark-streaked) nape, paler upperwing and darker tips to underside of primaries. **VOICE**
Vagrants here are silent. **HABITS** Plunge-dives in the manner of other *Sterna* terns. **STATUS
AND HABITAT** Widespread in North America, wintering on coasts. Vagrants here (almost
annual) are likely to turn up in late autumn or winter, and favour coasts.

BRÜNNICH'S GUILLEMOT

Uria lomvia │ TZ │ LENGTH 40–44cm

Similar to a Guillemot (*U. aalge*), compared to which all birds have a thicker, shorter bill (almost gull-like) with a striking white stripe along gape. Sexes are similar.

buoyant but swims rather low in the water; white on relatively short bill is visible in all plumages

1ST-WINTER

SUMMER

Compared to a Guillemot, the neck is thicker and plumage is darker overall. Vagrants here are most likely to be seen in non-breeding plumage. Non-breeding adult has a blackish hood, nape and upperparts, white underparts and a white wingbar (trailing margin to inner flight feathers). Note that the ear coverts are blackish and hence the dark hood is 'complete' (Guillemot has white ear coverts). Summer adult has an entirely black head, neck and upperparts, and white underparts. In 1st-winter plumage, resembles a winter adult but bill is shorter, throat is grubby and white gape stripe is less striking. Head shape can be distinctive, and often shows a peaked forecrown. **VOICE** Vagrants here are silent. **HABITS** Swims well and dives frequently. **STATUS AND HABITAT** An Arctic breeder that is pelagic in winter, mainly in northern seas. Vagrants here are likely to turn up after winter storms, and are sometimes rather sickly birds. There is a northerly bias to records.

PALLAS'S SANDGROUSE

Syrrhaptes paradoxus | LENGTH 30–42cm

Distinctive species. For observers not familiar with sandgrouse as a group, note the species' superficially gamebird-like appearance. Sexes are subtly dissimilar.

pale sandy
panel in
wings

Adult recalls a long-tailed, long-winged Grey Partridge (*Perdix perdix*). Has a mainly orange-buff head, bluish ear coverts and neck, and otherwise buffish-yellow underparts with a black belly patch; upperparts are buff with dark spots aligned to form bars. Female colours are duller than in male, and upperparts are more spotted. In flight, all birds show buff upperwing coverts that contrast with pale primaries (outer primaries have narrowly pointed projections), and pale and unmarked underwings. **VOICE** Vagrants here are silent. **HABITS** Walks with a shuffling gait, typical of sandgrouse. Flight is fast and direct. **STATUS AND HABITAT** Breeds on Asiatic steppes. A notorious wanderer; large irruptions reached here in 1863 and 1888, after which it bred. Nowadays, very rare.

ORIENTAL TURTLE DOVE

Streptopelia orientalis | LENGTH 30–35cm

Superficially similar to a Turtle Dove (*S. turtur*) but larger and bulkier. Two subspecies have occurred in Britain: *meena* and *orientalis*. Sexes are similar.

1ST-WINTER

Adults of both subspecies have shorter primary projections than Turtle Dove but in other respects are superficially similar to that species. Head, neck and underparts are blue-grey with a patch of black barring on neck; *meena* has a pinkish-buff flush on breast. Back and wing coverts are chestnut, with more extensive dark feather centres than in Turtle Dove. Tail is long and black-centred, the feather tips greyish in *orientalis* but white in *meena* (as in Turtle Dove), and the rump is greyer than in Turtle Dove. Juvenile/1st-winter is similar but colours are duller, back and wings appear scaly due to dark-centred, pale-edged feathers, and neck markings are absent. Overall, plumage of all birds is duller and darker than their Turtle Dove counterparts. **VOICE** Vagrants here are silent. **HABITS** Flight is fast and direct, with flicking wingbeats. **STATUS AND HABITAT** Breeds across N Asia and winters further south. Vagrants here are likely to turn up in autumn and early winter, and favour open country (they have also been noted at feeders).

MOURNING DOVE

Zenaida macroura | LENGTH 28–33cm

Recalls a slim-bodied, long-tailed Collared Dove
(*Streptopelia decaocto*) with particularly short legs.
Sexes are subtly dissimilar as adults.

Adult has pinkish-buff plumage overall. Upperwings, back and rump are buffish brown
with black spots on tertials and wing coverts. Head, neck and breast are paler buff, flushed
pink on breast and with iridescent bluish feathers on nape. Has a dark crescent on lower
margin of ear coverts, a dark bill and red legs. The tail is long and tapered. Outer-tail
feathers have white tips and black bases, creating a unique tail pattern. Female is similar
to male but less colourful on neck and breast. Juvenile/1st-
winter is similar to adult female but has a spotted and barred
appearance to back, neck and breast, and a pale face with
a dark line through eye. Legs are pink. **VOICE** Vagrants
here are mostly silent. **HABITS** Feeds on the ground,
walks with a jerky but rapid manner, and flies with
flicking wingbeats. **STATUS AND HABITAT**
Widespread across North America in the
breeding season, wintering south to
Mexico. Vagrants here are likely to
turn up in autumn and favour open
locations in coastal areas.

when feeding, often
adopts a rather
horizontal stance

1ST-WINTER

GREAT SPOTTED CUCKOO

Clamator glandarius | UK | LENGTH 35–39cm

crest often looks scruffy

Distinctive long-tailed bird. Sexes are similar; juveniles
are more strikingly marked than adults.

JUVENILE

Adult has a
grey cap and
shaggy crest, and
otherwise dark upperparts
adorned with white spots
on back and wing coverts.
Underparts are white, flushed
yellowish on throat and
neck. Bill is dark and slightly
downcurved, and legs are black.
In flight, the long, dark tail
shows pale feather tips; seen
from above, the dark wings show
2 white bars (aligned spots).
Juvenile/1st-winter is similar to
adult but cap and crest are neat and uniformly black, and wings show an orange-brown
panel on primaries, particularly striking in flight. **VOICE** Vagrants here are silent. **HABITS**
Nest parasite of Magpies (*Pica pica*) and other corvids. Flight is level, recalling a raptor or
Cuckoo (*Cuculus canorus*). On the ground, often hops with tail raised. **STATUS AND
HABITAT** Breeds in Iberia, and locally in the Mediterranean region; winters in Africa.
Vagrants here are likely to turn up in spring and autumn, and favour open coastal habitats.

BLACK-BILLED CUCKOO

Coccyzus erythropthalmus | LENGTH 28–31cm

Separable from the similar Yellow-billed Cuckoo on bill and orbital ring colours, and on tail pattern. Sexes are similar; vagrants here are likely to be immatures, which are subtly less colourful than adults.

All birds have grey-brown upperparts (crown is same colour as back) and whitish underparts. Flight feathers are buffish brown (not rufous), and note the uniformly dark bill and reddish orbital ring. Tail is long and wedge-shaped when fanned; upperside is brown with small white tips to feathers; underside is grey-brown with small white spots on feather tips, defined by sub-terminal black bands. Undertail coverts are yellowish buff (white on Yellow-billed). **VOICE** Vagrants here are silent. **HABITS** Unobtrusive. Feeds primarily on hairy caterpillars; vagrants in our region struggle to find suitable food. **STATUS AND HABITAT** Widespread breeder across temperate North America; winters in N South America. Vagrants here are likely to turn up in autumn, and favour coastal scrub and light woodland.

YELLOW-BILLED CUCKOO

Coccyzus americanus | LENGTH 29–32cm

Long-tailed bird that is superficially similar to its Black-billed cousin. Sexes are similar; vagrants here are likely to be 1st-winter birds, which are marginally duller than adult birds.

All birds have overall dark grey-brown upperparts, dull blue-grey on crown and darkest through eye (which has a yellow orbital ring). Rufous panel on primary feathers and rufous fringes to primary coverts are most obvious in flight. Underparts, including throat and undertail coverts, are whitish. Tail is long and wedge-shaped when spread; seen from above, tail appears mainly dark, but all feathers have striking white tips; seen from below, pale feather tips appear as large white spots against otherwise black tail feathers. Bill is downcurved with a yellow base to lower mandible. **VOICE** Vagrants here are usually silent. **HABITS** Vagrants in our region are often unobtrusive, and feed on large caterpillars and other insects. **STATUS AND HABITAT** Widespread breeder in North America that winters in South America. A more regular autumn vagrant than Black-billed.

1ST-WINTER

TENGMALM'S OWL

Aegolius funereus | LENGTH 35–43cm

Plump-bodied owl. Recalls a Little Owl (*Athene noctua*) but is larger, and has a proportionately large head and diagnostic rounded-oblong facial disc. Sexes are similar.

Adult and immature have rich brown plumage overall. Upperparts are marked with bold white spots, smallest and densest on head; underparts are whitish but heavily streaked with rufous brown. Facial disc is whitish with a dark border; yellow eyes are framed by a dark surround and white 'eyebrows', creating a 'startled' appearance. **VOICE** Vagrants here are silent. **HABITS** Strictly nocturnal and roosts in dense cover. **STATUS AND HABITAT** Breeds from Scandinavia eastwards and in central European mountain ranges. Mainly sedentary but wanders when food supplies are low. Vagrants here are likely to turn up in autumn and early winter.

SCOPS OWL

Otus scops | LENGTH 19–21cm

Tiny and unmistakable owl whose cryptic plumage pattern is a near-perfect match for tree bark. Colour forms exist but, given that, sexes are similar.

Overall plumage colour ranges from rufous brown to grey-brown depending on colour form. All birds have intricate dark markings on the feathers (streaks, cross-bars and vermiculations); large white spots align to form 'braces' on back. Facial disc is squarish and it has 'ear' tufts that can be raised. Eyes are yellow. In flight, wings are relatively long, broad and rounded at the tip. It is the only small owl to show cross-barring on underparts. **VOICE** Song (uttered after dark) is a diagnostic series of sonar blip-like notes, repeated every 2–3 seconds. **HABITS** Strictly nocturnal and roosts in deep cover in daytime. Adopts an upright, elongated posture when alarmed. **STATUS AND HABITAT** Breeds across S Europe and winters in Africa. Vagrants are most likely to turn up in spring; males sometimes sing.

SNOWY OWL

Bubo scandiacus | SO | LENGTH 55–65cm

staring yellow eyes

Huge and unmistakable owl that is often active in the daytime. Even sitting birds are usually conspicuous due to their white colour and size. Sexes are dissimilar.

FEMALE

JUVENILE

FEMALE

Adult male has mostly pure white plumage with feathered feet; yellow eyes can be seen at close range. Adult female and 1st-winter male are white overall but with grey spots on upperparts and grey barring below. All parts of juvenile/1st-winter female except head are heavily marked with dark barring. In flight, all birds have long, broad wings that are rounded at the tip. **VOICE** Vagrants here are mostly silent. **HABITS** Spends long periods sitting still, often in a hollow or against a boulder or bush. In flight, usually glides low over the ground. **STATUS AND HABITAT** An Arctic species. Mainly sedentary but immatures in particular are prone to wandering in autumn and winter; this is when vagrants usually turn up here. Has attempted to breed in Shetland, and solitary birds occasionally summer on Scottish islands or mountain tops.

COMMON NIGHTHAWK

Chordeiles minor | LENGTH 23–25cm

North American counterpart of the Nightjar
(*Caprimulgus europaeus*), with similar nocturnal habits.
Intricately marked plumage is a good match for tree
bark. Vagrants are likely to be immature (sexes similar).

white on wing
is noticeable
in flight

Immature has blackish-brown plumage overall. Upperparts are finely marked with black
and whitish lines and vermiculations. Throat is barred buff and underparts have dark brown
barring on a pale background. Primaries are mostly unmarked blackish with pale tips (in
Nightjar, primaries are brown and finely marked); white band near base of primaries is often
seen on resting birds and in flight (falls midway between primary tips and carpal joint; in
Nightjar it is closer to primary tips). Tail is forked (rounded in Nightjar). Adults are similar
but with a pale throat patch (buff in female, white in male; male also has a broad white sub-
terminal band on tail). **VOICE** Vagrants here are silent. **HABITS** Hawks insects on the wing,
in the manner of a Nightjar, sometimes at dusk as well as at night. Roosts on the ground or
on a tree branch, its camouflage making it hard to spot. **STATUS AND HABITAT** Breeds
across North America and winters in South America. Vagrants here are likely to turn up in
autumn and favour coastal habitats.

CHIMNEY SWIFT

Chaetura pelagica | LENGTH 12–13cm

Small North American swift. Compared to European swift species, it is appreciably smaller, with a different outline in flight. Sexes are similar.

Recognised in flight by its narrow, pointed wings (outerwing is noticeably broad), cigar-shaped body and short, square-ended tail. All birds have dark brown plumage, palest on the throat. Spiny tips to tail are visible only at very close range. **VOICE** Vagrants here are silent. **HABITS** Vagrants are only likely to be seen in flight. Active flight is speedy, with frequent changes in direction and style; wingbeats are shallow and rapid. Soaring and banking birds fan the tail but otherwise it is held closed. **STATUS AND HABITAT** Widespread breeder in North America that winters mainly in Amazonian South America. Vagrants here are likely to turn up in autumn, following westerly gales.

WHITE-THROATED NEEDLETAIL

Hirundapus caudacutus | NI | LENGTH 19–21cm

Relatively large swift (the size of an Alpine Swift), with rapid flight and superb aeronautical skills. Sexes are similar.

All birds have a dumpy body that tapers evenly at either end when seen in profile. Wings are broad-based and pointed. Has a striking white throat and small white patch on forehead, and a crescent-shaped white vent; body plumage is otherwise brown, palest on back. Upper surface of wings and tail have a bluish sheen. Tail is fanned when soaring or banking. **VOICE** Vagrants here are silent. **HABITS** Healthy vagrants are only ever seen in flight; they hawk insects on the wing. Flight is often rapid but occasionally much slower and relatively low to the ground. **STATUS AND HABITAT** Breeds in N and Central Asia and winters from Southeast Asia to Australia. Vagrants here are likely to turn up in spring; records have a northerly bias, with Scottish islands being favoured.

PALLID SWIFT

Apus pallidus | LENGTH 16–18cm

Very similar to a Swift (*A. apus*) – great attention to detail, and good views, are needed to separate the species. Sexes are similar.

Structural differences from Swift are subtle, but Pallid has broader wings, a larger head and a bulkier body. All birds have mainly brown plumage (subtly paler than Swift); in good light, note the pale throat and small dark 'mask' through the eye revealed against paler head. Seen in flight from below, underwing coverts and outer primaries are noticeably darker than inner primaries and secondaries. Seen from above, back appears darker than head and upperwings.

secondaries and inner primaries look pale from below

VOICE Vagrants here are silent. **HABITS** Vagrants are only likely to be seen in flight. Prolonged views alongside Swifts sometimes reveals subtly slower flight and more extended periods of gliding. **STATUS AND HABITAT** Breeds around the Mediterranean region and winters in Africa. Vagrants here are likely to turn up at migration times, mainly in spring.

PACIFIC SWIFT

Apus pacificus | LENGTH 18–19cm

Roughly the size of a Swift (*A. apus*), but with subtly different proportions and a diagnostic white rump. Sexes are similar.

Compared to a Swift, note the longer, more deeply forked tail; when tail is closed, this creates a longer-bodied appearance with a more attenuated rear end. In addition, wings are more slender than those of a Swift. All birds have overall dark grey-brown plumage, with a pale throat and a scaly appearance to breast and belly created by pale feather margins. **VOICE** Vagrants are mostly silent. **HABITS** Vagrants here are usually seen hawking insects, sometimes feeding low over water or grazing pasture. **STATUS AND HABITAT** Breeds in E Asia and winters from Southeast Asia to Australia. Most vagrants turn up in spring.

ALPINE SWIFT

Tachymarptis (Apus) melba │ AI │ LENGTH 20–23cm

Relatively large and impressive bird that invariably is seen in flight. Appreciably larger than a Swift (*A. apus*), with diagnostic markings on its underparts. Sexes are similar.

Has a crescent-shaped outline in gliding flight. Compared to Swift, wings are broader-based and body is bulkier. Seen in flight from below, note the contrast between the dark brown wings, rear end and collar, and white throat and belly. Upperparts are uniformly dark sooty brown. Flight often appears falcon-like. **VOICE** Vagrants here are silent. **HABITS** In active flight, wingbeats are slower than those of a Swift. **STATUS AND HABITAT** Breeds in S Europe and winters in Africa. Vagrants here (12 or so in a good year) usually turn up in spring and early summer, and favour coastal districts or freshwater habitats inland.

combination of
white throat and belly
make identification
straightforward

LITTLE SWIFT

Apus affinis │ LENGTH 12–13.5cm

Relatively small swift species; smaller even than a House Martin (*Delichon urbicum*). Has distinct and diagnostic markings and structure. Vagrants are invariably seen in flight. Sexes are similar.

neat white
rump

Compared to a Swift (*A. apus*), note the much smaller size; relatively short, broad wings; and broad, square-ended tail. All birds have blackish plumage except for a broad squarish white rump, which overlaps the sides (hence often visible from below). Throat is white. **VOICE** Vagrants here are silent. **HABITS** Flight pattern is much more fluttering than that of a Swift, and often recalls a House Martin. **STATUS AND HABITAT** Resident in, and partial summer migrant to, North Africa; some birds winter further south. Vagrants here are likely to turn up in spring and autumn, and favour coastal wetlands.

BELTED KINGFISHER

Megaceryle alcyon | LENGTH 31–34cm

Impressive, large kingfisher – the size of a Jackdaw
(*Corvus monedula*) – that is hard to confuse with anything
else. Often sits in the open, making observation
straightforward. Sexes are dissimilar.

JUVENILE

All birds have a blue-grey back, upperwings and tail,
with small white spots on wings. Head is blue-grey
with a white spot in front of eye, and a shaggy crest.
In male, head is separated from white underparts
by a blue-grey breast band; female has an
additional breast band below this, which is
orange-red and extends along flanks. In flight, all
birds show a contrast between white coverts and dark
flight feathers on underwing, and white wing patch
at base of primaries on upperwing. Juvenile is similar
to adult of respective sex but with reddish mottling on
otherwise blue breast band. **VOICE** Typical call is a loud,
harsh rattle. **HABITS** Usually feeds by diving
for fish from a perch or wire overlooking
water; sometimes hovers. **STATUS AND
HABITAT** Widespread breeder in North
America; northern birds migrate south in
autumn. Vagrants here are likely to turn
up in late autumn and winter, and favour
coastal habitats.

MALE

EUROPEAN ROLLER

Coracias garrulus | LENGTH 30–32cm

Colourful and unmistakable bird of crow-like proportions and size, with a powerful hook-tipped bill. Often perches in the open, making observation easy. Sexes are similar.

Adult has a blue head, neck and underparts, palest on the forehead and with a narrow dark patch through the eye. Back is chestnut and rump, tail and parts of the wing are bluish purple. In flight, wings look striking, the dark flight feathers contrasting with paler blue coverts; note also the dark tips to otherwise pale blue outer-tail feathers. Central tail feathers are chocolate brown. Juvenile/1st-winter has similar markings but colours are much duller. **VOICE** Vagrants here are usually silent. **HABITS** Often perches for extended periods on a dead branch or wire, scanning for prey, which includes large insects and lizards. **STATUS AND HABITAT** Breeds in S Europe and winters in Africa. Vagrants here (4 or 5 in a good year) are likely to turn up in spring and autumn, and favour dry, open habitats such as heaths.

no other bird of this size has such 'electric' blue plumage

BLUE-CHEEKED BEE-EATER

Merops persicus | LENGTH 28–32cm

Extremely colourful and distinctive bird that is
hard to confuse with anything other than a
European Bee-eater. Sexes are similar.

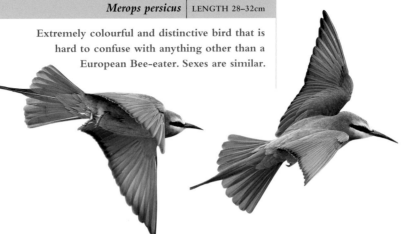

Adult has mainly bright green plumage with a reddish throat; blue face contains a dark stripe
through the eye, bordered above and below by white. Bill is long, downcurved and black,
and eye is bright red. Long central tail projections are most obvious in flight, as are long,
pointed wings. In flight, looks uniformly green from above; seen from below, underwings
are reddish with an even black trailing margin (black margin is broader on innerwing in
European Bee-eater). Juvenile/1st-winter is similar to adult but colours are duller and tail
projection is absent. **VOICE** Call is a rolling, trilling *prr-rrt*, similar to, but slightly higher-
pitched than that of European Bee-eater. **HABITS**
Flight is extremely aerobatic as it hunts insect
prey; also perches on dead branches. **STATUS
AND HABITAT** Breeds in North Africa
and Central Asia, and winters in Africa.
Vagrants here are likely to turn
up in spring and autumn, and
favour coastal locations.

EUROPEAN BEE-EATER

Merops apiaster | MZ | LENGTH 26–29cm

Stunningly beautiful bird, usually seen in flight. Its appearance is unmistakable and its call is readily identified. Sexes are similar.

Adult has a chestnut crown and nape, grading to yellow on the back and rump; upper surface of tail is green and there are 2 projecting central tail feathers. Underparts are blue except for black-bordered yellow throat. In flight, the broad-based, triangular wings show chestnut and blue on upper surface; underwings are pale with a black trailing margin, broader on innerwing. Close view of a perched bird reveals dark mask through eye and white forecrown. Juvenile/1st-winter is similar but colours are duller and tail projections are absent. **VOICE** Utters a bubbling *pruuupp* call, often in flight. **HABITS** Extremely aerobatic as it chases insect prey in flight. Sometimes perches on dead branches. **STATUS AND HABITAT** Widespread breeder in S Europe that winters in Africa. Has bred here on occasions but its status is mainly that of a spring and autumn vagrant. Small parties of birds are sometimes seen during spring migration.

almost every colour
of the rainbow is
represented in its
plumage

HOOPOE

Upupa epops | HP | LENGTH 25–28cm

An elegant bird with distinctive plumage
and a long downcurved bill. Unmistakable
when seen well. Sexes are similar.

All birds have mainly pale pinkish-brown plumage but with striking black and white barring on the wings and back; white rump is revealed in flight. Erectile crest of dark-barred pink feathers is raised in excitement. In flight, transformed by its broad wings into a striking black and white bird; this effect is emphasised by its slow, butterfly-like flight pattern. Tail is black with a broad white band. **VOICE** Utters a diagnostic *hoo-poo-poo* call. **HABITS** Creeps along the ground, often feeding in furrows, which can make it surprisingly difficult to spot. Bill is used to probe the ground for invertebrates. **STATUS AND HABITAT** Widespread breeder across warmer parts of mainland Europe; most birds winter in Africa. Vagrants here are likely to turn up in spring and autumn, and most records are coastal; favours areas of short grassland.

PHILADELPHIA VIREO

Vireo philadelphicus | LENGTH 11cm

vireos may bear a passing resemblance to warblers, but their chunky bills and habits make them more akin to shrikes

Short-billed, short-tailed and rather chunky bird, roughly the size of a *Phylloscopus* warbler. Sexes are similar.

Compared to a *Phylloscopus* warbler, has a relatively larger head, stouter bill and stronger plumage patterns. All birds have an olive-grey back and neck, and a greyish crown; the dark eye-stripe is framed above by a broad white supercilium and below by a white line in front of eye. Lores are dark. Underparts, including throat, are variably flushed yellow, appearing palest on belly. Bill is dark and legs are bluish. **VOICE** Call is a nasal *tchrrr*. **HABITS** Forages for insects in a more deliberate manner than most warblers. **STATUS AND HABITAT** Locally common breeder in North America that winters in South America. Vagrants here are likely to turn up in autumn in the west of our region and favour coastal habitats (scrub and light woodland).

RED-EYED VIREO

Vireo olivaceus | EV | LENGTH 13–14cm

Well-marked, stocky transatlantic vagrant that is unmistakable when seen well. Sexes are similar.

All birds have a yellowish-grey back, neck and wings. Head has a striking pattern comprising a dark blue-grey crown and long white supercilium, defined above and below by black lines (the latter forms a dark eye-stripe). Underparts, including throat, are whitish with a dull yellow wash on flanks and undertail. Note the beady red eye, rather long grey bill and blue legs. **VOICE** Call is a nasal *zz'nrrr*. **HABITS** Forages unobtrusively among foliage and gleans insects while hovering. Easily overlooked. **STATUS AND HABITAT** Widespread breeder in North America that winters in South America. One of the most regular transatlantic vagrants, with birds likely to occur here in autumn; there is a strong westerly bias to the records.

NUTCRACKER

Nucifraga caryocatactes | NC | LENGTH 32–35cm

Distinctive member of the crow family. Roughly
the size of a Jay (*Garrulus glandarius*) but with striking
markings and a long, stout bill. Sexes are similar.

white-spotted dark
plumage makes
identification
straightforward

All birds are brown overall with numerous white spots, these largest on the back, belly and
breast. Cap and flight feathers are uniformly dark, and tail is mostly dark, the feathers with
broad white tips. Note the pure white undertail coverts. Bill and legs are dark; Siberian birds
are slender-billed by comparison with their European counterparts. In flight, note the broad,
rounded wings and relatively long, rounded tail. **VOICE** Vagrants here are mostly silent.
HABITS Vagrants are usually not especially wary. They sometimes
feed on their usual food (hazelnuts and pine seeds) but also on
apples. **STATUS AND HABITAT** Mostly sedentary
resident of forests in European mountains and Siberia.
The Siberian ssp. *macrorhynchos* very occasionally irrupts
westwards, with vagrants sometimes arriving in Britain,
mainly in autumn and winter.

WOODCHAT SHRIKE

Lanius senator | OO | LENGTH 17–19cm

scaly-looking feathering on upperparts is a good identification feature

Bulky and well-marked bird that is almost unmistakable when seen well. Sexes are subtly dissimilar.

JUVENILE

FEMALE

MALE

Adult male has a chestnut cap and nape, a broad black mask running from forecrown through eye, and white underparts flushed faintly with peachy buff on flanks and breast. Has a striking white patch on scapulars, a white patch at base of primaries, and a buffish-white patch at base of bill. In flight, pale rump and white-margined black tail are obvious. Adult female is similar but black and chestnut elements of plumage are less intense, white patch at base of bill is more extensive, and has faint barring on underparts. Juvenile/1st-winter has scaly grey-brown upperparts, pale grey underparts with faint vermiculations, and a pale patch on scapulars. **VOICE** Vagrants here are mostly silent. **HABITS** Often perches on barbed-wire fences or low bushes, using these as lookouts. **STATUS AND HABITAT** Widespread breeder in S Europe that winters in Africa. Vagrants here (15–20 in a good year) are likely to turn up in spring and autumn, and favour areas of coastal scrub.

BROWN SHRIKE

Lanius cristatus | LENGTH 17.5–20cm

Adult has features in common with an adult
Isabelline Shrike; juvenile could be confused with
a juvenile Red-backed Shrike (*L. collurio*).
Sexes are subtly dissimilar.

All birds show, on average, stouter bills and a shorter primary projection than either Red-backed or Isabelline shrikes. Adult has a warm brown cap, back and rump, and a duller brown tail, with diagnostic short outer-tail feathers (the Turkestan race of Isabelline, ssp. *phoenicuroides*, shows a contrast between greyish-brown back and red tail). Facial pattern comprises a black mask and white supercilium. Underparts are mostly whitish, flushed with buffish yellow on breast and flanks. Female is duller than male, with scaly vermiculations on underparts. Plumage of 1st-winter is similar to that of adult female but back appears scaly; compared to juvenile/1st-winter Red-backed, note the warmer brown upperparts, blackish (not brown) tertials and short outer-tail feathers. General appearance of all birds is short-winged, long-tailed, large-headed and heavy-billed. **VOICE** Vagrants here are silent. **HABITS** Often perches in the open, like other shrikes. **STATUS AND HABITAT** Breeds in Siberia and winters in S Asia. Vagrants here are likely to turn up in autumn and early winter, and favour open country.

1ST-WINTER

ISABELLINE SHRIKE

Lanius isabellinus | IL | LENGTH 16.5–18cm

Two races could occur as vagrants. All birds have distinctive red tails; 1st-winters could be confused with 1st-winter Red-backed Shrikes (*L. collurio*). For each race, females are subtly less well marked than males.

SSP. *PHOENICUROIDES*

Adult ssp. *isabellinus* (Isabelline Shrike) has overall pale grey-buff upperparts and pale buff underparts. Note the black 'mask' through eye, black flight feathers and red tail.

Plumage of 1st-winter *isabellinus* is similar but slightly warmer brown overall; lacks black 'mask' and has subtle scaly effect on underparts. Compared to 1st-winter Red-backed, it is paler overall and has a redder tail; upperparts are unmarked (not barred and scaly-looking). Adult ssp. *phoenicuroides* (Turkestan Shrike) is similar to *isabellinus* but upperparts are darker grey-brown and it has a broader black 'mask', defined above and below by white. *Phoenicuroides* 1st-winter has greyer upperparts than *isabellinus* (but still unmarked) and a hint of a black 'mask'. **VOICE** Vagrants here are mostly silent. **HABITS** Often perches in the open like other shrikes. **STATUS AND HABITAT** Both subspecies breed from Central Asia eastwards, and winter in S Asia. Vagrants here are likely to turn up in autumn and early winter, and favour open country, usually on the coast.

SSP. *ISABELLINUS*

SSP. *ISABELLINUS*, 1ST-WINTER

red tail contrasts with otherwise rather sandy-grey plumage

LESSER GREY SHRIKE

Lanius minor | LENGTH 19–21cm

Elegant and well-marked bird. Recalls a Great
Grey Shrike (*L. excubitor*), but smaller and
with slightly different markings and
structure. Sexes are subtly dissimilar.

1ST-WINTER

FEMALE

Adult has mainly grey upperparts, white underparts, and black wings and tail. Compared to
a Great Grey, note the relatively longer primaries and shorter tail, and black patch through
eye that extends onto forehead; in addition, has more white on wings and hint of a rosy
flush to underparts, particularly in male. Juvenile/1st-winter is similar but
black eye patch does not extend onto forehead, and back and crown
appear scaly and faintly barred. Long primary projection is useful
for identification of juvenile/1st-winter birds. **VOICE** Vagrants
here are mostly silent. **HABITS** Often perches on wires and
fencelines. **STATUS AND HABITAT** Breeds in S and
E Europe and winters in Africa. Vagrants here (5 or
6 in a good year) are likely to occur in spring
and autumn; they favour open country,
usually near the coast.

MALE

SOUTHERN GREY SHRIKE

Lanius meridionalis | LENGTH 21–26cm

SSP. PALIDIROSTRIS

S European and Asiatic counterpart of the Great Grey Shrike (*L. excubitor*). Represented across its vast range by several subspecies, some of which may merit elevation to separate species status. Sexes are similar.

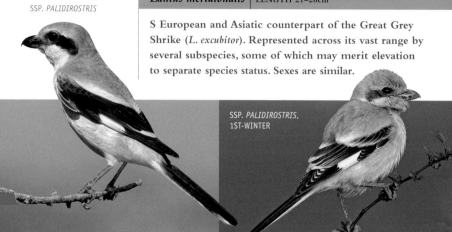

SSP. PALIDIROSTRIS, 1ST-WINTER

Each subspecies has a subtly different intensity of grey in its plumage, and a variable extent of black 'mask' and white on wings. Overall, most adults have a grey cap and back, white underparts and a black mask through eye; note the white patch on wings at base of primaries, and white sides to long black tail. Plumage of juvenile/1st-winter birds is similar, but has faint barring on underparts and black elements are washed out. So-called Steppe Grey Shrike (ssp. *palidirostris*) is distinctive, with a very stout bill that has a pale base in 1st-winter birds; also shows a greater extent of white on wing than other subspecies. **VOICE** Vagrants are usually silent. **HABITS** Often perches in the open. **STATUS AND HABITAT** Breeding range extends from S Europe eastwards across Central Asia. Some subspecies are mainly sedentary, while others wander outside the breeding season. Vagrants are likely to turn up here in autumn and early winter, and favour open country.

PENDULINE TIT

Remiz pendulinus | DT | LENGTH 10–11.5cm

MALE

Charming little wetland bird with a very slender, pointed bill. Sexes are subtly dissimilar.

Adult plumage pattern is vaguely reminiscent of that of a male Red-backed Shrike (*Lanius collurio*): reddish-brown back, blue-grey cap and nape, black 'mask' and white throat; underparts are peachy buff, most intense on the breast. Female is subtly duller and less colourful than male. Juvenile has a buffish-brown head and upperparts, and pale buffish-white underparts. Legs are dark in all birds. **VOICE** Call is a high-pitched, thin, whistling *tsiuu*. **HABITS** Feeds on seeds of Common Reed (*Phragmites australis*) and Bulrush (*Typha latifolia*). A very agile climber of slender stems.

STATUS AND HABITAT Widespread wetland bird across much of mainland Europe. Northern birds move south and wander outside the breeding season; consequently, vagrants here are likely to turn up in autumn and early winter. Some birds become long-stayers if they find suitable wetland habitat.

JUVENILE

adept at climbing up reed stems

RARE LARKS

Because they feed on the ground, larks are usually relatively easy to observe well with the aid of a telescope. Use the annotations on this Short-toed Lark photo to determine the key features to study. For comparison, Skylark is the default common lark species in Britain.

For the larger larks, absence or presence of a pale trailing edge to the wings in flight is a useful pointer.

Try to gauge the size of the bird – Short-toed is smaller than Skylark; the other rare larks are larger than that species

Look at the size and shape of the bill – in two rare species (Calandra and Bimaculated) it is massive; in Short-toed it is relatively smaller but distinctly pointed; in Crested it is long and pointed.

Does the head possess a distinct crest? Among rare British larks, only in Crested is this feature obvious.

Look at the wings to see if the tertials overlap the primaries.

SHORT-TOED LARK

Does the bird have well-marked median wing coverts? This feature is useful in the identification of some small lark species.

Are the underparts clean-looking and whitish, or streaked? Clean, mostly unmarked underparts are a good feature with Short-toed.

Look carefully to see if there is a dark patch on the side of the breast – very obvious in Calandra and Bimaculated; less obvious in many Short-toed individuals; absent in Crested.

CALANDRA LARK

Melanocorypha calandra | LENGTH 17.5–20cm

Large, chunky lark. Has a passing resemblance to an outsized Short-toed lark but its head and bill are proportionately much larger. Sexes are similar.

All birds have overall streaked greyish-brown upperparts and largely unstreaked white underparts. Note the striking black patch (variable in size) on side of breast, and pale supercilium and lores. Bill is large and yellowish brown, and legs are pinkish. In flight, shows diagnostic dark underwings with a contrasting white trailing edge; note the white sides to tail. **VOICE** Utters a rolling *schrrrip* call, similar to that of a Skylark (*Alauda arvensis*) but more buzzy. **HABITS** Feeds unobtrusively on the ground. Usually fairly wary. **STATUS AND HABITAT** Widespread in suitable open habitats across S Europe; mainly resident but nomadic to a degree in winter. Vagrants here are likely to turn up at migration times, mainly in spring, and favour areas of short grassland.

dark underwings are striking in flight; note white trailing edge

BIMACULATED LARK

Melanocorypha bimaculata | LENGTH 16–18cm

Superficially similar to a Calandra Lark and only marginally smaller than that species. Note the more striking, well-marked facial pattern. Sexes are similar.

Upperparts are streaked greyish-brown, underparts are white; has variable black patch on side of breast. Head has pale supercilium and dark lines, through eye (onto lores) and below eye; latter frames a pale eye-ring. Bill is large but more slender than in Calandra; upper mandible grey-brown, lower mandible yellow. Legs are pinkish. In flight, note brown (not blackish) underwings without a white trailing edge; has white tip (not sides) to tail. **VOICE** Utters a rolling, twittering *trrrrp* call. **HABITS** Posture is rather horizontal when feeding. **STATUS AND HABITAT** Breeds in arid terrain across Central Asia; winters from Middle East to S Asia. Vagrants here turn up mainly in spring, and favour bare ground.

BLACK LARK

Melanocorypha yeltoniensis | LENGTH 18–20.5cm

Large, plump lark. Sexes are dissimilar: the male is extremely distinctive and hard to confuse with any other species; by contrast, the female is rather nondescript.

MALE   FEMALE

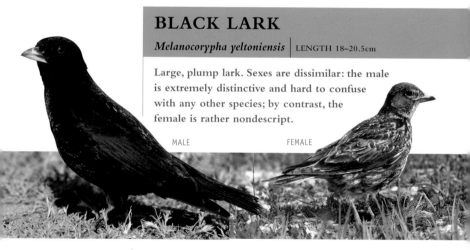

Adult male is black with pale feather margins on back and flanks, and very subtle rufous tinge to wings. Bill is pale pinkish grey and legs are dull pink. In flight, recalls a Starling (*Sturnus vulgaris*). Adult female is streaked grey-brown, darker above than below. Bill is pale straw colour and legs are dark. **VOICE** Vagrants are mostly silent. **HABITS** Feeds unobtrusively. Alert birds sometimes adopt an upright posture. **STATUS AND HABITAT** Breeds in steppe grasslands of Central Asia; at other times migratory and nomadic. Vagrants turn up mostly in spring and favour short grassland.

SHORT-TOED LARK

Calandrella brachydactyla | VL | LENGTH 14–16cm

Small, rather dumpy lark with a stubby, finch-like bill. Plumage is very 'clean-looking' by comparison with a Skylark (*Alauda arvensis*). Sexes are similar.

Short-toed is the most regularly occurring of the 'rare' lark species in Britain and Ireland

All birds have sandy-brown upperparts with faint streaking. Head has a streaked brown (sometimes reddish-brown) crown, a pale supercilium, brown cheeks and a whitish throat. Underparts are mainly whitish, but note the dark patch and faint streaking on side of breast. On closed wing, tertial feathers are long and mask the primaries; note also the row of dark-centred feathers with pale margins (median coverts). **VOICE** Utters a sharp *chrrrp-chrrrp* call. **HABITS** Unobtrusive and easy to overlook as it creeps along the ground in an almost mouse-like fashion. **STATUS AND HABITAT** Widespread breeder across S Europe that winters in Africa and S Asia. Vagrants here are likely to turn up in spring and autumn, and favour areas of short grassland and ploughed fields.

CRESTED LARK

Galerida cristata | LENGTH 17–19cm

Superficially similar to a Skylark (*Alauda arvensis*),
but with a much longer bill and a diagnostic long
crest (extended feathers are visible even when
the crest is flattened). Sexes are similar.

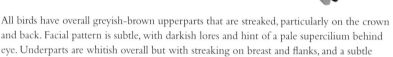

All birds have overall greyish-brown upperparts that are streaked, particularly on the crown
and back. Facial pattern is subtle, with darkish lores and hint of a pale supercilium behind
eye. Underparts are whitish overall but with streaking on breast and flanks, and a subtle
orange-buff flush to flanks. In flight, note the rufous-tinged
underwing coverts; compared to Skylark, note the lack
of a white trailing margin to wings and buff (not white)
outer-tail feathers. **VOICE** Call comprises a series of long,
thin, whistling *weeeeeluu* notes. **HABITS** Often runs along
the ground in short bursts. **STATUS AND HABITAT**
Widespread resident across much of mainland
Europe, often favouring roadside verges,
disturbed ground and industrial sites.
Vagrants here are likely to turn up
in spring and autumn, and
favour bare ground in
coastal locations.

CRAG MARTIN

Ptyonoprogne rupestris | LENGTH 14–15cm

**Relatively large swallow. Recalls a Sand Martin
(*Riparia riparia*), but is appreciably bulkier and
has distinctive plumage details that ensure
correct identification. Sexes are similar.**

white
tail
spots

Compared to a Sand Martin, has a bulkier
body and its triangular wings are broader-
based and more pointed. The short, broad
tail is sometimes fanned in flight, revealing
diagnostic white spots. All birds have grey-brown
upperparts and paler grey-buff underparts. Note the
dusky throat (white in Sand Martin) and absence of a dark
breast band (present in Sand Martin). Seen in flight from below, the rather pale grey-buff
underparts contrast with the dark underwing coverts and vent. **VOICE** Vagrants here are
mostly silent. **HABITS** Flight pattern is varied, alternating between gliding and circling, and
bouts of rapid wingbeats and direct flight. **STATUS AND HABITAT** Resident and partial
altitudinal migrant in S Europe. Vagrants here are likely to turn up in spring and autumn.

CLIFF SWALLOW

Petrochelidon pyrrhonota | LENGTH 13–14cm

**Compact swallow with relatively short, broad-based
triangular wings. Sexes are similar.**

Pale orange-buff rump (obvious
in flight) invites confusion with
a Red-rumped Swallow. Structural
differences allow separation, notably
Cliff Swallow's short, square-ended tail
(forked tail has long streamers in Red-rumped). Adult has a
bluish-black cap and white-streaked bluish-black back.
Note the pale collar, reddish-orange cheeks and dark throat;
forehead is buff. Rump is reddish buff and square-ended tail is
dark. Underparts are mostly pale with darker spots on undertail coverts. Juvenile/1st-winter
is duller than adult, with an unmarked back and a paler rump; reddish elements of adult's
facial plumage are buff. Throat is dark. **VOICE** Calls include various soft, twittering notes.
HABITS Catches flying insects on the wing. **STATUS AND HABITAT** Breeds in North
America, winters in South America; vagrants are likely to turn up in autumn on coasts.

RED-RUMPED SWALLOW

Cecropis daurica | VR | LENGTH 15–18cm

An attractive cousin to the Swallow (*Hirundo rustica*), from which it is readily distinguished at all times by its pale (sometimes reddish) rump. Sexes are similar.

Adult has mainly blue-black upperparts, except for the buffish-orange nape and cheeks, and pale rump. Underparts, including underwing, are mainly pale and streaked. Tail and tail coverts are black with a neat cut-off as though bird has been dipped, tail first, into a pot of black paint. Juvenile/1st-winter is similar but pale elements of plumage (particularly rump) are almost white, and tail streamers are rather short. In all ages always shows a pale, lightly streaked throat (ranges from salmon to deep red in Swallow and is always unstreaked). **VOICE** Vagrants here are mostly silent but have been heard to utter a harsh *chett* call. **HABITS** Vagrants here often associate with feeding Swallows and martins. **STATUS AND HABITAT** Widespread breeder in S Europe that winters in Africa. Vagrants here (15–20 in a good year) are likely to turn up in spring and autumn and favour coastal locations and freshwater marshes.

well-defined black tail and pale throat

RARE WARBLER GENERA

Warblers can be a challenge to identify, even for more experienced birdwatchers. Being able to place a mystery bird in a warbler genus is a useful first step in the identification process. Vocalisation is, of course, diagnostic with most species, but silent birds require careful observation of plumage to aid identification. Here are a few useful plumage pointers to aid recognition of the various genera of warblers.

Look for the presence or absence of a wingbar/wingbars.

The head pattern/extent of supercilium is useful in separating some species.

GENUS *PHYLLOSCOPUS*
These are small and relatively compact warblers; generally they are very active. The bill is rather small and thin, the primary projection of the wings varies according to species, the tail is subtly forked and the undertail coverts are relatively short. The sexes are usually similar in plumage terms.

YELLOW-BROWED WARBLER
Phylloscopus inornatus

Look at the colour of the undertail coverts - clean white in most, but buff or rusty coloured in Dusky and Radde's (often suffused with lemon in Chiffchaff and Willow Warbler).

GENUS *SYLVIA*
Characterised by a rounded head and medium-length wings, most have coloured eyes and eye-ring, and distinctive plumage features, for example coloured underparts, moustachial stripes or a short stout bill. The tail is relatively long and square-ended in most species, and some have white outer-tail feathers. In most species, the sexes are dissimilar.

RÜPPELL'S WARBLER
Sylvia rueppelli

GENUS *LOCUSTELLA*

These skulking warblers have a rather rounded head, relatively long wings, a long, broad and rounded tail and very long undertail coverts. The sexes are similar in plumage terms.

GENUS *ACROCEPHALUS*

Acrocephalus warblers have a distinctive elongated head shape, created by the sloping forehead and rather long bill. The wings are relatively short (compared to *Locustella* warblers for example). The tail is rather long and subtly rounded at the tip, and the undertail coverts are long (but not as long as in *Locustella* warblers). The sexes are similar in plumage terms.

RIVER
WARBLER
*Locustella
fluviatilis*

AQUATIC
WARBLER
*Acrocephalus
paludicola*

MELODIOUS WARBLER
Hippolais polyglotta

SYKES'S
WARBLER
Iduna rama

GENUS *HIPPOLAIS*

Two species are encountered regularly in Britain and both are relatively large by warbler standards. They have relatively stout, broad-based bills; pale lores create a rather plain-looking face. The tail is square-ended and the legs are stout.

GENUS *IDUNA*

Members of this genus were formerly placed in different genera (*Hippolais* and *Acrocephalus*). They range from small to large (in warbler terms), but all have broad-based bills and square-ended tails.

RARE *PHYLLOSCOPUS* WARBLERS

When confronted with a mystery *Phylloscopus* warbler, there are some key features that are worth concentrating on. Study the annotation on this Yellow-browed Warbler photo to hone your skills.

Check whether the bird has wingbars, and if so how many – feature is distinctive in Yellow-browed, Pallas's, Hume's, less so in Arctic and Greenish, and absent in most other species.

Check the wings for primary projection – for example, long in Arctic, short in Greenish.

Look for the presence or absence of a distinctive rump patch – bright yellow in Pallas's, but concolorous in other species.

YELLOW-BROWED WARBLER

Look for the presence or absence of a crown stripe – most distinctive in Pallas's but sometimes seen in Yellow-browed and Hume's too.

Study the boldness of the dark eyestripe – feature is most striking in Pallas's, almost lacking in both species of Bonelli's.

Study the colour of the underparts – most rare *Phylloscopus* warblers have clean-looking underparts; feathers are suffused with yellow in some species.

Leg colour can be a good feature – ranges from brightest in Yellow-browed to darkest in Hume's; be aware that shadows and bright sunshine can give a false impression of true colour.

WESTERN BONELLI'S WARBLER

Phylloscopus bonelli | IW | LENGTH 11–12cm

Delicate little warbler. Size and shape of a
Chiffchaff (*P. collybita*) but looks cleaner overall
and has pure white underparts. Sexes are similar.

rump is brighter
and more
colourful than in
Eastern Bonelli's
Warbler

Adult has greyish cap and nape, pale buff
lores and cheeks, grey-green upperparts,
whitish underparts and yellowish rump. Lack
of strong head pattern results in an 'open-faced'
look. Has an unbroken white eye-ring (the only
Phylloscopus warbler to show this). Wing feathers
have yellowish-green margins; pale green edges
to secondaries form a pale panel in folded wing.
Immature is similar but duller. **VOICE** Call is a disyllabic *hu-eet*. **HABITS** Forages for insects
among leaf foliage; sometimes hovers. **STATUS AND HABITAT** Widespread woodland
breeder in S Europe from Italy westwards; winters in Africa. Vagrants here (5–6 in a good year)
usually turn up in spring and autumn, and favour coastal woodland and scrub.

EASTERN BONELLI'S WARBLER

Phylloscopus orientalis | LENGTH 11–12cm

Clean-looking, rather pale warbler that is
very similar to Western Bonelli's; best separated
from that species by its call. Sexes are similar.

Adult has pale greyish cap and nape,
pale buff lores and cheeks, grey-green
upperparts, clean whitish underparts and
yellowish rump. Yellowish-green margins
of wing feathers are less colourful and less
extensive than in Western Bonelli's. In spring,
tertials and greater wing coverts are pale in
some birds, forming a panel. Immature is similar
but duller, with pale-edged dark tertials. **VOICE**
Call (best distinction from Western) is a single-note *tchip*. **HABITS** Searches for insects
among foliage; sometimes hovers. **STATUS AND HABITAT** Widespread woodland breeder
in S Europe, from Greece eastwards; winters in Africa. Vagrants here usually turn up in spring
and autumn, and favour coastal woodland and scrub.

GREENISH WARBLER

Phylloscopus trochiloides | LENGTH 9.5–10cm

single
short
wingbar

Similar size to a Chiffchaff (*P. collybita*) but with distinctive plumage features and vocalisation. Beware that potential exists for confusion with the more robust Arctic Warbler. Sexes are similar.

All birds have greyish-green upperparts, with a subtle pale wingbar and greyish-white underparts. Head has a narrow dark eye-stripe; pale supercilium is broadest behind eye, and extends onto forehead (stops short of forehead in Arctic Warbler). Bill is rather dainty; lower mandible is pale (dark-tipped in Arctic). Primary projection is short (⅔ length of exposed tertials) when compared to Arctic Warbler. **VOICE** Call is a disyllabic, wagtail-like *tsiu-lii*. Spring vagrants sometimes sing: a vibrant series of alternating notes often ending in a trill. **HABITS** Feeds like a Chiffchaff: active but not frantic. **STATUS AND HABITAT** Breeds from E Baltic States eastwards; winters in S Asia. Vagrants usually turn up in May or late summer, and favour coastal scrubby woodland.

ARCTIC WARBLER

Phylloscopus borealis | AP | LENGTH 11.5–13cm

two short
wingbars

Robust *Phylloscopus* warbler. Similar to, but appreciably more bulky than, a Greenish Warbler, and with subtle plumage and structural differences that allow separation. Sexes are similar.

All birds have overall greyish-green upperparts and greyish-white underparts, with dark speckling on cheek. Note the subtle pale wingbar (there is sometimes a hint of a 2nd one) and bold, dark eye-stripe; pale supercilium is well defined both behind eye and in front of it but stops short of forehead (continues to forehead in Greenish). Bill is relatively robust, the lower mandible pale and dark-tipped (uniformly pink in Greenish). Primary projection is long (equal to exposed tertials) when compared to that of Greenish Warbler. **VOICE** Call is a rather metallic, buzzing *przzz*. Song is a rapid trill, delivered at a constant pitch. **HABITS** Feeds in a deliberate, searching manner (not highly active like the Yellow-browed Warbler). **STATUS AND HABITAT** Widespread Arctic breeder from N Scandinavia eastwards; winters in southern Asia. Vagrants here are likely to turn up at migration times, mainly in autumn, and favour coastal scrub.

YELLOW-BROWED WARBLER

Phylloscopus inornatus │ YB │ LENGTH 9–10cm

Small, well-marked warbler. Its size, appearance and frenetic behaviour give it a passing resemblance to a Goldcrest (*Regulus regulus*). Sexes are similar.

All birds have bright olive-green upperparts and whitish underparts. Note the narrow, dark eye-stripe; broad, long yellow supercilium; and 2 pale yellow wingbars. Note that some birds, at some angles, show a hint of a pale crown stripe, inviting confusion with a Pallas's Leaf Warbler. Bill is needle-like with a pinkish base, and legs are pinkish. Compared to the similar Hume's Leaf Warbler, colours are brighter. Compared to Pallas's, crown stripe is indistinct at best (very bright in Pallas's) and rump is concolorous with back (lemon yellow in Pallas's). **VOICE** Vagrants are very vocal and utter an unmistakable drawn-out, disyllabic *tseu-eet*. They also occasionally utter a monosyllabic *tsveet* call, very reminiscent of that of a Coal Tit (*Periparus ater*). **HABITS** A fantastically active and acrobatic feeder, constantly foraging among foliage and sometimes hovering to pick insects from the undersurface of leaves. **STATUS AND HABITAT** Widespread breeder in Siberia that winters in S Asia. One of the most regularly recorded vagrants here, with numbers akin to a scarce passage migrant (200–300 in a good year), almost all discovered in autumn. Favours coastal scrub and woodland. Birds occasionally overwinter here.

yellow base to bill and pale legs

obvious double wingbar

HUME'S LEAF WARBLER

Phylloscopus humei | LENGTH 9–9.5cm

Recalls a drab Yellow-browed Warbler, with only subtle differences distinguishing the two. Note that some individuals (notably silent birds) will not be separable. Sexes are similar.

dark legs and bill

All birds have dull greyish-olive upperparts and rather grubby white underparts; some autumn birds show faint buff tinge to face, neck and flanks. Note the narrow, dark eye-stripe, broad, long, dull yellow supercilium, and 2 pale wingbars (tinged buff in some autumn birds). Bill is needle-like and dark, and legs are dark. **VOICE** Classic call is a shrill, monosyllabic *tsweet*. Not all vagrants call; repertoire of some birds includes calls similar to Yellow-browed. **HABITS** An active and acrobatic feeder; sometimes hovers to catch insects. **STATUS AND HABITAT** Breeds in Central Asia and winters in S Asia. Most vagrants turn up in autumn; some birds linger into early winter. Coastal scrub and woodland is favoured.

PALLAS'S LEAF WARBLER

Phylloscopus proregulus | PA | LENGTH 9–10cm

Tiny and energetic warbler that recalls a Firecrest (*Regulus ignicapilla*) or Yellow-browed Warbler in terms of size and behaviour. Sexes are similar.

All birds are olive-green above and whitish below with faintly dark-streaked cheeks. Stripy head pattern is striking and comprises a dark eye-stripe, bright yellowish supercilium, and pale median stripe on otherwise dark olive crown. Two pale wingbars are obvious, but pale rump is harder to discern except in hovering birds. **VOICE** Vagrants are mostly silent but occasionally utter a soft *tchuee* call. **HABITS** Active and acrobatic feeder, foraging among foliage; sometimes hovers. **STATUS AND HABITAT** Breeds in Siberia and winters in S Asia. Most vagrants turn up in late autumn (mid-Oct), and favour coastal scrub and woodland. Very occasionally overwinters.

pale rump and obvious crown stripe

RADDE'S WARBLER

Phylloscopus schwarzi | LENGTH 12–13cm

Relatively bulky, plump-bodied *Phylloscopus* warbler. Subtle plumage and structural features, and its habits, allow separation from the similar Dusky Warbler. Sexes are similar.

All birds have rather dingy-looking plumage overall. Upperparts are dark olive-brown while underparts are yellowish buff, palest on throat. Undertail coverts are warm yellowish buff (brighter than rest of underparts). Note the dark eye-stripe and long, pale supercilium, which is buffish in front of eye but whitish and brightest behind it (dullest behind eye in Dusky). Bill is noticeably short and stout (slender in Dusky), and legs are pale pinkish buff. **VOICE** Call is a soft *chip*. **HABITS** Prefers to keep in cover, in low vegetation. **STATUS AND HABITAT** Breeds in Siberian Asia and winters in S Asia. Vagrants here (6 in a good year) are likely to occur in late autumn, and favour scrub and open woodland on the coast.

DUSKY WARBLER

Phylloscopus fuscatus | UY | LENGTH 11–12cm

Recalls a sombre-looking Chiffchaff (*P. collybita*), but distinguished by subtly different plumage details and its call. These features also allow separation from the superficially similar Radde's Warbler. Sexes are similar.

In all birds, upperparts are dusky grey-brown, while underparts – including undertail coverts – are pale, grubby-looking buff. Note the dark eye-stripe and the long, pale supercilium, which is buffish behind eye but whitish and brightest in front of it (cf. Radde's Warbler). Bill is rather thin and legs are pale reddish brown. **VOICE** Call is a sharp *tchek*, similar to that of a Lesser Whitethroat (*Sylvia curruca*). Vagrants are usually vocal, often being detected initially by their call. **HABITS** Generally keeps in cover. Typically more mobile and active than Radde's Warbler, sometimes foraging at eye level or above in scrubby willows. **STATUS AND HABITAT** Breeds in Siberia and winters in S Asia. Vagrants here (perhaps 6 in a good year) are likely to turn up in autumn, and favour coastal woodland and scrub, often near water; a few individuals have overwintered in recent years.

SIBERIAN CHIFFCHAFF

Phylloscopus collybita tristis | LENGTH 11–12.5cm

Siberian subspecies of the Chiffchaff and separable from the nominate race only with great care using subtle differences in plumage and call. A possible contender for elevation to separate species status. Sexes are similar.

Compared to Chiffchaff, colours are washed out. All birds are grey-brown above (Chiffchaff, particularly autumn 1st-winter, is brighter, with yellowish-green tint to these areas). Wings usually have yellowish feather margins. Shows a rusty-buff wash to supercilium, ear coverts, and sides of neck and breast (subtly yellow in Chiffchaff). Bill and legs are black (dark reddish brown in Chiffchaff). **VOICE** Call is a soft, almost piping *huiip* (not a sharp, upslurred *hu-eet* as in Chiffchaff). **HABITS** Forages among foliage, like a Chiffchaff. **STATUS AND HABITAT** Breeds in Siberia and winters in India. Most vagrants turn up in late autumn, in coastal woodland and scrub; occasionally overwinters.

IBERIAN CHIFFCHAFF

Phylloscopus ibericus | LENGTH 11–12cm

Superficially similar to a Chiffchaff (*P. collybita*), separable only with great care using subtle differences in plumage and, importantly, song and call. Sexes are similar.

All birds are very similar in appearance to Chiffchaff, with greenish-yellow upperparts and clean-looking, pale underparts with a fresh yellow wash. Head has a narrow, dark eye-stripe and a pale, bright supercilium that is flushed yellow in front of eye. Legs are dark reddish brown. Main structural difference from Chiffchaff is the appreciably longer primary projection and longer tail. **VOICE** Song has been likened to a mixture of those of Chiffchaff and Willow Warbler (*P. trochilus*): comprises Chiffchaff-like notes repeated more rapidly, with interspersed accelerated sections, and whistling *chip-chip-chip-chuwee-chuwee-chuwee* notes. Call is a downslurred, piping *wee-eu*. **HABITS** Forages among foliage and twigs, in the manner of a Chiffchaff. **STATUS AND HABITAT** Breeds mainly in NW Iberia and is presumed to winter in West Africa. Vagrants here are usually detected in spring as singing males, favouring scrub and light woodland, mainly in the south.

RARE *SYLVIA* WARBLERS

When confronted with a mystery *Sylvia* warbler, note that some plumage features are more important than others when it comes to identification. Song is diagnostic, of course, and useful with some birds in spring; but encounters in autumn usually involve silent birds. Study the annotation on this Eastern Subalpine Warbler photo to improve your chances of a successful identification outcome.

Are the underparts entirely plain? If not, does the bird have barring towards the rear end (Barred) or faint spotting (Western Orphean)?

Study the primary projection – it is very short in species such as Spectacled, Asian Desert and Marmora's.

Are the undertail coverts plain or faintly spotted? Strong markings are a good indicator for Barred Warbler.

Look carefully at the colour of the eye-ring, if present – it is strikingly red or white in males of some species. Amongst common British warblers, the only species with a red eye-ring to rule out is Dartford Warbler; Whitethroat is the only common species with a striking white eye-ring.

Study the pattern and colours on the head – the colour of the throat and the extent and width of the moustache are important in many species.

EASTERN SUBALPINE WARBLER

BARRED WARBLER

Sylvia nisoria | RR | LENGTH 16–17cm

Bulky and relatively large-billed warbler. Adults are
unmistakable but seldom seen here. Immatures are more
regularly encountered and perhaps could be mistaken for
a Garden Warbler (*S. borin*). Sexes are subtly dissimilar.

1ST-WINTER

Adult male has blue-grey upperparts and pale underparts strongly marked with dark bars.
Has a yellow eye, pale wingbars and a pale tip to tail. Adult female is similar but eye colour
is duller and barring on underparts is less intense. Juvenile/1st-winter has grey-brown
upperparts, and pale underparts washed buff on breast and flanks. Compared to smaller
Garden Warbler, note the pale wingbars, subtle crescent-shaped
barring on flanks and undertail coverts, pale brown eye and
proportionately larger bill; head shape also often appears more
angular and less rounded. **VOICE** Utters a rattling *tchrrrr*
alarm call. **HABITS** Usually rather skulking and keeps
to deep cover of Bramble patches and the like,
emerging only very occasionally. **STATUS
AND HABITAT** Breeds from central
Europe eastwards and winters in Africa.
Status here is that of a scarce passage
migrant, seen mostly in autumn;
around 100–150 birds might
be found in a good year
and most records are
coastal.

has pale wingbars and very
subtle barring on flanks and
undertail coverts

1ST-WINTER

WESTERN ORPHEAN WARBLER

Sylvia hortensis | LENGTH 14.5–16cm

Large, bulky warbler. Hard to confuse when seen well and its size relative to other species can be confirmed. Sexes are subtly dissimilar.

Adult male has a dark cap with ear coverts a subtle shade darker. Upperparts are otherwise grey-brown, throat is white and underparts are whitish with a pinkish-buff flush to breast. Eye has a pale yellow iris, bill is stout and long, and legs are dark. Adult female is similar but cap is greyer, contrasting more strikingly with black ear coverts. Juvenile/1st-winter is similar to adult female but eye is dark. Potential exists for confusion between immature Lesser Whitethroat if size is not apparent. Structural and plumage differences also help with identification: Lesser Whitethroat has a small, thin bill by comparison and a relatively shorter primary projection (just over ½ of exposed tertials, compared to over ⅔ in Western Orphean). **VOICE** Call is a tongue-clicking *tzeck*, like that of a Blackcap (*S. atricapilla*). **HABITS** Generally rather secretive and stays mostly in cover. **STATUS AND HABITAT** Breeds from Iberia to Italy and winters in Africa. Vagrants here are likely to turn up at migration times, mostly in autumn, and favour coastal scrub.

1ST-WINTER

a thickset warbler with a stout bill; recalls
Lesser Whitethroat but appreciably larger

ASIAN DESERT WARBLER

Sylvia nana | LENGTH 11.5–12.5cm

**Charming and rather pale warbler.
If seen well, it is easy to identify and hard
to confuse with anything else. Sexes are similar.**

yellow
eye

Adult has grey-buff upperparts with subtly richer
chestnut ear coverts and dark centres to tertials. Rump
is chestnut brown, and tail is mostly a similar colour
except for dark feather centres and white outer-tail
feathers. Eye has a pale yellow iris, bill has a yellow
base, and legs are pinkish yellow. **VOICE** Call
is a rolling, chattering *chrrrrr*. **HABITS** Vagrants
often favour areas of relatively sparse, low-growing vegetation (like their breeding habitat).
They feed in cover but also in the open around the edges of small shrubs. **STATUS AND
HABITAT** Breeds in Central Asian steppes and winters further south, west to the Middle
East. Vagrants here are likely to turn up in spring and autumn, and favour coastal habitats.

MARMORA'S WARBLER

Sylvia sarda | LENGTH 13–14cm

**Compact and uniformly rather dark warbler that
is the size and shape of a Dartford Warbler (*S. undata*);
its primary projection is very short. Sexes are dissimilar.**

Adult male is overall dark blue-grey, palest
on centre of belly and with dark-spotted,
pale undertail coverts. Note the dark
lores and red eye-ring. Legs and base
of bill are yellowish pink. Female is similar
but lacks the dark lores. Juvenile/1st-winter is similar to

MALE

adult female but upperparts, wings and tail are tinged brown, eye-ring is less colourful, and
throat is noticeably pale; compared to an immature Dartford Warbler, it lacks any hint of
pinkish red on underparts and throat is paler. **VOICE** Utters a harsh *tcheck* call. Song is a
rapid series of warbling and trilling notes. **HABITS** Often keeps to the cover of low
vegetation, but occasionally pops up and perches. **STATUS AND HABITAT** Seemingly a
most unlikely contender for the British list: breeds on Corsica and Sardinia, and winters in
North Africa. Nevertheless, vagrants do turn up occasionally in spring and autumn, and have
even displayed territorial behaviour. They are likely to favour areas of short vegetation cover.

SPECTACLED WARBLER

Sylvia conspicillata | LENGTH 12–13cm

Tiny warbler that in some ways recalls a miniature Whitethroat (*S. communis*). Its very short primary projection is a good feature to look for. Sexes are dissimilar.

1ST-WINTER

FEMALE

MALE

Adult has a relatively large head with a blue-grey cap, white 'eyelids' or 'spectacles', extensive dark lores and a white throat. Nape is blue-grey, grading to grey-brown on back and rufous on wings. Primary projection is very short (½, or less, of the exposed tertials) and tertials have rufous edges and triangular black centres. Underparts are mainly pinkish buff, most intense on the breast; undertail coverts are white, as are outer-tail feathers. Legs and base of bill are yellowish. Adult female is similar but cap, ear coverts and nape are grey-brown (same colour as back), and 'spectacles' are less distinct. Juvenile/1st-winter is similar to adult female but upperparts, including cap, are warmer brown. **VOICE** Call is a buzzing *drrrr*. **HABITS** Usually feeds in low, tangled, thorny bushes and clumps, but sometimes emerges and perches, giving good views. **STATUS AND HABITAT** Breeds from Iberia to Italy, favouring low-growing Mediterranean scrub, and winters in Africa. Vagrants here are likely to turn up in spring and autumn, and favour coastal habitats.

RÜPPELL'S WARBLER

Sylvia rueppelli | LENGTH 12.5–13.5cm

**Striking and well-marked *Sylvia* warbler.
Sexes are dissimilar and males
are almost unmistakable.**

FEMALE

Adult male has mainly grey upperparts with striking
white margins to the dark tertials, secondaries and
wing coverts. Head pattern comprises a black crown
and cap, separated from black throat by a white
moustachial stripe. Note the red eye-ring. Dark bill
is slender and noticeably downcurved, with a pale
greyish base to lower mandible; legs are dull pink.
Adult female is similar, but back is warmer grey, cap
is grey and throat is greyish white, with hint of a
white moustachial stripe still discernible. Eye-ring
and leg colours are dull. Juvenile/1st-winter resembles
adult female although males sometimes show subtle dark spotting on throat.
VOICE Call is a *tzeck*, like that of a Blackcap (*S. atricapilla*). Song is a rapid
series of chattering and warbling notes. **HABITS** Outside the breeding
season, birds tend to skulk in cover, although singing males often perch
boldly in the open. **STATUS AND HABITAT** Breeds in the E
Mediterranean and winters in Africa. Vagrants here are likely to
turn up in spring and autumn, and favour coastal habitats.

MALE

SARDINIAN WARBLER

Sylvia melanocephala | LENGTH 13–14cm

Boldly marked *Sylvia* warbler. Sexes are dissimilar and males in particular are easy to identify if seen well.

FEMALE

MALE

Adult male has a black cap, white throat and striking red eye-ring. Back and wings are grey and tail is dark grey. Underparts are greyish white, palest on centre of belly and undertail coverts. Dark bill is thin with a grey base to lower mandible, and legs are pinkish. Adult female and juvenile/1st-winter have a grey cap, white throat and dull red eye-ring. Upperparts are buffish brown and underparts are buffish white, palest on centre of belly and undertail coverts. Has a moderate primary projection (½ of exposed tertials). **VOICE** Calls include a churring *drr-rrr-rrr…* and a sharp *tzeck*. Song is a rapid series of warbling and churring rattles, and whistling notes. **HABITS** Vagrants spend a lot of time feeding and skulking in cover, but occasionally perch out in the open. **STATUS AND HABITAT** Mainly a resident around the Mediterranean, but also a partial migrant. Vagrants here are likely to turn up in spring and autumn, and favour coastal scrub.

MALE

WESTERN SUBALPINE WARBLER

Sylvia inornata | LENGTH 12–13cm

Recalls a Dartford Warbler (*S. undata*). Similar to Eastern Subalpine Warbler; adult males can be separated, but other birds are problematic. Sexes are dissimilar.

1ST-WINTER

Adult male has blue-grey upperparts, except for the brownish margins to wing feathers. Has a subtle white 'moustache' and red eye-ring; throat, breast and flanks are reddish orange with a white centre to belly. Adult female and juvenile/1st-winter have a blue-grey cap, whitish-buff throat and hint of a pale 'moustache'. Back is grey-brown and wings have brown feather margins. Underparts are whitish buff, variably washed pinkish buff on breast and flanks, and sometimes on throat too. **VOICE** Utters a sharp, tongue-clicking *tcheck* alarm call. **HABITS** Spends a lot of time feeding and skulking in cover, but emerges and perches openly on occasions. **STATUS AND HABITAT** Formerly (and sometimes still) treated as a subspecies of Subalpine Warbler (*S. cantillans cantillans*) but treated here as a separate species. Breeds in SW Europe and winters in Africa. Vagrants here are likely to turn up in spring and autumn, and favour coastal scrub.

MALE

FEMALE

EASTERN SUBALPINE WARBLER

Sylvia cantillans | LENGTH 12–13cm

MALE

Very similar to a Western Subalpine Warbler. Adult males can be separated but many vagrants here are hard to assign to species level. Sexes are dissimilar.

Compared to similar Western Subalpine, male has grey-buff (not brown) margins to wing feathers, and more striking white 'moustache'; reddish orange on underparts is limited to throat and breast, with a paler wash on flanks; underparts are otherwise white. Adult female and juvenile/1st-winter are very similar to their Western Subalpine counterparts but margins of wing feathers are grey-buff not brown. **VOICE** Utters a sharp, tongue-clicking *tcheck* alarm call. **HABITS** Generally skulking, but emerges and perches openly on occasions. **STATUS AND HABITAT** Formerly (and sometimes still) treated as a subspecies of Subalpine Warbler (*S. cantillans albistriata*); treated here as a separate species. Breeds in SE Europe and winters in Africa. Vagrants here are likely to turn up in spring and autumn, and favour coastal scrub.

LESSER WHITETHROAT (ASIATIC RACES)

Sylvia curruca | LW | LENGTH 11.5–13.5cm

SSP. *HALIMODENDRI*

SSP. *MINULA*

Lesser Whitethroat is widespread across Asia in breeding season, represented by several subspecies. Some distinctive eastern races turn up as vagrants. Sexes are similar.

Superficially similar to British-breeding Lesser Whitethroat, with a grey cap, dark ear coverts and white throat; back is grey-brown and wings are brown. Underparts are pale, variably flushed grey-buff on flanks. Bill and legs are dark. Compared to standard British birds, ssp. *halimodendri* is paler and browner; ssp. *minula* is similarly pale but strikingly small with a small bill and short primary projection; ssp. *blythi* has brown tones to head, ear coverts and back (almost Whitethroat-like). **VOICE** Call is a tongue-clicking *tchek*. **HABITS** Usually rather unobtrusive and keeps to cover. **STATUS AND HABITAT** The various subspecies breed across Asia and winter in Africa and Asia. Vagrants here usually turn up in late autumn; has overwintered.

RARE *IDUNA* AND *HIPPOLAIS* WARBLERS

Iduna and *Hippolais* warblers are closely related and have a lot in common with one another in terms of plumage and structure. When confronted with a mystery individual, there are some key features that are worth concentrating on. Study the annotation on the Eastern Olivaceous and Icterine warbler photos shown here to hone your skills.

What size is the bird relative to other warblers? Members of the genus range from the size of a *Phylloscopus* warbler (for example, Booted) up to the size of a Great Reed Warbler (Thick-billed).

Study the lores to see if they are dark or pale. They are pale in Thick-billed Warbler, but dark in other species.

Note the bill size – that of Booted is particularly short, akin to the bill of a *Phylloscopus* warbler.

With small *Iduna* warblers, check the primary projection – shortest in Booted; longest in Eastern Olivaceous.

EASTERN OLIVACEOUS WARBLER
IDUNA PALLIDA

Does the bird have a pale wing panel? This feature is most obvious and reliable in Icterine. Beware that some Melodious also have a noticeable pale panel, so always check the primary projection (*see* below).

Check the primary projection – long in Icterine; relatively short in Melodious.

ICTERINE WARBLER
HIPPOLAIS ICTERINA

Look at the leg colour – blue in Icterine; pinkish brown in Melodious.

THICK-BILLED WARBLER

Iduna aedon | LENGTH 16–17.5cm

A large warbler, roughly the size and proportions of a Great Reed Warbler but unrelated to that species. Sexes are similar.

Compared to Great Reed Warbler, is marginally smaller and note the extremely short primary projection (½ the length of exposed tertials; equal to, or slightly longer than, tertials in Great Reed) and relatively stubby bill. All birds have grey-buff upperparts and whitish underparts with a buff wash to the flanks and undertail coverts. Has a plain-faced appearance due mainly to the pale lores (dark lores emphasise the pale supercilium in Great Reed). Bill is stout with a yellowish lower mandible, and legs are dark. Can look very shrike-like in the field. **VOICE** Utters a sharp *tchack* call. **HABITS** Usually keeps to the cover of foliage, making observation a challenge. **STATUS AND HABITAT** Breeds in Siberia and winters in India. Vagrants here are likely to turn up in spring and autumn, and favour coastal scrub.

BOOTED WARBLER

Iduna caligata | LENGTH 11–12.5cm

Small warbler, formerly placed in the genus *Hippolais* (along with Sykes's and Eastern Olivaceous warblers). The size of a *Phylloscopus* warbler but with proportions more akin to those of an *Acrocephalus*. Sexes are similar.

compared to a *Phylloscopus* warbler, is very pale – the colour of milky tea; note the slim proportions and relatively long tail; head appears proportionately smaller and more angular

A bird with grey-brown upperparts and pale underparts, whitest on throat and with a warm buff tinge to sides of breast and flanks. Subtly dark lores emphasise the pale supercilium, which is further emphasised by a dark brow above. Legs are pinkish brown and bill is mainly dark with a pale base. Compared to Sykes's, bill is smaller, with a dark tip to lower mandible, and primary projection is marginally shorter (½, or less, than length of exposed tertials, compared to ⅔ tertial length in Sykes's). Shows pale outer-tail feathers to its relatively short tail (tail is longer in Sykes's). **VOICE** Call is a tongue-clicking *tchrrk*. **HABITS** Prefers to feed in the cover of low bushes and shrubs. When agitated, sometimes flicks its tail and wings. **STATUS AND HABITAT** Breeds in Central Asia and winters in India. Vagrants here are likely to turn up in autumn and favour coastal habitats.

SYKES'S WARBLER

Iduna rama | LENGTH 11.5–13cm

compared to a *Phylloscopus* warbler, note the slim proportions and relatively long tail; head appears proportionately smaller and more angular

Very similar to, and formerly treated as a subspecies of, Booted Warbler. Fractionally larger than that species, and with subtle structural differences to aid identification. Sexes are similar.

Compared to Booted Warbler, Sykes's is on average paler. All birds have paler grey-brown upperparts and paler, almost silky-white underparts compared to Booted, and lack warm buff tinge to sides of breast and flanks. Pale supercilium is often fairly indistinct, fading just behind the eye (subtly longer in Booted), and dark brow is less distinct. Legs are brown (darker than Booted), and bill is mostly pale and appreciably longer and spikier than in Booted. Compared to Booted, primary projection is longer (⅔ tertial length). Shows pale outer-tail feathers. **VOICE** Call is a tongue-clicking *tchik*. **HABITS** Prefers to feed in the cover of bushes and shrubs. When agitated, sometimes flicks its tail. **STATUS AND HABITAT** Breeds in Central Asia and winters in India. Vagrants here are likely to turn up in autumn and favour coastal habitats.

EASTERN OLIVACEOUS WARBLER

Iduna pallida | LENGTH 12–13.5cm

Pale, rather nondescript warbler. Superficially like an *Acrocephalus* warbler, but slimmer, longer-tailed, and with a more elongated head and longer bill. Sexes are similar.

All birds have pale olive-grey upperparts with slightly dark, browner wings that sometimes show a pale panel (tertial feather margins). Underparts are whitish, with a faint buff tinge to sides of breast and flanks. Pale supercilium and pale lores emphasise open-faced look. Legs are pinkish brown and bill is relatively long, the lower mandible yellowish. Compared to Booted Warbler, primary projection is relatively long (around ⅔ tertial length). Shows pale outer-tail feathers. **VOICE** Call is a sharp *tchack*. Song recalls a cross between that of a Reed Warbler (*Acrocephalus scirpaceus*) and a Blackcap (*Sylvia atricapilla*). **HABITS** Usually keeps to the cover of bushes and shrubs. Active birds sometimes dip their tail downwards. **STATUS AND HABITAT** Breeds in SE Europe and winters in Africa. Vagrants here are likely to turn up at migration times, mainly in autumn, and favour coastal habitats.

ICTERINE WARBLER

Hippolais icterina | IC | LENGTH 12–13.5cm

Relatively large warbler with different proportions from a *Phylloscopus* warbler. Superficially similar to Melodious Warbler but separable using subtle plumage and structural differences. Sexes are similar.

Adult has greyish-green upperparts and pale yellow underparts. Pale lores contribute to its plain-faced appearance. Compared to Melodious, note the pale panel on wings (created by pale feather fringes; beware, however, that some Melodious can show this feature), blue-grey legs and long primary projection (equal to length of exposed tertials, or slightly less, compared to ½–⅔ tertial length in Melodious). Juvenile/1st-winter is similar but underparts are paler. Young birds can often appear surprisingly washed out. **VOICE** Utters a sharp *tchet* or rattling *tee-ter-tlueet*. Song is a rapid, fluty warble, with a rather 'nasal' tone; often includes elements of mimicry. **HABITS** Usually forages in the cover of tree-top foliage, making observation a challenge. Spring birds do occasionally sing. **STATUS AND HABITAT** Breeds from France to Scandinavia, eastwards across Europe and Asia; winters in Africa. Its status here is that of a scarce passage migrant in spring and autumn (50–100 in most years), with most turning up in coastal woodland and scrub.

pale wing panel is usually obvious, and is a good identification feature

long primary projection

bluish legs

MELODIOUS WARBLER

Hippolais polyglotta | ME | LENGTH 12–13cm

main confusion species for Melodious Warbler is its cousin the Icterine Warbler

Recalls a bulky, outsized juvenile/1st-winter Willow Warbler (*Phylloscopus trochilus*). But note proportionately large head, peaked (not rounded) crown, large, broad-based bill and pale lores.

Adult has uniform olive-green upperparts with a brownish hue to wings, which mostly lack Icterine's pale panel. Underparts are pale yellow, the colour most intense on throat and breast. Legs are greyish brown (blue-grey in Icterine). Compared to Icterine, primaries project only a short distance beyond tertials. Juvenile/1st-winter is similar but underparts are much paler; very pale yellow suffusion is confined to throat and breast. In all plumages, shares open-faced look of Icterine. **VOICE** Utters a sharp *tchet* call. Song is a series of very rapid warbling phrases, less 'nasal' in tone than that of Icterine. **HABITS** Usually keeps to the cover of dense bushes and shrubs.

STATUS AND HABITAT
Breeds across France, Iberia and Italy, and winters in Africa. Its status here is that of a scarce passage migrant, mainly in late summer and early autumn (40–50 in a good year). Migrants usually favour coastal scrub.

1ST-WINTER

short primary projection

RARE *LOCUSTELLA* AND *ACROCEPHALUS* WARBLERS

When confronted with mystery *Locustella* and *Acrocephalus* warblers, there are some key features that are worth concentrating on. Song is diagnostic, of course, and useful with some birds in spring; but encounters in autumn involve silent birds. Study the annotation on the River and Marsh warbler photos shown here to improve your chances of successful identification.

Study the upperparts carefully - unmarked in River and Savi's; streaked in Pallas's Grasshopper and Lanceolated.

RIVER WARBLER
Locustella fluviatilis

Are the undertail coverts strongly marked (streaked or pale-spotted as in Lanceolated and River warblers) or rather plain (as with Savi's Warbler)?

Note the size of the bird – Great Reed is large; other species are medium-sized warblers.

Does the bird have a prominent pale supercilium, and if so does it extend behind the eye? This feature is particularly useful with Blyth's Reed and Paddyfield warblers, in comparison with the common Reed Warbler.

Study the upperparts – streaked in Aquatic; plain in other species.

With plain, medium-sized *Acrocephalus* warblers, study the primary projection – short in Blyth's Reed and Paddyfield; long in Marsh.

MARSH WARBLER
Acrocephalus palustris

PALLAS'S GRASSHOPPER WARBLER

Locustella certhiola | LENGTH 13–14cm

Unobtrusive and generally secretive warbler. Immature (the plumage that is usually seen here) is very similar to a Grasshopper Warbler (*L. naevia*). Sexes are similar.

white
tertial
spots

Juvenile/1st-winter is streaked yellow-brown above, grading to reddish brown on rump; overall, colours are 'warmer' than in Grasshopper. Underparts are yellowish brown with faint streaking on breast; long undertail coverts are unmarked (undertail coverts of Grasshopper have dark streaks). Feathers of rounded tail have dark sub-terminal marks and white tips (feathers are unmarked and brown in Grasshopper). Tertials are white-tipped. Often shows a greyish cowl on nape. **VOICE** Calls include a soft *tchick*, but vagrants here are typically silent. **HABITS** Secretive; prefers to creep through tangled stems rather than venture into the open. **STATUS AND HABITAT** Breeds in Siberia and winters in S Asia. Vagrants here turn up in autumn; only those at locations with little cover are likely to be discovered.

LANCEOLATED WARBLER

Locustella lanceolata | LENGTH 11.5–12.5cm

Well-marked warbler whose unobtrusive (borderline secretive) habits make it a challenge to observe. Sexes are similar; typically seen here in immature plumage.

heavily streaked flanks
and undertail coverts

Compared to Grasshopper (*L. naevia*) and Pallas's Grasshopper warblers, note proportionately shorter tail and smaller size. Juvenile/1st-winter has streaked olive-brown upperparts and only marginally paler underparts. Extensive dark streaking on back, and dark feather centres on wing coverts and wing feathers (tertials in particular), are striking. Underparts are streaked, and dark spots are particularly bold on undertail coverts. **VOICE** Calls include a soft *tchick*, but vagrants here are typically silent. **HABITS** Secretive; keeps to the cover of dense, low vegetation. **STATUS AND HABITAT** Breeds in Siberia and winters in S Asia. Vagrants here turn up in autumn; only those at locations with little cover are likely to be discovered.

RIVER WARBLER

Locustella fluviatilis | VW | LENGTH 14.5–16cm

Stocky warbler with rather undistinguished plumage. Easiest to detect by its song; fortunately, vagrants sometimes sing for extended periods. Sexes are similar.

streaked throat

All birds are unmarked dark olive-brown above and olive-buff below, palest on centre of belly, and with subtle dark streaking on throat and upper breast. Note pale tips to extremely long undertail coverts, which reach nearly to tip of tail. **VOICE** Song is a mechanical-sounding, endlessly repeated series of *tze-tze-tze…* notes. Call is a slightly buzzing *zrrr*. **HABITS** Singing birds are not especially shy but typically perch at least in partial cover. **STATUS AND HABITAT** Breeds from E Europe eastwards and winters in Africa. Vagrants here (typically singing birds) are usually detected in spring and favour overgrown wetland habitats.

unstreaked throat

SAVI'S WARBLER

Locustella luscinioides | VI | ENGTH 13.5–15cm

Superficially like a Reed Warbler (*Acrocephalus scirpaceus*), and shares the same habitat preferences. Hard to observe and usually detected by its song. Sexes are similar.

Best separated from Reed Warbler by song. In structural terms note longer undertail coverts, extending well beyond primary tips on folded wing (equal to, or only slightly longer, in Reed), and proportionately smaller head. All birds are unmarked, warm buffish brown above (with concolorous rump); have a whitish throat and otherwise plain buffish-white underparts (with subtle, pale fringes to undertail coverts), palest on centre of belly. **VOICE** Song is an endless, rather mechanical-sounding rattle, reminiscent of a bush-cricket's 'song'; it is too high-pitched for many people to be able to hear. Call is a sharp *kvit*. **HABITS** Singing birds often climb up reed stems. However, because favoured habitat is dense, views are typically partial. **STATUS AND HABITAT** Widespread but local breeder across Europe, on edge of breeding range in SE England; winters in Africa. Vagrants here are likely to turn up in spring and favour extensive reedbeds.

ZITTING CISTICOLA

Cisticola juncidis | FZ | LENGTH 10–11cm

heavily streaked crown

Small, delicate-looking warbler. Recalls a tiny Sedge Warbler (*Acrocephalus schoenobaenus*), but unlike that species its head lacks any distinctive markings or patterns. Sexes are similar.

All birds are buff-brown above, heavily streaked on crown, nape and back, and subtly more orange-buff on rump and centre of tail. Face is pale buffish brown (with pale lores) and only faintly streaked. Underparts, including throat, are whitish, flushed buff on flanks. Tail feathers have dark sub-terminal marks and white tips, easiest to see when fanned in flight. Bill is slender and legs are pinkish. **VOICE** Call is a shrill *tchip*. Song is an endlessly repeated *tzip-tzip-tzip…*, delivered in undulating (yoyo-like) flight. **HABITS** Usually keeps to the cover of low grassy vegetation. **STATUS AND HABITAT** Locally common breeding resident across S Europe; range extends to coastal NW France. Vagrants here are likely to turn up in spring and autumn, and favour tussocky coastal meadows.

AQUATIC WARBLER

Acrocephalus paludicola | AQ | LENGTH 11.5–13cm

pale central crown stripe

Well-marked warbler, seen here in immature plumage. Superficially similar to a Sedge Warbler but separable by studying the patterns on the head and back. Sexes are similar, and adults are similar to immatures.

Has warm yellow-buff upperparts, heavily marked with bold dark and pale stripes on back, and dark-centred tertials and wing coverts. Head pattern is diagnostic: narrow, dark stripe behind eye (lores are pale); bold, pale yellow-buff supercilium; and dark crown with central bold, pale stripe. Underparts are whitish, flushed yellow-buff on breast and flanks. **VOICE** Call is a tongue-clicking *tchak*. **HABITS** Secretive; keeps to the cover of low vegetation, particularly tussocks of sedges and rushes. **STATUS AND HABITAT** Breeds very locally in E Europe and winters in West Africa. Vagrants turn up in autumn and favour coastal wetland habitats.

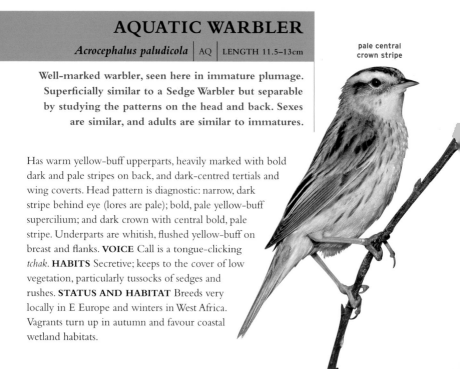

PADDYFIELD WARBLER

Acrocephalus agricola | PY | LENGTH 12–13.5cm

pale supercilium and dark eye stripe

Very similar to a Reed Warbler (*A. scirpaceus*), and to the British rarities Blyth's Reed and Marsh warblers. Note the subtly distinctive head pattern and very short primary projection. Sexes are similar.

Adult is overall buffish-brown above, grading to warm reddish brown on lower back and rump, and with dark centres to tertials. Head pattern comprises a dark eye-stripe, and pale supercilium emphasised by dark upper border. Underparts are whitish, flushed buffish orange on chest and flanks. Eye has a yellowish iris. Juvenile/1st-winter is similar but colours are less intense, and head markings are less distinct. **VOICE** Call is a soft *tche*. Song is a rapid series of warbling phrases containing mimicry of other bird songs. **HABITS** Usually keeps to the cover of dense wetland vegetation. **STATUS AND HABITAT** Breeds from Black Sea eastwards and winters in India. Vagrants here turn up in autumn and favour coastal wetlands.

BLYTH'S REED WARBLER

Acrocephalus dumetorum | LENGTH 12.5–14cm

bulging pale lores

Similar to Reed (*A. scirpaceus*) and Marsh warblers. Separable only with great care; combination of short primary projection and unremarkable plumage patterns aids identification. Sexes are similar.

Has unmarked greyish-brown upperparts (Reed is 'warmer' reddish brown), with unmarked tertials. Head pattern comprises a subtle, pale supercilium and dark lores. Underparts are pale grey-buff, palest and whitest on throat. Legs are dull grey-brown (darker than in Reed or Marsh). **VOICE** Call is a tongue-clicking *tzeck*, like a Blackcap (*Sylvia atricapilla*). Song (sung after dark) is a slowly delivered series of repeated phrases with much mimicry of other species. **HABITS** Vagrants usually keep to the cover of low scrub. **STATUS AND HABITAT** Breeds from Baltic states eastwards and winters in India; favours drier habitats than its relatives. Vagrants turn up in spring and autumn and favour coastal scrub.

MARSH WARBLER

Acrocephalus palustris | MW | LENGTH 13–14cm

Superficially very similar to a Reed Warbler
(*A. scirpaceus*) but separable using song and subtle
plumage and structural differences. Sexes are similar.

Adult has grey-brown
upperparts (typically not as
'warm' as Reed), including the
rump. Underparts are whitish,
suffused pale yellow on breast
and flanks. Face shows a subtle,
pale supercilium (as in Reed).
Legs are pinkish (as in Reed) but
bill is appreciably shorter. Note
the long primary projection (equal to, or greater than, exposed tertials, compared to equal
to or slightly shorter in Reed, and much shorter in Blyth's Reed and Paddyfield warblers).
Juvenile/1st-winter is similar to adult but upperparts are warmer brown and rump is very
subtly reddish brown; pale underparts are washed with buff. **VOICE** Utters a sharp *tche* call.
Song is rich and varied, and includes amazing mimicry of both other European songbirds
and species from its African wintering grounds. **HABITS** Usually forages in the cover of
bushes and scrub. **STATUS AND HABITAT** Rare summer breeder and passage migrant to
Britain; winters in Africa. Territorial birds favour subtly different habitats from Reed Warbler:
lush growth of rank waterside vegetation rather than reedbeds.

on average, primary projection is appreciably longer than most Reed Warblers,
and always noticeably longer than both Blyth's Reed and Paddyfield warblers

GREAT REED WARBLER

Acrocephalus arundinaceus | QW | LENGTH 17–20cm

Similar to a Reed Warbler (*A. scirpaceus*) but
appreciably larger, and with a relatively longer
and much stouter bill. Song is a useful aid to
identification. Sexes are similar.

All birds have sandy-brown upperparts, darkest on crown and
most rufous on rump. Head pattern comprises a subtly dark
eye-stripe and pale supercilium that is broadest in front of eye.
Underparts are pale buff with a rufous-yellow wash to flanks.
Legs are usually dark brown. Has a long primary projection
(equal to, or slightly longer than, exposed tertials). **VOICE**
Call is a sharp *tchik*. Song is slower and much louder than that
of Reed, with a croaking, almost frog-like quality. **HABITS**
Invariably discovered in reedbeds. Generally hard to observe,
but occasionally clambers up reed stems or moves into more
open bushes. **STATUS AND HABITAT** Widespread breeder
across mainland Europe that winters in Africa. Vagrants here
are likely to turn up in spring and autumn, with spring arrivals
often particularly vocal.

CEDAR WAXWING

Bombycilla cedrorum | LENGTH 16–19cm

**Superficially similar to a Waxwing (*B. garrulus*) but
slightly smaller, with a distinctive crest and soft-looking
orange-buff plumage. Subtle differences in markings
allow separation of the two. Sexes are similar.**

Adult has overall orange-buff plumage, palest on underparts and white on undertail
(Waxwing has a rufous undertail). Note the black 'mask', defined above and below by a
white line. Often shows a yellowish flush to belly (pinkish in Waxwing). Wings are dark and
almost unmarked except for white inner edge to tertials and red wax-like feather projections
(Waxwing has yellow or white tips to primaries and coverts).
In flight, and in common with Waxwing, has a silhouette
like a Starling (*Sturnus vulgaris*). Similar juvenile/1st-winter
lacks red waxy wing projections. **VOICE** Utters piercing *tzeee*
call notes. **HABITS** Vagrants here are likely to join flocks of
Waxwings and feed in a similar manner. **STATUS AND
HABITAT** Widespread breeder in North America; nomadic
and generally moves south outside the breeding season.
Vagrants here are likely to turn up in late autumn and
winter, when they are found with Waxwing flocks in
urban settings.

pale
undertail
coverts

WALLCREEPER

Tichodroma muraria | LENGTH 15.5–17cm

Stunning little bird that is easy to recognise when feeding and unmistakable in flight. Associated with rugged and rocky locations. Sexes are similar.

Non-breeding birds (plumage likely to be seen here) are overall soft grey above, with whitish throat and upper breast (breeding male has black throat and breast), and otherwise pale grey underparts. Bill is long, black and downcurved, and legs are stout and black. Lower margin of wings in resting bird is deep maroon; transformed in flight into broad, round wings with maroon centres, dark margins and large white spots near primary tips. Note white tips to outer-tail feathers. **VOICE** Vagrants are silent. **HABITS** Climbs up rock faces; probes in crevices for invertebrates. **STATUS AND HABITAT** Breeds in Alps and Pyrenees. Altitudinal migrant in winter, sometimes wandering further afield. Most vagrants turn up here in winter and favour coastal cliffs and quarries.

SHORT-TOED TREECREEPER

Certhia brachydactyla | TH | LENGTH 12–13cm

Very similar to a Treecreeper (*C. familiaris*), with only subtle plumage and structural differences existing between these closely related species. Voice is an additional aid to identification. Sexes are similar.

All birds have streaked brown upperparts. Underparts are grubby white (darker than in Treecreeper) with a strong buffish wash to flanks. Needle-like bill is appreciably longer than that of Treecreeper and hind claw is shorter. Pale wingbar is even-sided (margin looks jagged in Treecreeper). Alula is more extensively white and in good views is a useful aid to identification (whole of leading edge is white; in Treecreeper, only tip is white). **VOICE** Utters a rather piercing *zeeht* call, quite unlike that of a Treecreeper. Song is shorter and more piercing than that of a Treecreeper. **HABITS** Feeds in the manner of a Treecreeper, climbing trunks and probing with its bill for invertebrates. **STATUS AND HABITAT** Widespread breeder across mainland Europe. Mainly sedentary but wanders occasionally. Vagrants here are likely to turn up outside the breeding season and favour coastal scrub and woodland.

RARE THRUSHES, CHATS AND FLYCATCHERS

A variety of rare thrushes, chats and flycatchers turn up each year, with origins as far afield as North America and Siberia. Some species are bold and relatively showy, making for easy observation, while others are distinctly secretive. If sightings are occasional and brief, it pays to focus on the important features for identification. Use these annotated photos to hone your skills. For comparison, Song Thrush and Redwing are probably the most useful default common thrushes to refer to; Robin and Spotted Flycatcher help with other birds.

Size can be useful – North American *Catharus* thrushes are appreciably smaller than a Song Thrush; most other rare thrushes are the same size or larger.

Facial pattern and colour can provide vital clues to identity – pay attention to features such as cheek colour, presence or absence of a pale eye-ring, and throat colour and markings.

Colours and patterns on the body are important – for example, look for scaly markings, or note differences in colour between the back versus the breast and belly. Any colour or patterning in the tail, as seen when a bird is flying away, can be useful identification features.

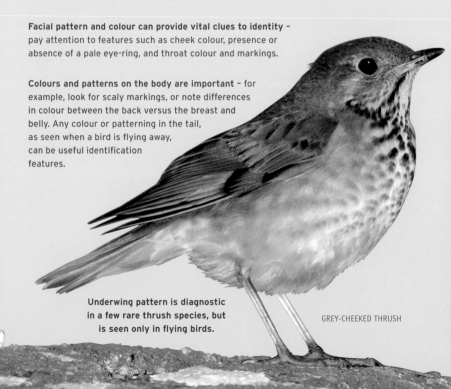

Underwing pattern is diagnostic in a few rare thrush species, but is seen only in flying birds.

GREY-CHEEKED THRUSH

Note the colour of the tail, particularly relative to the colour of the lower back – in some species the two are contrastingly different.

Check for any patterns on the tail – for example, Rufous Bush Chat has black and white markings at the tail tip, while Red-breasted Flycatcher has a white patch at the side of the tail-base.

Study the facial pattern – features such as throat, moustache and supercilium colour can be useful and are sometimes diagnostic.

RED-BREASTED FLYCATCHER

Look for the presence or absence of wingbars.

Study the habits of the bird – does it perch like a flycatcher, or hop along the ground like a Bluethroat?

HERMIT THRUSH

Catharus guttatus | LENGTH 15–17cm

Well-marked songbird that recalls a miniature Song Thrush (*Turdus philomelos*). Separated from the other 3 vagrant members of genus *Catharus* by subtle differences in markings and overall colour. Sexes are similar.

rufous tail and rump

All birds have overall olive-brown upperparts except for the contrasting reddish-brown rump and tail. Note the rufous panel on primaries, faint pale tips to covert feathers, white eye-ring, and white throat bordered by a black lateral line. Underparts are whitish, subtly washed yellowish and heavily dark-spotted on breast. Undertail coverts are buffish white. **VOICE** Call is a muted *tchuck-tchuck*. **HABITS** Generally secretive and keeps to dense cover, making it hard to observe. Forages among leaf litter. **STATUS AND HABITAT** Widespread breeder in North America that winters in southern states and Central America. Vagrants here are likely to turn up in autumn, and favour coastal scrub and woodland.

SWAINSON'S THRUSH

Catharus ustulatus | LENGTH 16–18cm

buff lores and eye-ring

Similar to other *Catharus* thrushes. Its overall colour and pale buff 'spectacles' (eye-ring and line continuing to base of bill) are reliable identification features. Sexes are similar.

All birds have overall olive-brown upperparts, including tail. Buff (not grey) cheeks allow separation from Grey-cheeked Thrush. Juvenile/1st-winter birds (typically those seen here) have pale tips to wing-covert feathers. Pale buff throat is bordered by a dark line and lores are buff. Underparts are otherwise pale with a yellow-buff wash and dark spots on breast, subtle grey spots on lower breast and olive-grey flanks. **VOICE** Call is a sharp *quiirp*. **HABITS** Spends long periods foraging in cover among leaf litter, periodically emerging into the open. **STATUS AND HABITAT** Widespread North American breeder that winters in South America. Vagrants here are likely to turn up in autumn, and favour coastal woodland and scrub.

GREY-CHEEKED THRUSH

Catharus minimus | LENGTH 15–17cm

Another small thrush. Separated from the similar Swainson's Thrush by its greyish (not olive-brown) upperparts, grey (not buffish) cheeks and absence of buff 'spectacles'. Sexes are similar.

cold grey cheeks

Upperparts, including tail, are grey-brown. Has an indistinct, pale grey eye-ring and greyish cheeks and grey lores. Juvenile/1st-winter birds (typically those seen here) have pale tips to wing-covert feathers. Whitish throat is bordered by dark line that defines pale malar stripe. Breast is washed yellow-buff and heavily marked with dark spots; underparts are otherwise pale except for pale grey spots on lower breast and grey flanks. **VOICE** Call is a rather nasal *piuup*. **HABITS** Generally secretive. Forages among leaf litter for invertebrates. **STATUS AND HABITAT** Widespread North American breeder that winters in N South America. Vagrants usually turn up in autumn, and favour coastal woodland and scrub.

VEERY

Catharus fuscescens | LENGTH 15–17cm

The least spotted of the *Catharus* thrushes. Its warm plumage tones and understated markings help separate it from its near relatives. Sexes are similar.

warm rufous upperparts and tail

All birds have mainly reddish-brown upperparts. Juvenile/1st-winter birds (typically those seen here) have pale tips to wing-covert feathers. Face is grey-brown and faintly marked, and pale buff throat is bordered by a brown line. Breast is yellow-buff with brown spots, grading to greyish white on rest of underparts; flanks are washed grey, and note the faint grey spots on lower breast and flanks. Shares the striking dark and white underwing pattern common to all *Catharus* thrushes. **VOICE** Call is a sharp *veer*. **HABITS** Generally rather secretive. Forages among leaf litter for invertebrates. **STATUS AND HABITAT** Widespread North American breeder wintering in South America. Vagrants are likely to turn up in autumn, and favour coastal woodland and scrub.

AMERICAN ROBIN

Turdus migratorius | AR | LENGTH 22–25cm

**Well-marked, distinctive thrush with the habits
of a Blackbird (*T. merula*) or Song Thrush
(*T. philomelos*). Sexes are subtly dissimilar.**

1ST-WINTER

Adult male has a grey-brown back, rump
and wings, grading to almost black on
head and neck. Eye is framed above and
below by white 'eyelids', and throat is
variably streaked black and white. Tail is
dark brown, and underparts are mostly
orange-red but contrastingly white on
belly and undertail. In flight, note the
reddish underwing coverts. Legs are dull
pinkish and bill is yellowish. Adult female
and juvenile/1st-winter birds are similar
but less colourful overall, with more white
on throat, and underparts have pale feather fringes, creating a
scaly look. **VOICE** Calls include a sharp *puup*, and a high,
thin trill given in flight. **HABITS** Forages in leaf litter
and short grassland for invertebrates. **STATUS AND
HABITAT** Widespread across North America,
northern breeders moving south in autumn.
Vagrants here are likely to turn up in
autumn, and favour coastal grassland
and open woodland.

MALE

EYEBROWED THRUSH

obvious white supercilium

Turdus obscurus | LENGTH 20.5–23cm

Well-marked thrush, the size of a Redwing (*T. iliacus*). Vagrants sometimes associate with flocks of that species. Sexes are subtly dissimilar.

Adult male has grey head with black loral stripe emphasised by white supercilium and white crescent below that extends to chin. Upperparts are otherwise grey-brown and underparts are flushed peachy buff, except for white undertail and centre to belly. Adult female and juvenile/1st-winter birds are similar but with less intense grey colour on head; 1st-winter birds have pale tips to greater coverts. All birds have a slender yellowish bill and dull pink legs. In flight, note pale underwing. **VOICE** Call is a thin, Redwing-like *tsseer*. **HABITS** Vagrants often favour open, grassy habitats. **STATUS AND HABITAT** Breeds in Siberia and winters in S Asia. Most vagrants appear in autumn and early winter, and favour open country or light woodland.

MALE

spotted underparts and rufous wing panel

DUSKY THRUSH

Turdus eunomus | LENGTH 21–14cm

Distinctive, well-marked thrush that is hard to confuse if seen well. Sexes are subtly dissimilar.

FEMALE

Adult male has grey-brown back and reddish brown on wings. Head pattern comprises black crown, nape, ear coverts, lores and malar stripe, with contrasting white face, throat and supercilium. Underparts are otherwise white, with black breast band and neat black spotting on flanks. Adult female and juvenile/1st-winter birds show less contrast in plumage; in particular, dark elements of head pattern and breast band are less intense. All birds have a slim yellowish bill and dull pink legs. In flight, note rusty-red underwing coverts. **VOICE** Calls include a *tchack-chack*, like Fieldfare (*T. pilaris*). **HABITS** Vagrants often favour open, grassy habitats. **STATUS AND HABITAT** Breeds in Siberia and winters in S Asia. Most vagrants turn up in autumn and early winter and favour open country.

BLACK-THROATED THRUSH

Turdus atrogularis | XC | LENGTH 23–25.5cm

Large thrush, the size of a Blackbird (*T. merula*). Sexes are dissimilar. Adult male is distinctive but other plumages are rather nondescript.

FEMALE

cold pale underparts

MALE

Adult male has grey-brown upperparts, including tail. Face, throat and upper breast are black but underparts are otherwise white. Bill is yellow-based and dark-tipped, and legs are dull pink. Adult female and juvenile/1st-winter birds are grey-brown above. Face is grey, throat is white, upper breast is variably marked with dark spots, and flanks have subtle grey-buff spotting; 1st-winter birds have pale tips to greater coverts. Shows orange underwing coverts in flight. **VOICE** Calls include a sharp *tchep-tchep-tchep…* and a shrill, buzzing *kverr*. **HABITS** Typically forages in short grassland. **STATUS AND HABITAT** Breeds in Siberia and winters in S Asia. Most vagrants turn up in autumn and winter, among flocks of Redwings (*T. iliacus*) and Fieldfares (*T. pilaris*) in open country.

SIBERIAN THRUSH

Geokichla sibirica | LENGTH 20–21.5cm

Well-marked thrush, the size of a Redwing (*Turdus iliacus*). Sexes are dissimilar. Male is unmistakable and other plumages are relatively distinctive.

MALE

Adult male is overall grey-black with striking white supercilium, white centre to lower belly and white spotting on undertail coverts. In flight, note black and white banded pattern on underwings. Female has brown upperparts overall; brown ear coverts are framed by pale buff. Underparts are whitish but heavily marked

with dark crescent-shaped feather margins, creating a scaly appearance. Juvenile/1st-winter birds resemble adult counterparts, although male shows less contrast. In all ages, dark bill has a hint of yellow at base, and legs are dull yellow. **VOICE** Call is a shrill *tziit*. **HABITS** Shy and secretive; keeps to the cover of dense bushes. **STATUS AND HABITAT** Breeds in Siberia and winters in S Asia. Most vagrants turn up in autumn, and favour coastal scrub.

WHITE'S THRUSH

Zoothera dauma | LENGTH 27–31cm

Large thrush. Vaguely reminiscent of a juvenile Mistle Thrush (*Turdus viscivorus*), but its extremely scaly-looking plumage allows certain identification. Sexes are similar.

All birds have a yellow-buff ground colour, heavily marked all over with black crescent-shaped feather margins that create a scaly appearance. Dark crescents on back are emphasised by white sub-terminal markings. Bill is proportionately long (for a thrush) and dark, and legs are pinkish. In flight, note the bold black and white banded pattern on underwings, the strong black and yellow-buff upperwing pattern, and the white tips to otherwise dark tail feathers. **VOICE** Vagrants here are silent. **HABITS** Generally rather secretive and keeps to the cover of dense bushes for much of the time. **STATUS AND HABITAT** Breeds in Siberia and winters in S Asia, where it favours dense forest. Vagrants here are likely to turn up in autumn, and favour scrub and light woodland where cover is available.

ROSE-COLOURED STARLING

Pastor roseus │ OE │ LENGTH 20–22cm

IMMATURE

**Distinctive relative of the Starling
(*S. vulgaris*), and separable from that
species at all times. Sexes are similar.**

IMMATURE

yellow
bill

Adult is unmistakable: the bright pinkish
back and underparts contrast with the
otherwise dark head, neck, wings and tail.
Head has a shaggy crest that can be raised
or flattened. In good light, dark elements
of plumage have a metallic sheen. Bill
and legs are pinkish. Juvenile/1st-winter
has pale buffish-grey plumage, palest on
throat, a yellow bill (dark on immature Starling) and pinkish
legs. **VOICE** Utters various Starling-like squawking and
chattering calls. **HABITS** Vagrants here often associate
with Starling flocks and are occasionally seen in
gardens at feeders. **STATUS AND HABITAT**
Breeds from E Europe eastwards and winters
in Southeast Asia. Vagrants here (10–15
in most years) are likely to turn up
in autumn and winter. Some
individuals become long-
stayers if they find a reliable
food source and a flock
of Starlings with
which to associate.

adult's pink and black plumage
make it unmistakable

RED-FLANKED BLUETAIL

Tarsiger cyanurus | LENGTH 13–14cm

Rather compact, round-bodied chat with a diagnostic combination of orange-red flanks and a blue tail. Sexes are dissimilar.

Vagrants here are likely to be seen in 1st-winter plumage: grey-brown head, back and wings, and striking blue tail. Has a white throat, a grey-brown breast that grades to grubby white on belly, and an orange-red flush on flanks. Bill and legs are dark. In adult male, grey-brown elements of upperparts are replaced by dull blue. Adult female resembles juvenile/1st-winter. **VOICE** Utters a whistling alarm call. **HABITS** Vagrants here are usually rather perky, often perching in the open and fly-catching from prominent perches; generally tolerant of human observers. **STATUS AND HABITAT** Breeds in Siberia and winters in Southeast Asia. Vagrants here are likely to turn up in autumn, and favour coastal scrub and open woodland.

1ST-WINTER

1ST-WINTER

1ST-WINTER

blue tail is diagnostic in a bird of this size

SIBERIAN BLUE ROBIN

Larvivora cyane | LENGTH 12–13cm

Compact thrush-like bird with a short tail that shows
some blue in all plumages. Sexes are dissimilar.

FEMALE

Adult male is unmistakable. Has mainly bright blue
upperparts, including its tail, the lower margins of which
are well defined and blackish, showing a clear division from
the pure white underparts (including throat and undertail).
Bill has a pinkish base, and legs are proportionally large
and pink. Adult female and juvenile/1st-winter are brown
above, with a rufous tint to wings; underparts are grey-
brown, flushed rufous on cheeks, lores and breast, which normally shows indistinct dark
crescents. Tail and rump often have some blue. **VOICE** Vagrants here are mostly silent.
HABITS Secretive and a real challenge to see well. Usually keeps to the cover of tangled
undergrowth. **STATUS AND HABITAT** Breeds in Siberia and winters in Southeast Asia.
Vagrants here are likely to turn up in autumn, and favour coastal scrub and woodland.

RUFOUS BUSH CHAT

Cercotrichas galactotes | LENGTH 15–17cm

Warm-plumaged chat with a relatively long
reddish tail, and a proportionately large
head and stout bill. Sexes are similar.

rufous tail

All birds (of the subspecies that has occurred
here – ssp. *galactotes*, from Iberia and
North Africa) have reddish-buff
upperparts that are darkest on
crown and wings. Head pattern comprises a dark eye-stripe,
bold pale supercilium and pale ear coverts, outlined by dark
feathering. Tail is rufous overall, the feathers with white tips
and black sub-terminal markings. Underparts are overall
very pale, flushed buff on breast. Bill is pinkish and slightly
downcurved, and legs are stout and pink. **VOICE** Utters a sharp *tchu*. **HABITS** Often flicks
its tail upwards and very occasionally also fans it. Usually forages on the ground, often in
undergrowth. **STATUS AND HABITAT** Widespread breeder from North Africa to Middle
East; winters in sub-Saharan Africa. Vagrants turn up in spring and autumn, in coastal scrub.

RUFOUS-TAILED ROBIN

Larvivora sibilans | LENGTH 12–13cm

scaly
underparts

Similar (and related) to the Thrush Nightingale, but appreciably smaller (the size of a Robin, *Erithacus rubecula*) and with a proportionately shorter tail and larger head and eyes. Sexes are similar.

In 1st-winter birds (plumage most likely to be seen here), upperparts are warm brown and wings and tail rufous. Note the pale eye-ring surrounding the large eye. Underparts are pale overall, but feathers on throat and breast have subtle brown fringes that create a distinctive pale-spotted appearance (in contrast, Nightingale, *L. megarhynchos*, has overall unmarked underparts while Thrush Nightingale is at best dark-mottled on breast). Bill is dark and legs are pink. **VOICE** Vagrants here are mostly silent. **HABITS** Generally rather shy and retiring, keeping to the cover of undergrowth. **STATUS AND HABITAT** Breeds across N Asia and winters in Southeast Asia. Vagrants here are likely to turn up in autumn and favour coastal scrub.

SIBERIAN RUBYTHROAT

Calliope calliope | LENGTH 14.5–16cm

Chat whose proportions recall a large, plump Robin. Sexes are similar. Adults are unmistakable; immature identification is more challenging.

MALE

Adult is grey-brown above, including tail. Head pattern comprises white supercilium and sub-moustachial stripe, dark lores and black-framed red throat. Colours are more intense in males than females. Underparts are grey-buff. Juvenile/1st-winter resembles adult but throat patch is greyish white and sub-moustachial stripe is buffish white. All birds have a plain brown tail. **VOICE** Utters a thin, high-pitched, whistling *tsi-uu*. **HABITS** Shy; keeps to cover, emerging into the open only occasionally. **STATUS AND HABITAT** Breeds in Siberia and winters in Southeast Asia. Vagrants turn up in autumn and favour coastal scrub.

THRUSH NIGHTINGALE

Luscinia luscinia | FN | LENGTH 15–17cm

Superficially very similar to a Nightingale
(*L. megarhynchos*) and separable only
with care. Sexes are similar.

All birds have overall grey-brown upperparts (warm rufous brown in
Nightingale) with a subtle rufous tinge to tail. Face and side of neck
can appear greyish, and often show a mottled band of grey-brown
on breast, this usually extending onto flanks. Undertail coverts
sometimes appear faintly spotted (unmarked in Nightingale).
Extremely close views (or good-quality digital images) reveal
subtle differences between wing formula of Nightingale
and Thrush Nightingale: former has a long 1st primary
and 7 primary tips extending beyond tertials; latter has
a short 1st primary and 8 primary tips extending
beyond tertials. **VOICE** Utters a whistling
alarm call. Song is less musical than that
of Nightingale, but louder and with more
'throaty' whistles and more pronounced
clicking trills. **HABITS** Generally
secretive, keeping to the cover of
undergrowth. **STATUS AND
HABITAT** Breeds from NE
Europe eastwards and winters
in Africa. Vagrants here are
likely to turn up in spring
and autumn, and favour
coastal scrub.

MALE, SUMMER

BLUETHROAT

Luscinia svecica | BU | LENGTH 13–14cm

Perky, compact bird, the size of a Robin (*Erithacus rubecula*). Distinctive in all plumages but adult males are stunningly beautiful. Red sides to base of tail are diagnostic in all birds.

MALE, RED-SPOTTED

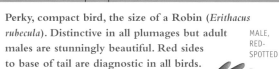

Adult male has mainly grey-brown upperparts and whitish underparts. Head pattern comprises a white supercilium and blue throat and breast, bordered below by concentric bands of black, white and red. Most birds show either a white or a red spot in centre to throat, depending on the race. In autumn, blue colour is partially masked by pale feather fringes. Similar juvenile/1st-winter male has a creamy-white throat and supercilium; blue colour is restricted to band on lower throat. Females resemble juvenile/1st-winter male, but supercilium, throat and sub-moustachial stripe are white, not creamy; adult females have variable but limited blue on throat, whereas blue is absent in 1st-winter females. In all plumages, dark tail shows a rusty-red base. **VOICE** Utters a sharp *tchick* call. **HABITS** Often feeds on the ground. Not particularly shy – some migrants are remarkably tame. **STATUS AND HABITAT** Widespread breeder across N and central Europe; winters in Southeast Asia. Its status here is that of a scarce passage migrant (100 or so in most years); generally turns up in short grassland and scrub on coasts.

distinctive tail pattern in all ages

MALE, 1ST-WINTER

FEMALE, 1ST-WINTER

WHITE-THROATED ROBIN

Irania gutturalis | LENGTH 16.5–18cm

**Thrush-like bird that is only marginally
smaller than a Redwing (*Turdus iliacus*).
Sexes are dissimilar, and the male in
particular is unmistakable.**

FEMALE

Adult male has mainly blue-grey
upperparts with a dark tail. Head
pattern comprises a white supercilium,
a black face and a white centre to
throat, which is framed on its lower
margin by black. Breast and flanks are
reddish orange, grading to white on
lower belly and undertail. Adult female
and juvenile/1st-winter are grey-buff overall with a
black tail, orange-flushed flanks, and a pale throat and
sub-moustachial stripe. **VOICE** Calls include a soft,
disyllabic *tchu-itt*. **HABITS** Generally shy but
often feeds on the ground at the margins of
cover, allowing occasional views. **STATUS
AND HABITAT** Breeds from Turkey
eastwards and winters in Africa.
Vagrants here are likely to turn
up in spring and autumn, and
favour coastal scrub.

MALE

COLLARED FLYCATCHER

Ficedula albicollis | LENGTH 12–13.5cm

Distinctive black and white bird. Superficially similar to a Pied Flycatcher (*F. hypoleuca*); adult male is relatively easy to separate from that species, but adult female and immatures are more of a challenge. Sexes are dissimilar.

FEMALE

Summer adult male has mainly black upperparts and white underparts, with a complete white collar, a whitish rump, and a bold white patch on otherwise black wings; white patch at base of bill is larger than in Pied. Autumn adult male, adult female (at all times) and juvenile/1st-winter birds are very similar to their Pied counterparts, with mainly brown upperparts and white underparts. The main difference lies in the larger size of white patch at base of primaries, which almost reaches wing edge (falls well short on Pied). Some juvenile/1st-winter birds may also show a median-covert wingbar and a greyish wash on the nape. **VOICE** Utters a sharp *tik* call repeatedly when alarmed. Song comprises a series of whistling notes. **HABITS** Similar to Pied: perches on branches and makes fly-catching sorties before returning to perch. **STATUS AND HABITAT** Breeds from E Europe eastwards and winters in Africa. Migrants here are likely to turn up in spring and autumn, and favour coastal woodland. Spring males provide the best opportunities for certain identification.

large white primary patch almost reaches leading edge of wing

MALE

RED-BREASTED FLYCATCHER

Ficedula parva | FY | LENGTH 11–12cm

Charming and compact little bird. All birds have
striking white sides to their otherwise black tail, a
feature shared only with the Taiga Flycatcher. Sexes are
dissimilar.

TAIGA FLYCATCHER,
1ST-WINTER

RED-BREASTED FLYCATCHER,
1ST-WINTER

Adult male has a brown back, blue-grey face, orange-red throat and upper breast, and
whitish underparts; note the relatively large, dark eye surrounded by a whitish eye-ring.
Adult female has entirely brown upperparts and whitish underparts, tinged buffish brown on
sides of breast. In juvenile/1st-winter plumage, resembles adult female but throat and breast
are washed buffish, and has pale tips to wing coverts, forming a thin
wingbar. Bill has a pale-based lower mandible in all birds (cf.
Taiga). **VOICE** Utters a rattling call like that of a Wren
(*Troglodytes troglodytes*). **HABITS** Fly-catches from lookout
perches in the tree canopy, undertaking aerial sorties.
Sometimes flicks its wings and cocks its tail. **STATUS
AND HABITAT** Breeds from E Europe eastwards
and winters in India and Southeast Asia. A
scarce passage migrant here, with 70–100
recorded in a good year, almost all in
autumn. Usually turns up in
patches of woodland
near the coast.

MALE

TAIGA FLYCATCHER MALE

obvious grey wash on upper breast

BROWN FLYCATCHER

1ST-WINTER

TAIGA FLYCATCHER

Ficedula albicilla | LENGTH 11–12.5cm

Very similar to a Red-breasted Flycatcher. Sexes are dissimilar. Adult male is distinctive from its Red-breasted counterpart, but other plumages are separable only with great care.

Adult male is grey-brown above with white sides to otherwise black tail. Compared to male Red-breasted, orange-red is restricted to throat (not extending to breast), defined by grey breast band that grades into white underparts. To separate female and juvenile/1st-winter birds from their Red-breasted counterparts, look for: 'colder', greyer upperparts, including face; whitish (not buffish) throat; grey wash on breast (no hint of buff); and black (not dark grey) uppertail coverts. Bill is black in all birds (cf. Red-breasted). **VOICE** Loud buzzing call is quite different from Red-breasted's rattling call. **HABITS** Fly-catches from lookout perch. **STATUS AND HABITAT** Breeds in Siberia and winters in S Asia. Most vagrants turn up in autumn, in coastal woodland.

BROWN FLYCATCHER

Muscicapa dauurica | LENGTH 12–13cm

Recalls a plain-looking Spotted Flycatcher (*M. striata*), but note the proportionately large head and eye, and short tail. Sexes are similar.

Adult has unmarked grey-brown upperparts, including crown and forehead (these are streaked in Spotted). The pale eye-surround and lores create a 'spectacled' effect. Throat is white and breast and flanks are washed uniformly with grey-buff (these are subtly streaked in Spotted); underparts are otherwise whitish. Similar juvenile/1st-winter has pale buff margins to inner flight feathers and to wing coverts, the latter creating a wingbar. In all ages it has a broad yellow-orange base to bill, best seen from below. **VOICE** Utters a thin *tzii* call. **HABITS** Perches in tree canopy, making aerial sorties after insects. **STATUS AND HABITAT** Breeds across Siberia and winters in S Asia. Vagrants turn up in autumn and favour coastal woodland.

ROCK THRUSH

Monticola saxatilis | OH | LENGTH 17–20cm

Thrush-like bird with a relatively short
tail. Sexes are dissimilar: male is striking and
colourful; other plumages, while dowdy,
are still well marked and distinctive.

MALE   FEMALE

All birds have a dark-centred red tail. Adult male has a blue head, white back and dark wings.
Underparts are orange-red. Bill and legs are dark. Adult female, immatures and winter male
have scaly-looking brown upperparts and orange-flushed underparts, the feathers with dark
margins, creating a scaly-looking appearance. **VOICE** Calls include a shrill *wee-chuk*, the last
note like 2 stones being knocked together. **HABITS** Generally a shy and wary species and a
master of concealment among rocks and boulders. **STATUS AND HABITAT** Breeds in the
mountains of S Europe and winters in Africa. Vagrants here are likely to turn up in spring
and autumn, and favour rugged and rocky coastal habitats with plenty of cover in the form
of crags and boulders. Generally, most vagrants here are seen only fleetingly.

BLUE ROCK THRUSH

Monticola solitarius | LENGTH 21–23cm

**Thrush-like bird with a particularly long bill.
Sexes are dissimilar. Male's blue coloration
is not always easy to discern in poor light.**

1ST-WINTER

MALE

Adult male has mainly uniformly dull blue plumage with brown wings. Bill and legs are
dark. Juvenile/1st-winter male is similar but feathers on underparts have pale tips and
dark sub-terminal bands, creating a scaly appearance; feathers on back and wings have pale
margins. Adult female is overall brown, darkest and uniform on upperparts; underparts are
paler buff but heavily marked with fine, dark markings on throat, and dark barring on breast
and belly. Tail is plain brown. **VOICE** Calls include a fluty *tiu-tee* and a vibrant *wee-tchuk-
tchuk*, the latter notes like 2 stones being knocked together. **HABITS** Generally shy and
wary. Views intruders by peeping over rocky outcrops, and conceals itself behind boulders if
alarmed. **STATUS AND HABITAT** Mainly sedentary resident of rocky terrain and cliffsides
in S Europe. Vagrants here are likely to turn up in spring and autumn in coastal regions.

REDSTART (EASTERN RACE)

Phoenicurus phoenicurus samamiscus | LENGTH 14cm

Redstart is represented by several subspecies across its wide breeding range; distinctive eastern ssp. *samamiscus* occasionally turns up here. Sexes are dissimilar.

large white wing patch

Adult male *samamiscus* recalls male British ssp. *phoenicurus*, with blue-grey upperparts, black face and mainly orange-red underparts. But note white panel on wings, subtly darker upperparts and more neatly defined white border to crown. Female and juvenile/1st-winter are similar to their *phoenicurus* counterparts (grey-brown above, orange-flushed pale below) with a hint of male's pale panel on wings. **VOICE** Utters a soft *huiit* call and a sharp ticking when alarmed. **HABITS** Perched birds pump tail up and down. **STATUS AND HABITAT** Breeds from SE Europe eastwards and winters in Africa. Vagrants turn up in spring and autumn, on coasts.

EASTERN BLACK REDSTART

Phoenicurus ochruros phoenicuroides | LENGTH 14cm

Black Redstart is represented by several subspecies across its wide breeding range; eastern ssp. *phoenicuroides* occasionally turns up here. Sexes are dissimilar.

Eastern Black Redstart could potentially be confused with an eastern race Redstart, but note the absence of white on face and wings

Adult male has dark slate-grey upperparts, head and breast, and orange-red underparts. 1st-winter male is similar but with pale tips to body feathers and pale rufous tips to wing feathers. Legs and bill are dark. Adult female and juvenile/1st-winter birds have rather uniform grey-brown body plumage. **VOICE** Utters a whistling svit, or *svit-it-it* call. **HABITS** Often quivers tail. **STATUS AND HABITAT** Breeds across central Asia and winters in S Asia. Vagrants are likely to turn up in autumn or early winter, on coasts; has overwintered.

SIBERIAN STONECHAT

Saxicola maurus | LENGTH 11–13cm

CASPIAN, 1ST-WINTER

Superficially similar to a Stonechat (*S. rubicola*) and only relatively recently elevated to separate species status. Sexes are dissimilar. In all plumages, note the pale, unmarked rump and larger white wing patch.

Adult male has a blackish hood, separated from blackish back and wings by a broad white collar. Underparts are mainly pale, flushed orange on breast. In ssp. *maurus*, tail is uniformly black and contrasts with white rump. In ssp. *variegatus* (so-called Caspian Stonechat), tail and rump pattern is like that of a Wheatear (*Oenanthe oenanthe*), with a black terminal band and central bar to tail, and white rump and tail sides. In other plumages, both races are much paler than their Stonechat counterparts, with very pale, unmarked rumps (those of Stonechat are always darker and heavily streaked). **VOICE** Utters a harsh *tchak* call, like 2 pebbles being knocked together. **HABITS** Often perches on fence wires or Bramble clumps. **STATUS AND HABITAT** Ssp. *maurus* breeds across Siberia and ssp. *variegatus* breeds west of the Caspian Sea; both winter from the Middle East to S Asia. Vagrants here are likely to turn up in spring and autumn; they favour areas of scrub, mainly around the coast.

MALE

RARE WHEATEARS

A number of interesting wheatear species turn up in Britain each year, arriving from southern and eastern Europe or even further afield. They tend to feed out in the open, so observers are usually in little doubt that they are looking at a wheatear species of some sort. But there are similarities between the various rare species, and with the default common species in Britain, Northern Wheatear. Use the annotations on this Desert Wheatear photo to identify the key features.

Study the colours and patterns on the back.

Posture can provide clues – in most species, standing birds adopt a moderately upright stance, but in Isabelline the posture is near vertical, usually with the neck stretched.

Study the tail – uniformly black in Desert; with black and white patterns in other species (the proportion of black compared to white will help with identification, for example Black-eared Wheatear).

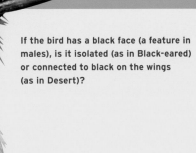

If the bird has a black face (a feature in males), is it isolated (as in Black-eared) or connected to black on the wings (as in Desert)?

Uniformly plain, sandy birds are contenders for Isabelline, but beware confusion with 1st-winter Northern Wheatear.

DESERT WHEATEAR

PIED WHEATEAR

Oenanthe pleschanka | PI | LENGTH 14–16.5cm

FEMALE

Well-marked wheatear. Sexes are dissimilar. Males are striking and straightforward to identify; females and immatures are more challenging and can be confused with their Black-eared Wheatear counterparts.

All birds have a black 'T' marking on otherwise white tail and rump; terminal band is not uniform in width and black extends up tail sides. Adult male has a black face and throat, connected to black back and wings. Crown and nape are whitish, and underparts are otherwise white, flushed with peachy buff on breast. Head and upperparts of juvenile/1st-winter male are grey-brown, with hint of a pale supercilium; underparts are pale, flushed peachy orange on breast. It is very similar to its Black-eared counterpart, but plumage is 'colder' grey and pale feather tips create a scaly appearance. Females have grey-brown upperparts, head and breast; the latter is separated by dark streaking from the grubby white underparts. When ruffled by wind, mantle feathers of younger birds and females show paler-edged dark centres (on Black-eared, mantle feathers are plain). **VOICE** Utters a loud buzzing call, and a whistling *wee-tchik*, the last note like 2 stones being knocked together. **HABITS** Often perches on boulders, posts or low bushes. **STATUS AND HABITAT** Breeds from E Europe eastwards and winters in Africa. Vagrants here are likely to turn up in spring and autumn, and favour open coastal habitats.

1ST-WINTER

the extent of black in the male's plumage makes identification straightforward

MALE

BLACK-EARED WHEATEAR

Oenanthe hispanica | LENGTH 13.5–15.5cm

FEMALE *MELANOLEUCA*, PALE-THROATED

Has a complicated set of plumage variations. Separated into eastern (ssp. *melanoleuca*) and western (ssp. *hispanica*) races, both sexes of which occur as dissimilar black-throated and pale-throated forms.

MALE *HISPANICA*, 1ST-WINTER

All birds have a black 'T' marking on otherwise white tail and rump; terminal band is not uniform in width and black extends up tail sides. Adult males have black wings and either an entirely black face and throat, or a black 'mask' (lores to ear coverts). Crown, nape and back are pale, variably flushed peachy buff (most intense in ssp. *hispanica*). Underparts are pale, flushed yellow-buff on breast. Adult female has mainly buffish-brown upperparts with dark brown wings. Either face and throat are dark, or throat can be pale; underparts are otherwise buffish white, flushed orange-buff on breast. In general, ssp. *hispanica* has a shorter primary projection than ssp. *melanoleuca*. **VOICE** Calls include a chirruping buzz, and a shrill, whistling *tchweerp*. **HABITS** Often perches on boulders, posts or low bushes. **STATUS AND HABITAT** Breeds across S Europe and winters in Africa. Vagrants here are likely to turn up in spring and autumn, and favour open coastal habitats.

MALE *MELANOLEUCA*, PALE-THROATED

MALE *HISPANICA*, PALE-THROATED

MALE *MELANOLEUCA*, BLACK-THROATED

MALE *HISPANICA*, DARK-THROATED

DESERT WHEATEAR

Oenanthe deserti | LENGTH 14.5–15.5cm

Rather plump-bodied wheatear with a slender,
needle-like bill. All birds have a diagnostic (for a
wheatear) uniformly black tail. Sexes are dissimilar.

1ST-WINTER

Adult male has sandy-brown
upperparts, and a black face and
throat that 'connect' via a black
line to black wings. Note the
white supercilium and scapulars.
Underparts are whitish, flushed
sandy buff on breast. (By comparison,
adult male black-throated form of
Black-eared has separate areas of
black on face and wings, and a
different tail pattern.) Plumage pattern of juvenile/1st-winter male is similar to adult male,
but pale feather tips render black elements less striking. Females have sandy-brown
upperparts, including face, and white underparts, including throat. **VOICE** Calls include a
sharp *tsik* and a whistling *tsee-a*. **HABITS** Vagrants often allow
close observation. **STATUS AND HABITAT** Breeding range
extends from North Africa through the Middle East to
Central Asia; winters from North Africa to SW
Asia. Vagrants here are likely to turn up in late
autumn or early winter, and favour open
coastal habitats.

good identification features include
the uniformly black tail, and black
wings 'connected' to the black face

MALE

ISABELLINE WHEATEAR

Oenanthe isabellina | LENGTH 15–16.5cm

Relatively large, pale wheatear. Potential exists
for confusion with a juvenile/1st-winter Wheatear
(*O. oenanthe*). Sexes are similar.

Adult has pale sandy-buff upperparts,
including wing coverts (in Wheatear,
wing coverts are as dark as flight
feathers). Note the broad, uniformly
white supercilium (in Wheatear,
supercilium is buff in front of eye).
Face, breast and flanks are subtly
flushed buffish yellow and underparts
are otherwise whitish. Tail pattern
comprises a broad black terminal
band (much broader than in Wheatear) and a short central
black band. Note the dark alula, contrasting with otherwise
pale feathers on closed wing. Male has darker lores than
female. In 1st-winter plumage, resembles adult female but
with pale margins to wing feathers. **VOICE** Calls
include a sharp *tchiup*. **HABITS** Usually adopts a much
more upright posture than other wheatears, with
neck stretched. **STATUS AND HABITAT** Breeds
from SE Europe eastwards across Central Asia;
winters in Africa and SW Asia. Vagrants here are
likely to turn up in spring and autumn,
and favour open coastal habitats.

upright stance, uniformly pale
body plumage and dark alula
are typical of the species

seen in flight, note the broader
terminal black band on the tail
when compared to Wheatear

YELLOW WAGTAIL (VAGRANT RACES)

Motacilla flava | YW | LENGTH 15–16cm

Represented across its extensive breeding range by many subspecies, the males of which have distinctive head patterns. Sexes are dissimilar.

SUPERCILIARIS

FELDEGG

Females cannot be separated reliably in the field; descriptions hereafter refer to males. Default is British breeding Yellow Wagtail (ssp. *flavissima*) with yellow face and subtly dark crown, ear coverts and lores. With other vagrant subspecies, note colours of crown, ear coverts and throat, and presence or absence of supercilium. Lacking a supercilium: Black-headed (ssp. *feldegg*) has black cap and yellow throat; Grey-headed (ssp. *thunbergi*) has grey cap, black lores and ear coverts, and yellow throat; Ashy-headed (ssp. *cinereocapilla*) recalls Grey-headed but has white throat. With a white supercilium: Blue-headed (ssp. *flava*) has blue-grey crown, lores and ear coverts, and white band bordering yellow throat; intergrade Blue-headed/Black-headed (ssp. *dombrowski*) has grey crown, dark grey lores and ear coverts, and yellow throat; Spanish (ssp. *iberiae*) has blue-grey crown, dark grey lores and ear coverts, and white throat; ssp. *superciliaris* has black crown, lores and ear coverts, yellow throat and supercilium flushed yellow at front and rear. Other intergrades include so-called 'Channel Wagtail', now considered an intergrade between Yellow and Blue-headed sspp.; resembles a washed-out Blue-headed with a yellow throat. **VOICE** Most sspp. utter a distinctive *tsree-ee* call. Call of Black-headed is a more rasping *brrzee-ee*. **HABITS** Feeds on insects, in short grassland. **STATUS AND HABITS** Widespread breeder across Europe and Asia; winters in Africa and S Asia. Vagrants turn up in spring and autumn and favour short grassland.

DOMBROWSKI

FLAVISSIMA

IBERIAE

FLAVA

CINEREOCAPILLA

MALE, BLUE-HEADED

THUNBERGI

CITRINE WAGTAIL

Motacilla citreola | LENGTH 15–17cm

1st-winter birds are as lacking in colour as a 1st-winter Pied Wagtail (*Motacilla alba yarrellii*)

1ST-WINTER

note completely pale surround to ear coverts

Well-marked wagtail. Sexes are dissimilar. Summer adult male is unmistakable, and other plumages are separable from their Yellow Wagtail counterparts with care.

Summer adult male has a lemon-yellow head, neck and underparts. Back is grey, and note the black collar and 2 striking white wingbars on otherwise blackish wings. Adult female is similar, but yellow colour is less intense and grey on back continues to nape and crown; note also the greyish ear coverts. In juvenile/1st-winter bird, upperparts are essentially grey and underparts whitish, including the undertail coverts. Note the 2 striking white wingbars; ear coverts are entirely bordered with white or yellowish white. (In juvenile/1st-winter Yellow Wagtail, undertail coverts are yellow and ear coverts are not framed with white.) **VOICE** Flight call is a thin, buzzing *sreee*. **HABITS** Feeds actively on insects. **STATUS AND HABITAT** Breeds across N Asia and winters from the Middle East to S Asia. Vagrants here are likely to turn up in spring and autumn, and favour freshwater margins.

MALE

RARE PIPITS

To the untutored eye, all pipits can look confusingly similar to one another. But the more you study the group, the more differences become apparent. Of the seven species of rare pipit that turn up in Britain regularly, three are appreciably larger than the default common species, Meadow Pipit. The remaining pipits are a similar size but all have distinctive markings. Use this annotated Olive-backed Pipit photo to hone your identification skills.

A black and white spot at the rear of the ear coverts is unique to Olive-backed.

Study the face pattern – dark or pale lores, the prominence and colour of the supercilium, and throat colour are all useful features.

Assess the colour and brightness of the wingbars – with larger pipits, the shape of dark centres to the median coverts can provide clues to identity.

Look for the presence of bold mantle stripes – particularly striking in Red-throated and Pechora.

Hind claw length can be important but the feature is often hard to discern with birds feeding in grass.

OLIVE-BACKED PIPIT

Among the larger pipits, bill size can provide a clue to identity – smallest in Blyth's; largest in Richard's.

Pipits are usually fairly vocal, even in autumn. The calls – usually delivered in flight, or on take-off – are diagnostic in some species.

RICHARD'S PIPIT

Anthus richardi | PR | LENGTH 17–20cm

of all the rare, large pipit species to occur here, Richard's is the most regular

Appreciably larger than a Meadow Pipit (almost the size of a Song Thrush, *Turdus philomelos*), with a proportionately much longer tail and legs, and a particularly long hind claw. Sexes are similar.

All birds have heavily streaked buffish-brown upperparts. Flanks and streaked breast are flushed with peach-buff; underparts are otherwise whitish. Facial pattern comprises a bold, pale supercilium and rather pale lores. In juvenile/1st-winter birds, pale fringes to wing coverts form 2 pale wingbars; median coverts have dark tapering and pointed centres. In all birds, bill is extremely stout, and legs are very long. Potential exists for confusion with Tawny and Blyth's pipits; pay particular attention to facial pattern (cf. Tawny), length of hind claw, relative size of bill and tail length (cf. Tawny and Blyth's), and extent of white in outer-tail feathers (cf. Blyth's). **VOICE** Flight call is a diagnostic loud *pschreep*, like that of a House Sparrow (*Passer domesticus*). **HABITS** Often feeds in quite long grass, disappearing from view for lengthy periods. Frequently adopts a rather upright posture. **STATUS AND HABITAT** Breeds in Siberia and winters in S Asia. Vagrants here are likely to turn up at migration times, mainly in late autumn and early winter, and favour coastal grassland.

large bill and pale lores

1ST-WINTER

TAWNY PIPIT

Anthus campestris | TI | LENGTH 15.5–18cm

Another large pipit. Adult has distinctive pale and mainly unmarked plumage; 1st-winter bird could be confused with a Richard's Pipit. Sexes are similar.

often seen in open habitats when can appear surprisingly wagtail-like

Adult has pale sandy-buff upperparts, with at best only subtle and indistinct streaking. Note the obvious median wing coverts, which have dark centres and pale margins that form an obvious blackish bar. Face is overall pale but with dark lores (cf. Richard's and Blyth's) and a dark eye-stripe. Underparts are mostly whitish, subtly flushed buff on sides of breast and flanks. Legs are long, but not as long as Richard's, and hind claw is shorter. In juvenile/1st-winter plumage, shares adult's facial pattern and overall pale colour, but upperparts and breast are lightly streaked. **VOICE** Calls include a shrill *tsche-erp* like that of a Yellow Wagtail, and a *tchirrp* like that of a House Sparrow (*Passer domesticus*). **HABITS** Feeds actively, searching for insects on grassy habitats. Can look surprisingly wagtail-like. **STATUS AND HABITAT** Widespread breeder across mainland Europe that winters in Africa. Vagrants here are likely to turn up in spring and autumn, and favour areas of short coastal grassland.

SUMMER

slender bill and dark lores

can look surprisingly long-tailed

WINTER

BLYTH'S PIPIT

Anthus godlewskii | LENGTH 15.5–17cm

happily forages in long
grass, only rarely
venturing into the open

slender bill
and pale
lores

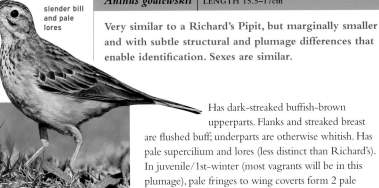

Very similar to a Richard's Pipit, but marginally smaller
and with subtle structural and plumage differences that
enable identification. Sexes are similar.

Has dark-streaked buffish-brown
upperparts. Flanks and streaked breast
are flushed buff; underparts are otherwise whitish. Has
pale supercilium and lores (less distinct than Richard's).
In juvenile/1st-winter (most vagrants will be in this
plumage), pale fringes to wing coverts form 2 pale
wingbars (more obvious than Richard's). Adult's median
wing coverts have squarish dark centres (tapering and pointed in Richard's). Compared to
Richard's, bill is smaller, tail, legs and hind claw are shorter, and white in outer-tail feathers is
less extensive. **VOICE** Flight call is a loud *schreep*, subtly softer than Richard's. Also utters a
Yellow Wagtail-like *speeoo* call. **HABITS** Forages for insects in grassland. Rather skulking;
often creeps through vegetation. **STATUS AND HABITAT** Breeds in Central Asia and
winters in S Asia. Vagrants are likely to turn up in autumn, in coastal grassland.

PECHORA PIPIT

Anthus gustavi | LENGTH 14–15cm

a generally secretive
and skulking species;
records tend to come
from locations with
limited cover; they have
a northerly bias

Small, boldly marked pipit that could perhaps be
confused with a 1st-winter Red-throated Pipit.
Structural and plumage differences allow identification.
Sexes are similar.

Diagnostically, relatively short tertials
allow at least 3 primaries to project
on closed wing (primaries are mostly
concealed by tertials in other pipits). Streaked brown
upperparts have bold white mantle stripes and striking
white wingbars. Underparts are whitish overall, boldly
streaked on breast and flanks, with yellow-buff flush to
breast. Bill is stouter than Red-throated's and pinkish
(not yellow) at base. Pale on outer-tail feathers is more extensive than in Red-throated;
colour is dull white (bright white in Red-throated). **VOICE** A buzzing, rattling *dzee*.
HABITS Creeps like a mouse through vegetation. **STATUS AND HABITAT** Breeds in
Siberia and winters in S Asia. Vagrants turn up mainly in autumn, in coastal grassland.

OLIVE-BACKED PIPIT

Anthus hodgsoni | OV | LENGTH 14–16cm

As well marked as a Tree Pipit (*A. trivialis*). Plumage details allow separation from that species, and from Meadow Pipit (*A. pratensis*). Sexes are similar.

has a characteristic, almost bobbing gait, emphasised by tail being pumped up and down

very distinctive head pattern with obvious white ear spot

1ST-WINTER

1ST-WINTER

All birds have olive-brown upperparts that are only faintly streaked. Whitish underparts are flushed warm buff on breast, and boldly streaked on breast and flanks. Head pattern is diagnostic: has a bold, pale supercilium that is buff in front of eye but whitish behind, and defined above by a narrow black border; note the white and black patch on the ear coverts. **VOICE** Call is a thin *tseep*. **HABITS** Tail is often pumped up and down as the bird walks. **STATUS AND HABITAT** Breeds in Siberia and Central Asia, and winters in S Asia. Vagrants here (4 or 5 in a good year) are likely to turn up in autumn and favour short coastal grassland.

RED-THROATED PIPIT

Anthus cervinus | VP | LENGTH 14–15cm

breeding birds are
unmistakable;
1st-winter birds have
very 'stripy' backs

A distinctive pipit that is easy to identify in some
plumages. Adults are particularly striking and even
1st-winter birds are well marked. Sexes are similar.

In adults, face, neck and breast are variably suffused with reddish orange. Colour is most
intense in spring and summer, and males are more striking than females; at other times of year
both sexes may show a hint of reddish buff on face and throat. Has bold white and dark stripes
on back, and clean white underparts with distinct streaking on flanks. In juvenile/1st-winter
plumage, lacks any reddish coloration and has more streaking on underparts, which are pale
yellowish white. In all ages has unmarked lores. **VOICE** Flight call is a thin, high-pitched *pssee*.
HABITS Feeds very actively in grassland, foraging for insects. **STATUS AND HABITAT**
Breeding range extends eastwards from N Scandinavia; winters mainly in
Africa. Vagrants are likely to turn up in spring and autumn, and
favour damp coastal grassland and freshwater margins.

1ST-WINTER

SPRING

BUFF-BELLIED PIPIT

Anthus rubescens | LENGTH 15–16cm

bill is thinner and more
needle-like than in Rock
and Water pipits; shows
complete white eye-ring

Size and shape of Rock (*A. petrosus*) and Water (*A. spinoletta*) pipits, with plumage elements of Meadow Pipit (*A. pratensis*). Size and pale lores are a good combination of identification features. Sexes are similar.

In autumn and winter, ssp. *rubescens* (from North America) is buffish above with, at best, faint dark streaking. Pale-looking face created by pale lores (dark in Rock and Water) and indistinct markings; has unbroken white orbital ring. Underparts are pale buff, flushed darker and streaked on breast and flanks. In autumn and winter, ssp. *japonicus* (from Asia) has subtly paler underparts, dark patch on side of breast, and bolder streaking. In summer plumage, all birds are grey-buff above, with yellow-buff face and underparts, and thrush-like spots on breast. **VOICE** Utters a single-note *pseet* call; tone recalls Meadow Pipit. **HABITS** Feeds actively like other pipits. **STATUS AND HABITAT** Breeds across N North America and East Asia; winters south of breeding range. Vagrants turn up in autumn and winter, on freshwater margins.

1ST-WINTER

ALPINE ACCENTOR

Prunella collaris | LENGTH 15–17.5cm

Marginally larger than the superficially similar Dunnock (*P. modularis*), and with distinctive plumage features that allow certain identification. Sexes are similar.

All birds have a streaked grey-brown back; blackish greater coverts create a dark wing panel, defined by 2 white wingbars. Head is bluish grey, the whitish throat marked with dense black spots that align to create bars. Breast is bluish grey, grading to streaked reddish brown on flanks and belly. Note the yellow base to the narrowly pointed bill. **VOICE** Utters a slightly trilling *drrrp* call. **HABITS** Feeds unobtrusively, searching for insects in tufts of vegetation and among stones and scree. **STATUS AND HABITAT** Breeds in mountains of S and central Europe; mainly sedentary but a partial altitudinal migrant that sometimes wanders outside the breeding season. Vagrants here are likely to turn up in spring and autumn, and favour bare coastal habitats.

FEMALE

some females
show a hint of
male's breast
and flank
streaking

MALE

SPANISH SPARROW

Passer hispaniolensis | LENGTH 14–16cm

**Has the proportions and habits of a House Sparrow
(*P. domesticus*). Sexes are dissimilar; only the male
has distinctive plumage.**

Adult male has black-streaked back and reddish-brown
wings with bold white wingbar. Has reddish-brown
cap, thin white supercilium (broken above eye), white face,
and black throat and breast, grading to black-streaked white
underparts. Adult female is almost identical to female House
Sparrow: brown upperparts with buff streaks, pale grey
below, and with pale buff supercilium behind eye. **VOICE**
Chirping calls are subtly higher-pitched than House Sparrow.
HABITS Vagrants associate with House Sparrow colonies.
STATUS AND HABITAT Locally common S Europe; mainly
resident in west, but eastern birds migrate south in autumn.
Vagrants turn up in spring and autumn, favouring gardens and
scrub.

TRUMPETER FINCH

Bucanetes githagineus | LENGTH 11.5–13cm

**Rather small, long-winged finch with a relatively large
head and thick neck, and a proportionately large, red
bill. Call is distinctive. Sexes are dissimilar in summer.**

Adult summer male has a grey head and buffish-brown back, both
variably flushed with pink; rump is pink. Wing feathers are dark
but have pink margins. Throat is pinkish grey and underparts are
otherwise buffish white, variably flushed pink. Legs and bill are
pinkish red. Adult female and non-breeding male have overall
paler, greyer plumage but still show a hint of pink flushing and a
pale pink rump. **VOICE** Utters a strange nasal bugling call, *neeerp*,
rather like a toy trumpet. **HABITS** Feeds unobtrusively among
low vegetation. **STATUS AND HABITAT** Mainly resident in
deserts of North Africa and the Middle East. Vagrants here
are likely to turn up at migration times, particularly in
spring, and favour coastal sites with short vegetation.

SERIN

Serinus serinus | NS | LENGTH 11–12cm

Small, dumpy-bodied finch with a proportionally large head and thick neck, and small, stubby grey bill. All birds have a pale yellow rump. Sexes are dissimilar.

all birds have at least some yellow in their plumage, particularly on the rump; this feature is easiest to see in flight

Adult male has a dark-streaked yellowish-green back, and dark wings with 2 white wingbars. Head and breast are overall bright yellow, with a streaked crown and ear coverts; latter are framed above by a long, broad, pale supercilium. Underparts are otherwise white with bold, dark streaking on flanks. Other plumages of both sexes are similar to adult male, but with variable degrees of yellow on head and breast; autumn female is only subtly flushed yellow. **VOICE** Calls include a silvery *diddle-iddle-lip* trill and a buzzing *de-drree*. Song is a rapid jingling, recalling a speeded-up Corn Bunting (*Emberiza calandra*) song. Spring males sometimes sing from tall trees. **HABITS** Vagrants often feed unobtrusively in weedy arable fields. **STATUS AND HABITAT** Widespread breeder in mainland Europe that winters mainly around the Mediterranean. Vagrants here are likely to turn up in spring and autumn, and favour coastal locations.

MALE

MALE

FEMALE

ARCTIC REDPOLL

Acanthis hornemanni | AL | LENGTH 12–14cm

Similar to Common Redpoll (*A. flammea*) and identification is not always easy; but a pale bird with a tiny bill is a contender for this species

Rump is diagnostically almost white and unstreaked; bill is extremely small and stubby. Occurs as two subspecies: Coue's Arctic Redpoll (ssp. *exilipes*); and Hornemann's Arctic Redpoll (ssp. *hornemanni*).

Plumage shows considerable overlap in appearance between sexes and at different ages and times of year. All birds have broadly streaked, very pale grey-brown upperparts (paler overall than in Common) with a bold white wingbar on otherwise dark wings. Rump is obviously white, clean and largely unstreaked. Head has a small black bib, red forecrown and pale ear coverts (these are dark-streaked in Common). Whitish underparts show little or no streaking except in 1st-winter birds (especially females), which also have a warmer buff wash to head, breast and back. Undertail coverts are largely unstreaked but can show a few fine, dark streaks (not as broad as in Common). Hornemann's is larger and overall whiter than Coue's. **VOICE** Utters a rattling *chek-chek-chek* call in flight. **HABITS** Vagrants usually feed on birch and alder seeds, often with other redpoll species. **STATUS AND HABITAT** A northerly species: Coue's breeds from Arctic Scandinavia eastwards; Hornemann's breeds in North America. Vagrants here are likely to turn up in autumn and winter, and favour open woodland.

COUE'S   HORNEMANN'S

TWO-BARRED CROSSBILL

Loxia leucoptera | PD | LENGTH 14.5–16cm

FEMALE

Plump-bodied finch. The combination of
cross-tipped mandibles and bold white wingbars
makes for easy recognition. Sexes are dissimilar.

in young birds, white spots
on tertials are a good
pointer to identification

JUVENILE

Adult male has overall bright pinkish-red plumage, palest and greyest on belly and flanks.
Dark wings have 2 broad white wingbars and broad white tips to the tertials; tail is blackish.
Similar 1st-year has overall bright pinkish-yellow plumage. Females of all ages have streaked,
dull olive-yellow plumage overall but with a pale yellow rump; dark wings show a similar
pattern to male. Juvenile/1st-winter is brownish and heavily streaked, paler below than
above; wingbars are less distinct than on adult. In all birds, bill is appreciably more slender
than in other crossbill species. Beware variant forms of Common Crossbill (*L. curvirostra*) that
have 2 pale wingbars, although in that species wingbars are always
much less striking and bill is appreciably stouter. **VOICE** Calls
include a sharp *tchip-tchip* and a nasal trumpeting note. Song
is a series of vibrating trills and whistles. **HABITS** Extracts
seeds from conifer cones, particularly those of larches.
STATUS AND HABITAT Breeds from N
Scandinavia eastwards. Generally sedentary but
flocks wander if food crop fails. Vagrants here
are likely to turn up in autumn and
winter, and usually associate with
Common Crossbill flocks in
conifer woodland.

MALE

PARROT CROSSBILL

Loxia pytyopsittacus | PC | LENGTH 16–18cm

plumage colour is not useful in separating Crossbill species; bill size and shape are the most reliable features

Confusingly similar to both the Common (*L. curvirostra*) and Scottish (*L. scotica*) crossbills, and separable from those species only with great care. Bill size and shape offer the best clues. Sexes are dissimilar.

All birds have deep, powerful-looking bills, the mandibles of which overlap at the tip, but not to the extent seen in most Common Crossbills; bill is uniformly thick along much of its length (tapers more evenly in Common) and can show an obvious gonys at base of lower mandible. Head and neck also look proportionately large. Adult male has mainly dull red plumage, while that of adult females is yellowish green. Immatures have duller colours than adults of their respective sexes, while juveniles are brownish and streaked. **VOICE** Call is a loud *tchip-tchip*. Song is a series of vibrating trills and whistles. **HABITS** Extracts seeds from conifer cones in the manner of other crossbills. **STATUS AND HABITAT** Breeds from Scandinavia eastwards. Mainly sedentary within its range, although nomadic locally outside the breeding season in search of food. Occasionally irruptive if food crop fails; vagrants are likely to turn up here in late summer and autumn, sometimes in good numbers, and favour conifer woodland. Typically these birds remain for the winter; the species has been known to breed here.

FEMALE

MALE

PINE GROSBEAK

Pinicola enucleator | LENGTH 19–22cm

Large, plump-bodied finch with a
stout, stubby bill and a considerable
amount of white on its wings.
Sexes are dissimilar.

plumage recalls that of
smaller Two-barred
Crossbill but bill is stubby
without overlapping,
crossed mandible tips

FEMALE

MALE

Adult male has overall pinkish-red plumage with varying amounts of grey
on flanks and belly. Note the subtly dark eye-stripe. Tail is dark; blackish
wings have 2 striking white wingbars and white margins to tertials and greater
coverts. Adult female and juvenile/1st-year birds of both sexes have similar
plumage patterns to adult male, but plumage is overall greyish with varying amounts
of olive-yellow on head, back and rump. **VOICE** Call is whistling *piew*. **HABITS** Feeds
on buds, seeds and fruits. Not especially wary. **STATUS AND HABITAT** Breeds from
Scandinavia eastwards. Mainly resident but its range usually extends southwards in winter.
Vagrants here are likely to turn up in autumn and early winter, and favour coastal scrub and
woodland. There is a northerly and north-easterly bias to records.

COMMON ROSEFINCH

Erythrina erythrina | SQ | LENGTH 14–15cm

Robust little finch with a proportionately stout bill. Sexes are dissimilar: adult male is colourful and distinctive, but most birds seen here have sombre, nondescript plumage.

thin double wingbars and dark beady eye

JUVENILE

MALE

Adult male has a red head, breast and rump. Underparts are whitish and back, and tail and wings are brown; note the 2 subtly pale pinkish-buff wingbars. Adult female and 1st-summer male have streaked, mainly brown plumage, but note the 2 pale buff wingbars and streaked pale underparts. Juvenile/1st-winter is similar to adult female but plumage is overall more buffish. **VOICE** Utters a *tchu-ee* call like that of a Greenfinch (*Chloris chloris*). Song is a whistling *weed-ya, weed-ya, viu*. **HABITS** Vagrants are typically rather elusive, keeping to cover and seldom showing themselves for long. **STATUS AND HABITAT** Breeding range extends eastwards from E Europe; winters in India. Its status here is that of a regular vagrant (or perhaps a scarce passage migrant); 100 or so birds are recorded in a good year. Singing males have been noted in spring but birds are most likely to turn up in autumn, favouring coastal scrub and weedy fields.

ROSE-BREASTED GROSBEAK

Pheucticus ludovicianus | LENGTH 17.5–20cm

Distinctively marked songbird whose large bill has the proportions of that of a Hawfinch (*Coccothraustes coccothraustes*). Sexes are dissimilar as adults, but vagrants here are likely to be seen in 1st-winter plumage.

In 1st-winter birds, upperparts are mostly streaked brown with 2 white wingbars; male has a white base to primaries that creates a short additional bar. Head has a broad, pale supercilium, a dark brown crown with a narrow central pale stripe, and a white half-collar that almost frames the dark ear coverts. Underparts are pale overall but with bold, dark streaking; male sometimes has a hint of red on breast. In all birds, underwing coverts are yellowish and bill is pink. **VOICE** Call is a sharp *piik*. **HABITS** Often feeds unobtrusively in cover and can be surprisingly hard to spot in dappled foliage. Diet includes insects, but blackberries are often popular with vagrants here. **STATUS AND HABITAT** Widespread breeder in North America that winters in Central America. Vagrants here are likely to turn up in autumn, and favour coastal scrub and gardens.

1ST-WINTER

MALE, 1ST-WINTER, MOULTING

in recent years, a Rose-breasted Grosbeak overwintered, albeit briefly, on the Isles of Scilly; its plumage was more colourful than typical individuals seen in autumn

SCARLET TANAGER

Piranga olivacea | LENGTH 15.5–17cm

Sexes are dissimilar as adults, but vagrants seen here are likely to be 1st-winter birds, whose plumage colours are reminiscent of an immature Greenfinch (*Chloris chloris*), which has a long and pointed bill.

1st-winter is unmarked yellowish green overall, paler below than above, and with darker brown wings and tail. Bill is pinkish and legs are pinkish blue. On average, male is brighter than female and has darker wings and tail. Other plumages are unlikely to be encountered here, but adult female and non-breeding male are similar to their 1st-winter counterparts; breeding male has bright red plumage with black wings and tail. **VOICE** Utters a tongue-smacking *tchh-brrr* call. **HABITS** Rather unobtrusive and easily overlooked among dappled foliage. **STATUS AND HABITAT** Widespread breeder in North America that winters mainly in South America. Vagrants here are likely to turn up in autumn and favour coastal scrub.

1ST-WINTER

IPSWICH
SPARROW

SAVANNAH SPARROW

Passerculus sandwichensis | LENGTH 14–16cm

North American bunting relative, of which ssp. *princeps* (sometimes referred to as the Ipswich Sparrow) has turned up here. Sexes are similar.

All birds have sandy-brown upperparts with bold, dark streaking on back. Inner flight feathers and greater coverts are subtly more reddish brown, and note the 2 indistinct, pale wingbars. Head pattern comprises a darkish brown crown with a subtle pale central stripe, a dark line behind eye and a yellowish supercilium. The pale moustachial stripe and throat are separated by a dark malar stripe. Underparts are pale but with reddish-brown streaks on breast and flanks. Tail is buffish brown. **VOICE** Call is a thin *stip*. **HABITS** Usually unobtrusive and feeds in low vegetation, but sometimes perches in bush if flushed. **STATUS AND HABITAT** Widespread breeder in North America that winters on the Atlantic coast. Vagrants here are likely to turn up in autumn or spring, and favour coastal grassland and weedy fields.

SONG SPARROW

Melospiza melodia | LENGTH 13–15cm

Well-marked North American bunting relative. Has a relatively long tail; central breast spot (not always obvious) is a good identification feature. Sexes are similar.

North American 'sparrows' are related to our buntings, a fact that becomes obvious when you look at their structure and habits

All birds have a dark-streaked brown back, reddish-brown wings and tail, and 2 pale wingbars. Head pattern comprises a brown crown with a pale central stripe, and a greyish face overall; dark brown line behind eye emphasises the pale grey supercilium. Has a pale moustachial stripe and throat, separated by a dark malar stripe. Underparts are whitish overall, flushed brown on flanks; bold, dark streaks usually merge to create the impression of a dark central spot. **VOICE** Call is a flat *cheerp*. **HABITS** Feeds on the ground and in scrub. **STATUS AND HABITAT** Widespread in North America, where northern birds move south outside the breeding season. Vagrants here are most likely to turn up in spring, coinciding with migration times, and favour coastal scrub.

WHITE-CROWNED SPARROW

Zonotrichia leucophrys | LENGTH 15–16cm

Well-marked, distinctive North American bunting relative that is almost unmistakable when seen well. Sexes are similar.

distinctive head pattern

All birds have dark-streaked brown back and reddish-brown wings with 2 white wingbars. Head pattern comprises black crown with white central stripe, black stripe behind eye, and white supercilium that is broad behind eye. Plumage is otherwise mostly grey-buff, subtly flushed brown on flanks. Tail and rump are grey-brown. Bill and legs are dull pinkish orange. **VOICE** Call is sharp *pink*. **HABITS** Not especially wary; feeds in the open. **STATUS AND HABITAT** Widespread breeder in North America; winters in southern states and Central America. Vagrants turn up in spring and autumn, favouring scrub; has overwintered.

white throat and
yellow lores

WHITE-THROATED SPARROW

Zonotrichia albicollis | LENGTH 15–17cm

Well-marked North American bunting relative, unmistakable when seen well. Sexes are similar.

Adult has a dark-streaked brown back and reddish-brown wings with 2 white wingbars; rump and tail are grey-brown. Head pattern comprises a dark crown with a white central stripe, a broad pale supercilium (white behind eye, yellow-buff in front), a black-framed white throat and grey cheeks. Underparts are grey, palest on belly and undertail coverts. Similar juvenile/1st-winter is subtly duller overall, with less distinct markings and colours. **VOICE** Call is a sharp *cheenk*. **HABITS** Often feeds on the ground but retreats regularly to cover. **STATUS AND HABITAT** Widespread breeder in North America that winters mainly in the southeast. Vagrants here are most likely to turn up in winter and spring, and favour scrub and light woodland.

DARK-EYED JUNCO

Junco hyemalis | JU | LENGTH 13.5–14.5cm

Grey and white North American bunting relative. Sexes differ but all birds share a similar overall plumage pattern.

Adult male has mostly dark grey plumage except for the white belly and undertail coverts. Bill and legs are pink. Adult female and all juvenile/1st-winter birds are similar to adult male, but grey elements of plumage are tinged rufous, especially on crown and wings. All birds have a dark eye and white outer-tail feathers. **VOICE** Call is tongue-smacking *tchht*. **HABITS** Hops along the ground and flicks its tail while feeding; returns regularly to the cover of bushes and scrub. **STATUS AND HABITAT** Widespread in North America, with most birds wintering south of their breeding range. Vagrants here are most likely to turn up in winter and spring, and favour coniferous and mixed woodland and scrub.

RARE BUNTINGS

Many buntings are highly migratory, and several Asian and southern European species turn up in Britain, mostly in autumn but occasionally in spring too. Most have striking markings and colours, but many are flighty or keep in cover for much of the time. If glimpses are brief it pays to know what to look for – to help distinguish the rare species, and to separate them from the default common species in Britain, Yellowhammer and Reed Bunting. Use the annotations on this Ortolan Bunting photo to help hone your skills.

Head pattern and colour can give vital clues – some species have a striking eye-stripe and supercilium; in others, throat and moustache colour can be diagnostic, particularly in males.

Bill colour can be useful. Many rare buntings have greyish bills (like the common British species) but several species have pink bills.

If a pale eye-ring is present, note the colour (yellow in Ortolan, white in Cretzschmar's, for example).

Look for the presence and colour of wingbars.

Note the colour of the back, and whether it is plain or streaked.

ORTOLAN BUNTING

Note whether or not the bird has white outer-tail feathers.

ROCK BUNTING

Emberiza cia | LENGTH 15–16.5cm

Well-marked bunting with a particularly striking head pattern. Sexes are dissimilar.

FEMALE

Adult male has a dark-streaked reddish-brown back. Wings are reddish brown overall, but with grey lesser coverts and 2 white wingbars. Head is grey overall with a pattern that comprises a black frame to ear coverts (eye-stripe, linked to moustachial stripe) and black lines on sides of crown. Throat is grey with a clear demarcation from otherwise reddish-brown underparts. Adult female and juvenile/1st-winter birds are similar to adult male but with muted colours and a less distinct head pattern. All birds show white sides to tail. **VOICE** Call is a thin *tsi*. **HABITS** Feeds unobtrusively and hence easily overlooked. **STATUS AND HABITAT** Widespread in mountains of S Europe; mainly resident but shows some dispersal and altitudinal migration outside the breeding season. Vagrants here are likely to turn up in spring and autumn, and favour barren, rocky coastal habitats.

MALE

although a Rock Bunting's body plumage shares similarities with other rare species (Ortolan and Cretzschmar's in particular) the pattern on the head is unique and diagnostic

CRETZSCHMAR'S BUNTING

Emberiza caesia | LENGTH 14–15.5cm

**Attractive bunting. Sexes are subtly dissimilar
and adult male is particularly colourful. Similar to
an Ortolan Bunting but separable by studying
the colours on the head in particular.**

In all plumages, note the diagnostic combination of a white
eye-ring, pink bill, and orange-red throat and sub-moustachial
stripe. Adult male has a mainly blue-grey head, neck
and breast; orange-red colour on the head is intense.
Upperparts are brown and streaked, and underparts
are orange-brown and show a clear demarcation
from the blue-grey breast. Adult female and
1st-winter birds have similar plumage patterns
to adult male but colours are muted, and
1st-winters have streaking on breast and
flanks. In 1st-winter plumage very like
an Ortolan, but has a whiter throat
and eye-ring and a warmer brown
rump. **VOICE** Utters
a shrill, almost sparrow-like
tchiup. Song is a sweet-
sounding *tswe-tswe-tswe-tswee*
(likened by some to the start
of Beethoven's 5th Symphony).
HABITS Usually feeds
unobtrusively, foraging
among clumps of low
vegetation and between
stones and boulders.
**STATUS AND
HABITAT** Breeding
range is restricted to
Greece, Turkey and
parts of the Middle East;
winters in Africa. Vagrants
here are likely to turn up
in spring and autumn, and
favour rugged and rocky
coastal habitats.

MALE

FEMALE

ORTOLAN BUNTING

Emberiza hortulana | OB | LENGTH 15–16cm

although scarce, Ortolan occurs far more regularly in Britain than Cretzschmar's Bunting, which remains a great rarity

Distinctive bunting. Sexes are subtly dissimilar and adult male is particularly striking and colourful.

1ST-WINTER

FEMALE

In all plumages, note the diagnostic combination of a pale yellow eye-ring, pink bill, and yellow throat and sub-moustachial stripe. Adult male has a mainly greenish-grey head, neck and breast; yellow colour on the head is intense. Upperparts are brown and streaked, and underparts are orange-brown and show a clear demarcation from the greenish-grey breast. Adult female and 1st-winter birds have similar plumage patterns to male but with muted colours; juvenile/1st-winter birds have streaking on breast and flanks. **VOICE** Calls include a thin *tsee*, a tongue-clicking *tchiup* and a liquid *plett*. Song is a rather rasping *tswe-tswe-tswe-tchue* (its tone is reminiscent of the song of a Yellowhammer, *E. citrinella*). **HABITS** Usually feeds low to the ground, making it easily overlooked, and generally rather shy. **STATUS AND HABITAT** Widespread breeder in mainland Europe that winters in Africa. Its status here is that of a regular passage migrant (50 or more recorded in a good year). Most turn up in autumn, and favour short coastal grassland and weedy fields.

MALE

YELLOW-BROWED BUNTING

Emberiza chrysophrys | LENGTH 14–15.5cm

Well-marked and distinctive bunting. If seen well, it is hard to confuse with any related species. Likely to be seen here in 1st-winter plumage, when sexes are similar.

1st-winter has dark-streaked grey-brown back and reddish-tinged rump. Head pattern comprises black crown with narrow white median stripe, broad pale supercilium flushed yellow in front of eye, dark-framed brown ear coverts with white spot near rear, and white moustachial stripe. Underparts are mostly white, with subtle buff tinge to breast and faint dark streaks on breast and flanks. Adult female is similar; adult male is similar but black elements on head are more intense and ear coverts are black. All birds have pink bill and legs. **VOICE** Call is a thin, shrill *tzik*. **HABITS** Usually keeps to the cover of vegetation. **STATUS AND HABITAT** Breeds in Siberia and winters in S Asia. Vagrants usually turn up in autumn, and favour coastal fields and scrub.

RUSTIC BUNTING

Emberiza rustica | LENGTH 13–15cm

broad chestnut streaking on flanks

MALE

Most records of this distinctive bunting relate to 1st-winter birds. Useful identification features include colours and markings on underparts and rump. Sexes are similar in 1st-winter plumage, subtly dissimilar as adults.

1ST-WINTER

1st-winter is warm brown above, dark-streaked on back, unmarked on rump; has 2 pale wingbars. Head pattern comprises pale supercilium and sub-moustachial stripe, and pale spot towards rear of dark-margined ear coverts. White throat is bordered by dark malar stripe; otherwise mostly whitish underparts have reddish-brown streaks on breast and flanks. Summer adult (rare here) is unmistakable, with black and white markings on head, reddish neck, breast and streaks on flanks, and white underparts; male is brighter than female. All birds have pinkish bill and legs. **VOICE** Call is a thin *tsip*. **HABITS** Forages for seeds and insects in short vegetation.
STATUS AND HABITAT Breeds from Scandinavia eastwards across Asia; winters in S Asia. Most vagrants turn up in autumn, in coastal grassland and fields.

open-faced appearance

LITTLE BUNTING

Emberiza pusilla | LJ | LENGTH 12–14cm

Small, well-marked bunting that could perhaps be confused with an immature or female Reed Bunting (*E. schoeniclus*). Specific plumage details allow certain identification on close inspection. Sexes are similar.

Has a dark-streaked brown back, and brown wings marked with 2 pale wingbars. Diagnostic head pattern comprises plain reddish-brown face and throat, pale reddish-brown median stripe to dark crown, and narrow black border to rear part of ear coverts; pale eye-ring is striking and pale spot towards rear of ear coverts can usually be discerned. Underparts are mainly whitish with narrow streaking on breast and flanks. Bill is grey and legs are pink. **VOICE** Call is a sharp *tzik*. **HABITS** Feeds unobtrusively on the ground; shuffles along with a rather horizontal posture. **STATUS AND HABITAT** Breeds in Siberia and winters in S Asia. Vagrants here (20–30 in a good year) turn up mainly in autumn, in coastal fields.

YELLOW-BREASTED BUNTING

Emberiza aureola | LENGTH 14–16cm

Likely to be seen here in 1st-winter plumage, when sexes are similar. At this time, possibility exists for confusion with a non-breeding Yellowhammer (*E. citrinella*).

1st-winter is buffish-brown above, heavily streaked on back; note 2 white wingbars. Head pattern comprises pale supercilium and centre to crown, pale buff ear coverts, framed by dark sides to crown, and dark eye-stripe that connects with dark moustachial stripe. Whitish throat grades to otherwise subtly lemon-yellow underparts, with dark streaking on flanks. Bill and legs are pink. Adults are unlikely to be seen here, but summer male has chestnut upperparts, black face and breast band, yellow chest and underparts, and white patch on wings. Adult female is similar but less colourful. **VOICE** Call is a sharp *tsick*. **HABITS** Forages on the ground for insects and seeds. **STATUS AND HABITAT** Breeds across N Central Asia and winters in Southeast Asia. Vagrants turn up mainly in autumn, in coastal grassland and fields.

BLACK-FACED BUNTING

Emberiza spodocephala | LENGTH 14–15.5cm

MALE

Rather plain-looking but nevertheless distinctive bunting. Adults, the sexes of which are subtly dissimilar, look markedly different from 1st-winter birds.

1st-winter has dark-streaked reddish-brown back and unmarked brown rump; wings show 2 indistinct pale wingbars. Head pattern comprises greenish-grey cap with dark lores, variably pale yellow supercilium behind eye, and yellow throat. Underparts are pale with variable yellow tinge and dark streaks on flanks. Adult male has blue-grey head and neck with dark lores. Upperparts are otherwise brown and dark-streaked, and underparts are flushed yellow with streaking on flanks. Adult female is less well marked; head pattern is reminiscent of 1st-winter. Bill and legs pink in all birds. **VOICE** Calls include a thin *tzip*. **HABITS** Usually keeps near to the cover of bushes. **STATUS AND HABITAT** Breeds in Siberia and winters in south Asia. Vagrants turn up mainly in autumn, in coastal scrub.

FEMALE

PINE BUNTING

Emberiza leucocephalos | EL | LENGTH 16–17.5cm

Large bunting with the size and proportions of a Yellowhammer (*E. citrinella*). Sexes are dissimilar; male is particularly striking.

lacks any yellow hues

Summer adult male has reddish-buff upperparts with dark streaks on back; wings have 2 subtle, pale wingbars. Head pattern comprises black-framed white ear coverts, black-bordered white crown, and otherwise chestnut head. Underparts are whitish, flushed reddish buff and streaked on breast and flanks. Bill is grey and legs are dull pink. Summer adult female is similar but colours and pattern on head are less striking, and throat is pale. Winter adults and 1st-winter birds have indistinct head patterns and greyish-white underparts with rufous-tinged dark streaks on breast and flanks. **VOICE** Rasping *sziff* call is similar to that of Yellowhammer. **HABITS** Forages on the ground. **STATUS AND HABITAT** Breeds in Siberia and winters in S Asia. Vagrants turn up in spring and autumn, in coastal grassland and scrub.

1ST-WINTER

MALE

BLACK-HEADED BUNTING

Emberiza melanocephala | LENGTH 15–17cm

**can show ghosting of
male's head pattern**

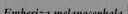

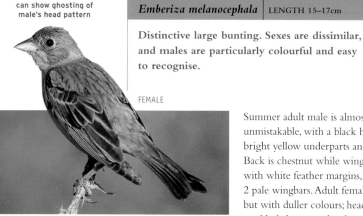

FEMALE

Distinctive large bunting. Sexes are dissimilar,
and males are particularly colourful and easy
to recognise.

Summer adult male is almost
unmistakable, with a black hood and
bright yellow underparts and neck.
Back is chestnut while wings are dark
with white feather margins, creating
2 pale wingbars. Adult female is similar
but with duller colours; head is greyish,
not black, but note the clean, unstreaked
yellowish underparts. In 1st-winter plumage, recalls an adult female but colours are duller still,
and ear coverts are paler than streaked crown, so the appearance of a dark hood is reduced.
All birds have a large grey bill. Beware escaped Red-headed Buntings (*E. bruniceps*): 1st-winter
and adult female birds are very difficult to separate from their Black-headed counterparts.
Longer primary projection, ghosting of black hood, longer bill and obviously streaked crown
are all good features for Black-headed. **VOICE** Song is a trilling mix of rasping, fluty notes,
descending in pitch from start to finish. Calls include a shrill
tchiurp. **HABITS** Spring males often sing from prominent perches.
STATUS AND HABITAT Breeds from SE Europe eastwards,
and winters in India. Vagrants here are likely to turn up at
migration times, mainly in spring, and favour
coastal scrub.

**no other bunting shares the male's
combination of black cap, chestnut
back and yellow underparts**

**by bunting
standards, bill is
proportionately
large**

MALE

PALLAS'S REED BUNTING

Emberiza pallasi | LENGTH 12–13.5cm

Similar to, but appreciably smaller than, a Reed Bunting
(*E. schoeniclus*), and with subtly different plumages and a
proportionately much shorter tail. Sexes are dissimilar;
most likely to be seen here in 1st-winter plumage.

FEMALE

Plumages of 1st-winter and female have an overall
much colder, paler yellow-buff ground colour to upperparts
(including nape) than Reed (which is a richer chestnut brown). Back is
dark-streaked and note the 2 subtly pale buff wingbars; lesser coverts are pale
grey-buff (reddish brown in Reed). Head pattern is similar to that of a similar-aged
Reed, but note the uniformly buffish-brown crown (darker and with a pale median
stripe in Reed). Underparts are pale buff with very little streaking. Bill is pinkish (dark
grey in Reed). Adult male has a similar plumage pattern to male Reed, but brown elements
of that species' plumage are pale grey-buff. **VOICE** Calls include a sparrow-like *tchiurp*.
HABITS Forages on the ground and clambers through low wetland vegetation. **STATUS
AND HABITAT** Breeds in Siberia and winters in Southeast Asia. Vagrants here are likely
to turn up at migration times (mostly autumn), and favour coastal wetlands and fields.

BOBOLINK

Dolichonyx oryzivorus | LENGTH 16–18cm

1ST-WINTER

Chunky, rather finch- or sparrow-like bird
with a stout bill and diagnostic pointed tips to
tail feathers. Vagrants here are likely to be seen
in 1st-winter plumage, sexes of which are similar.

1st-winter is warm buffish brown overall, with dark
streaking on back, and dark centres and buff margins
to wing coverts and tertials. Tail feathers are
extremely pointed. Head pattern comprises
dark stripe behind eye and dark crown with
a pale central stripe. Throat is pale and underparts are
otherwise pale buff, with subtle dark streaking on flanks.
Adult breeding male (unlikely to be seen here) has mostly black plumage but with a buff nape,
white rump and white 'shoulder' patch. Adult female recalls a 1st-winter bird, but markings
are bolder. **VOICE** Call is a rather harsh *tchukt*. In flight, utters a distinctive *pink* call. **HABITS**
Usually forages on the ground like a House Sparrow (*Passer domesticus*) or Skylark (*Alauda
arvensis*). **STATUS AND HABITAT** Widespread breeder in North America that winters in
South America. Vagrants here are likely to turn up in autumn, in coastal grassland.

BROWN-HEADED COWBIRD

Molothrus ater | LENGTH 18–19cm

Slim, long-bodied bird. Sexes are dissimilar; likely to be seen here in 1st-winter plumage, when it vaguely recalls a long-tailed immature Starling (*Sturnus vulgaris*). Note the distinctive stout, conical greyish bill.

1ST-WINTER

Plumage of 1st-winter birds is overall rather uniform brown, darkest on wings and tail; note the subtly pale throat and fine, streaked underparts. Adult birds are unlikely to be seen here, but female is similar to 1st-winter birds; adult male has mostly blackish plumage with a green sheen, and a rich brown hood. Legs are dark in all birds. **VOICE** Call is rattling *krrrk*. **HABITS** Usually feeds on the ground in the manner of a foraging Starling. **STATUS AND HABITAT** Widespread breeder in North America; wanders outside the breeding season and northern birds migrate south. Vagrants here are likely to turn up in autumn and favour coastal grassland.

BALTIMORE ORIOLE

Icterus galbula | LENGTH 18cm

Colourful, slim-bodied bird. Proportions are rather like those of a Starling, but note the relatively long tail and long, pointed bill. Sexes are dissimilar; vagrants here are likely to be seen in 1st-winter plumage.

In 1st-winter plumage, has a grey-brown back and wings, the latter with 2 white wingbars, the upper one broadest. Plumage is otherwise yellowish; female is paler overall than male. Adults are unlikely to be seen here, however adult female recalls a 1st-winter but with variable black mottling on head; adult male has striking orange and black plumage. Bill and legs are greyish in all birds. **VOICE** Utters a rattling call. **HABITS** Feeds unobtrusively in foliage and can be surprisingly difficult to spot. **STATUS AND HABITAT** Widespread breeder in North America that winters mainly in Central and South America. Vagrants here are likely to turn up in autumn and favour coastal scrub.

1ST-WINTER

OVENBIRD

Seiurus aurocapilla | LENGTH 15cm

Plump, mainly terrestrial North American warbler that recalls a miniature thrush in its appearance and habits. The combination of crown pattern and large eye with a striking white eye-ring is diagnostic. Sexes are similar.

feeds on the ground, often in deep woodland shade, so easy to overlook

1ST-WINTER

All birds have mostly olive-brown upperparts and wings (1st-winter birds have 2 subtly pale wingbars). Head pattern comprises a striking black-bordered orange crown, olive-brown face with a white eye-ring, and white throat with a black malar stripe. Underparts are otherwise mostly white with bold black spots and streaks on breast and flanks. Legs are pinkish.

VOICE Call is a sharp *tsik*. **HABITS** Forages among leaf litter for invertebrates. **STATUS AND HABITAT** Widespread North American breeder that winters mainly in Central America. Vagrants here are likely to turn up in autumn and favour coastal woodland.

NORTHERN WATERTHRUSH

Parkesia noveboracensis | LENGTH 14cm

Unusual North American warbler that recalls a miniature thrush. Its appearance and behaviour make identification relatively straightforward. Sexes are similar.

some birds have remained here for some time and have been known to overwinter (on Isles of Scilly)

1ST-WINTER

All birds have mostly dark olive-brown upperparts, including wings and tail. Note the long, bold supercilium that is buffish along its length. Underparts are whitish overall with a variable yellow wash, particularly on breast and flanks, and bold, dark streaks on throat and all areas of underparts except undertail coverts. Legs are stout and dull pink, and bill is pink-based. **VOICE** Call is a thin, sharp *tzip*.

HABITS Often found near water, typically foraging along muddy margins, constantly pumping its tail up and down. **STATUS AND HABITAT** Widespread North American breeder that winters in Central America and N South America. Vagrants here are likely to turn up in autumn, and favour coastal damp woodland and scrub.

BLACK-AND-WHITE WARBLER

Mniotilta varia | LENGTH 12cm

has been known to
overwinter, mixing with
other winter birds notably
Blue Tits (*Cyanistes
caeruleus*)

1ST-WINTER

**Unmistakable North American warbler. Legs are dark, and
has relatively long, slightly downcurved bill. Likely to be
seen here in 1st-winter plumage; sexes are subtly dissimilar.**

1st-winter is striped black and white, palest on
underparts, and with 2 white wingbars. Head pattern
comprises black stripe behind eye, and black crown
with white central stripe. Female 1st-winter
has less intense black markings than male
1st-winter, and buffish wash to cheeks
and underparts (particularly flanks). Adults
(unlikely to be seen here) have more intense markings
than 1st-winter birds. **VOICE** Call is sharp *tchak*.
HABITS Feeds like a Treecreeper (*Certhia familiaris*), moving along branches, sometimes upside
down, investigating nooks and crannies for invertebrates. **STATUS AND HABITAT**
Widespread North American breeder; winters mainly in Central America. Vagrants here are
likely to turn up in autumn, in coastal woodland and scrub.

TENNESSEE WARBLER

Oreothlypis peregrina | LENGTH 12cm

1ST-WINTER

**North American warbler with rather clean-looking
plumage and dark legs. Likely to be seen here in
1st-winter plumage, the sexes of which are similar.**

Recalls a *Phylloscopus* warbler, but note the more compact
body, proportionately larger head and shorter tail, and more
conical bill. In 1st-winter plumage, has a dull yellowish-
green back and rump, and yellowish-tinged brown wings
with 2 subtly pale wingbars. Has a grey cap, dark lores and
pale supercilium. Throat and underparts are whitish with
a faint yellowish tinge to breast and flanks. Undertail coverts are always paler than
rest of underparts. Adults (unlikely to be seen here) are more intensely colourful
and more clearly marked than 1st-winter birds. **VOICE** Call is a tongue-smacking *tchht*.
HABITS Feeds actively, hunting for invertebrates among foliage. **STATUS AND HABITAT**
Fairly widespread North American breeder that winters in Central and South America.
Vagrants here are likely to turn up in autumn, and favour coastal scrub and woodland.

COMMON YELLOWTHROAT

Geothlypis trichas | LENGTH 12cm

**Colourful North American warbler. Sexes are
dissimilar but all birds have a distinctive yellow
throat; vagrants here are likely to be 1st-winter birds.**

1ST-WINTER

In 1st-winter plumage, has an olive-grey nape, back,
wings and tail, tinged yellow, especially on wings. Face
is olive-grey, tinged with yellow, and throat and breast
are unmarked yellow. Underparts are otherwise pale
olive-grey, flushed yellow, particularly on flanks and
undertail coverts. Adults are unlikely to be seen here
but adult female is similar to 1st-winter; adult male
has a diagnostic black mask. All birds have a stout bill
and pinkish legs. **VOICE** Call is a tongue-smacking
tchet. **HABITS** Generally secretive, keeping to the
cover of low vegetation. **STATUS AND HABITAT**
Widespread North American breeder that winters
mainly in Central and South America. Vagrants here
are likely to turn up in autumn, and favour coastal
grassy and wetland habitats.

MALE

NORTHERN PARULA

Setophaga americana | LENGTH 11cm

**Distinctive small, colourful North American
warbler. Hard to confuse with any other species
if seen well. Likely to be seen here in 1st-winter
plumage, the sexes of which are similar.**

a combination of colourful
plumage and striking white
wingbars make
identification
straightforward

1ST-WINTER

In 1st-winter plumage, has mainly bluish-grey upperparts with
a greenish patch on the back, and 2 striking white wingbars.
Face is bluish grey and dark eye has white 'eyelids'. Throat and
breast are flushed yellow, grading to white on belly and undertail.
Lower mandible is yellow and legs are dull orange. Adults
(unlikely to be seen here) are more intensely colourful and more
clearly marked than 1st-winter birds. **VOICE** Call is a sharp *tzip*.
HABITS Very active and often forages high in tree tops, making observation a challenge.
STATUS AND HABITAT Widespread North American breeder that winters in Central
America. Vagrants here are likely to turn up in autumn, and favour coastal woodland and scrub.

AMERICAN REDSTART

Setophaga ruticilla | AD | LENGTH 14cm

with a passing
resemblance to an Old
World flycatcher, this
species' tail markings are
unique and diagnostic

**Strikingly colourful North American warbler with
a proportionately long, well-marked tail. Likely to
be seen here in 1st-winter plumage.**

In 1st-winter plumage, has a greenish-grey back, and darker brown wings with a striking
yellow wingbar. Greenish-grey tail has extensive yellow sides (basal ⅔ of length). Head is
greyish, grading to greyish white on rest of underparts, which have a yellow flush on sides of
breast and undertail coverts. Legs and bill are dark in all birds. Adults (unlikely to be seen
here) are more intensely colourful and more clearly marked than 1st-winter birds. **VOICE**
Call is a thin *chip*. **HABITS** An active feeder that often fans its tail. **STATUS AND HABITAT**
Widespread breeder in North America that winters mainly in Central and South America.
Vagrants here are likely to turn up in autumn, and favour coastal woodland and scrub.

1ST-WINTER

MALE

BLACKBURNIAN WARBLER

Setophaga fusca | LENGTH 14cm

1ST-WINTER

Well-marked North American warbler. Vagrants here are likely to be seen in 1st-winter plumage.

In 1st-winter plumage, has an olive-brown back with distinctive pale braces and brown wings marked with 2 striking white wingbars. Head pattern comprises an olive-brown crown; olive-buff ear coverts are framed by yellow (supercilium above and throat below). Yellow on throat extends to breast and grades to white overall on rest of underparts, flushed yellow and streaked on flanks. Adults (unlikely to be seen here) are more intensely colourful and more clearly marked than 1st-winter birds. In all birds, legs are dull brown with yellowish feet, and bill has a pinkish base. **VOICE** Call is a sharp *tsik*. **HABITS** Active warbler that forages for insects high in tree tops. **STATUS AND HABITAT** Widespread breeder in North America that winters in South America. Vagrants here are likely to turn up in autumn, and favour coastal woodland and scrub.

YELLOW WARBLER

Setophaga petechia | LENGTH 12cm

Colourful and aptly named North American warbler. Likely to be seen here in 1st-winter plumage.

1ST-WINTER

In 1st-winter plumage, has olive-yellow upperparts overall; wings are subtly browner (tertials are darkest and have white margins) and show 2 indistinct pale wingbars. Shows distinctive yellow inner webs on spread tail. Head is uniformly dull yellow (with a contrasting dark eye), and throat and rest of underparts are yellowish. Brighter 1st-winter birds with red on the breast are likely to be males. Adults (unlikely to be seen here) are more intensely colourful and more clearly marked than 1st-winter birds. Bill is dark and legs are dull brown in all birds. **VOICE** Call is sharp *tchup*. **HABITS** Favours waterside bushes and commonly feeds rather low; often flicks its tail. **STATUS AND HABITAT** Widespread breeder in North America that winters in South America. Vagrants here are likely to turn up in autumn, and favour coastal woodland and scrub.

combination of striking
wingbars and yellow flush
to head and breast make
identification fairly
straightforward

BLACKPOLL WARBLER

Setophaga striata | LENGTH 14cm

A well-marked species, and one of the most regular North American warblers to cross the Atlantic. Vagrants here are likely to be seen in 1st-winter plumage.

1ST-WINTER

In 1st-winter plumage, has olive-yellow upperparts with dark streaking on back. Crown and ear coverts are olive-yellow, and supercilium and throat are brighter yellow. Yellow on throat extends to breast and grades to white on rest of underparts, including undertail coverts; breast and flanks are streaked. Adults (unlikely to be seen here) are more intensely colourful and more clearly marked than 1st-winter birds, and male has a black crown. All birds have a stout orange-based bill, and orange legs and feet. **VOICE** Call is a sharp *chip*. **HABITS** Feeds in a slower, more deliberate manner than many other warblers. **STATUS AND HABITAT** Widespread breeder in E North America that winters in N South America. Vagrants here are likely to turn up in autumn, and favour coastal woodland and scrub.

spread tail shows
large white spots

YELLOW-RUMPED WARBLER

Setophaga coronata | LENGTH 14cm

North American warbler. Vagrants here are likely to be ssp. *coronata* in 1st-winter plumage, which is rather nondescript apart from the diagnostic yellow rump.

1ST-WINTER

In 1st-winter plumage, has grey-buff upperparts that are subtly dark-streaked on back; wings are blackish with white feather margins and show 2 bold wingbars. Head is mostly uniform grey-buff, grading to whitish on throat. Underparts are overall greyish white, streaked on breast, flushed and streaked yellow on flanks, and whitish on undertail coverts. Bright 1st-winters with blue on wing coverts and yellow on crown are likely to be males. Adults (unlikely to be seen here) are more intensely colourful and more clearly marked than 1st-winter birds. Bill and legs are dark in all birds. **VOICE** Call is a soft *tchep*. **HABITS** Forages among foliage for invertebrates. **STATUS AND HABITAT** Widespread breeder in North America that winters in South America. Vagrants here are likely to turn up in autumn, and favour coastal woodland and scrub.

RAREST OF THE RARE

Collin BTO Guide to Rare Birds deals with scarce and rare birds in Britain and Ireland. Based on submitted records, the status and occurrence of these species is determined by adjudicators on the subject: the British Birds Rarities Committee (BBRC) in Britain; and the Irish Rare Birds Committee (IRBC) in Ireland.

The main section of the book deals with species that have been recorded, in the main, four times or more at the time of writing (September 2014). In addition, there are a number of other genuinely wild birds that have also been recorded in Britain and Ireland; these species are listed below. They include: species that have been recorded, in the main, three times or fewer (as of September 2014); species whose status and records are still the subject of discussion, hence the number of records cannot be determined precisely at the moment; and one extinct species.

RAREST OF THE RARE RECORDED IN BRITAIN AND IRELAND (AS OF SEPTEMBER 2014)

White-winged Scoter *Melanitta deglandi* – North America.
One British record, from northeast Scotland, Murcar, 11–23 June 2011.
One Irish record, from County Kerry, Rossbeigh, 1 February–11 April 2011.

Yellow-nosed Albatross *Thalassarche chlororhynchos* – South Atlantic.
One British record involving an immature bird. Initially discovered at Brean Down in Somerset, it was taken into care on 29 June 2007 and released the following day. What was assumed to be the same bird turned up on Carsington Water, Derbyshire, on 2 July, and then later that day at Manor Farm fishing lakes near Messingham, Lincolnshire; it stayed until the following day. The wider birdwatching community was not aware of its presence until after the event.

MADEIRAN STORM-PETREL

It may seem like the Madeiran Storm-petrel (*Oceanodroma castro*) has suddenly disappeared off the British birdwatching radar. In fact, it is now recognised as being part of a species 'complex' comprising three Macaronesian-breeding *Oceanodroma* species; its companion species are the Cape Verde Storm-petrel (*O. jabejabe*) and Monteiro's Storm-petrel (*O. monteiroi*). These are almost impossible to distinguish in the field, and the British Ornithologists' Union has decided that sightings of individuals in British waters cannot be assigned to any of the three species. Collectively, they are embraced within the Band-rumped Storm-petrel complex, and this is how they are treated in the main section of the book (*see* p. 59). The one record of a Madeiran Storm-petrel in Ireland – from County May, Blackrock Light, 18 October 1931, is currently under review by the Irish Rare Birds Committee.

EGYPTIAN VULTURE

Capped Petrel
Pterodroma hasitata
– Caribbean.
Two British records, the most
recent from East Yorkshire,
Barmston, tideline corpse, long
dead, 16 December 1984.

Scopoli's Shearwater *Calonectris diomedea*
– Mediterranean.
One British record, from the Isles of Scilly,
10km south of St Mary's, 4 July 2009.

St Mary's, 7
December 2007.

Frigate Petrel *Pelagodroma marina*
– southern oceans.
One British record, prior to 1950.

Double-crested Cormorant *Phalacrocorax
auritus* – North America.
One British record, from Cleveland/County
Durham, Billingham, 11 January–26 April
1989.
One Irish record, from County Galway,
Nimmo's Pier, 18 November 1995–6
January 1996.

Ascension Frigatebird *Fregata aquila*
– South Atlantic.
Two British records, the most recent
from Argyll, Islay, 5 July 2013.

Magnificent Frigatebird *Fregata magnificens*
– Atlantic and Pacific coasts of the Americas.
Two British records, the most recent from
Shropshire, near Whitchurch, taken into care
7 November 2005, died 9 November 2005;
now in the Natural History Museum, Tring.

Great Blue Heron
Ardea herodias – North America.
One British record, from the Isles of Scilly,

Egyptian Vulture *Neophron percnopterus*
– southern Europe, Africa, the Middle
East and India.
Two British records, prior to 1950.

Greater Spotted Eagle *Aquila clanga*
– Asia.
Twelve British records, prior to 1950.
Two Irish records, of two birds shot in
County Cork, near Youghal, January 1845.

Allen's Gallinule *Porphyrio alleni*
– Africa.
Two British records, the most recent
from Dorset, Portland, found moribund,
10 February 2002.

Macqueen's Bustard *Chlamydotis macquenii*
– Sinai Peninsula to Mongolia.
Four records prior to 1950, one since,
Suffolk, Hinton, 25 November–29
December 1962.

Little Whimbrel *Numenius minutus*
– Asia.
Two British records, the most recent from
Norfolk, Cley next the Sea, 24 August–3
September 1985.

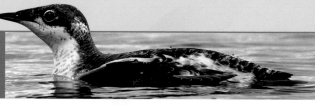

LONG-BILLED MURRELET
Brachyramphus perdix
– North Pacific

One British record, from Devon, Dawlish, 10–17 November 2006.

The appearance in 2006 of a Long-billed Murrelet caused a sensation in ornithological circles, and thousands of birdwatchers flocked to Dawlish in Devon to see the bird. They thronged along the seawall and the bird provided memorable views for much of its time. It often fed close to shore, bobbing up among the breaking waves, much to the delight of onlookers.

Eskimo Curlew *Numenius borealis*
– North America.
Four British records, prior to 1950. One Irish record, prior to 1950. Now considered globally extinct.

Grey-tailed Tattler *Tringa brevipes*
– North America.
Two British records, the most recent from Moray and Nairn, Burghead Bay, 27 November–27 December 1994.

Tufted Puffin *Fratercula cirrhata*
– North Pacific.
One British record, from Kent, Oare Marshes, 16 September 2009.

Ancient Murrelet *Synthliboramphus antiquus* – North Pacific.
One British record from Devon, Lundy, initially 27 May–26 June 1990, and last seen there 30 March–29 April 1992.

Great Auk *Pinguinus impennis*
– northern seas.
Now extinct; last record in the British Isles from the Outer Hebrides, St Kilda, July 1844.

Aleutian Tern *Onychoprion aleuticus*
– North Pacific.
One British record, from Northumberland, Farne Islands, 28–29 May 1979.

Cabot's Tern *Sterna acuflavida* – North America.
One British record, from Herefordshire, Newhouse Wood, found freshly dead, 8 November 1984.

Royal Tern *Sterna (Thalasseus) maxima* – North America and Mauritania.
Five British records of two or three individuals, the most recent from Caernarfonshire, Porth Ceiriad, 15 June 2009.
One Irish record from County Cork, Clonakilty, 7 June 2009.

Pallas's Gull *Larus ichthyaetus* – Russia.
One British record, prior to 1950.

Glaucous-winged Gull *Larus glaucescens*
– North America.
Two British records, the most recent from Cleveland/County Durham, 31 December 2008–10 January 2009.

PALLAS'S GULL

Hawk Owl *Surnia ulula* – northern Holarctic.
Three British records, the most recent from Shetland, Mainland, Frakkafield, 12–13 September 1983; the same individual was later on Bressay, 20–21 September 1983.

Red-necked Nightjar *Caprimulgus ruficollis* – Iberia and North Africa.
One British record, prior to 1950.

Egyptian Nightjar *Caprimulgus aegyptius* – North Africa and the Middle East.

HAWK OWL

Two British records, the most recent from Dorset, Portland, 10 June 1984.

Yellow-bellied Sapsucker *Sphyrapicus varius* – North America.
One British record, from the Isles of Scilly, Tresco, 26 September–6 October 1975.
One Irish record, from County Cork, Cape Clear Island, trapped and ringed, 16–19 October 1988.

American Kestrel *Falco sparverius* – North America.
Two British records, the most recent from Cornwall, Bearah Tor, 13–28 June 1976.

Amur Falcon *Falco amurensis* – Asia.
One British record, from East Yorkshire, Tophill Low, 14–15 October 2008.

Eastern Phoebe *Sayornis phoebe* – North America.
One British record, from Devon, Lundy, 24–25 April 1987.

Alder Flycatcher *Empidonax alnorum* – North America.
Two British records, the most recent from Norfolk, Blakeney Point, 25–27 September 2010.

LONG-TAILED SHRIKE

Yellow-throated Vireo
Vireo flavifrons – North America.
One British record, from Cornwall,
Kenidjack, 20–27 September 1990.

Long-tailed Shrike *Lanius schach*
– Asia.
One British record, from the Outer
Hebrides, South Uist, Howbeg and
Howmore, 3–4 November 2000.

Masked Shrike *Lanius nubius*
– the Middle East.
Two British records, the most
recent from the Isles of Scilly,
St Mary's, 1 November 2006.

White-winged Lark *Melanocorypha
leucoptera* – Asia.
Two British records, the most recent from
Norfolk, King's Lynn, 22–24 October 1981.

Lesser Short-toed Lark
Calandrella rufescens –
Mediterranean, the
Middle East and Asia.
One British record,
from Dorset,
Portland, 2 May
1992.

LESSER
SHORT-TOED
LARK

Tree Swallow *Tachycineta bicolor*
– North America.
Two British records, the most recent from
Shetland, Unst, 29 May 2002.

Purple Martin *Progne subis*
– North America.
One British record, from the Outer
Hebrides, Lewis, 5–6 September 2004.

Eastern-crowned Warbler *Phylloscopus
coronatus* – Asia.
Two British records, the most recent from
Hertfordshire, Hilfield Park, 30 October
2011.

Green Warbler *Phylloscopus nitidus*
– Asia.
One British record, from the Isles of Scilly,
St Mary's, 26 September–4 October 1983.

Olive-tree Warbler *Hippolais olivetorum*
– eastern Mediterranean and the Middle
East.
One British record, from Shetland,
Mainland, 16 August 2006.

Red-breasted Nuthatch *Sitta canadensis*
– North America.
One British record, from Norfolk, Holkham,
13 October 1989–6 May 1990.

Northern Mockingbird *Mimus polyglottos*
– North America.
Two British records, the most recent from
Essex, Horsey Island, 17–23 May 1988.

Brown Thrasher *Toxostoma rufum*
– North America.
One British record, from Dorset, Durlston
Head, 5 February 1966.

Grey Catbird *Dumetella carolinensis*
– North America.
One British record, from Anglesey, South
Stack, 4–6 October 2001.
One Irish record, from County Cork, Cape
Clear Island, 4 November 1986.

Varied Thrush *Ixoreus naevius*
– North America.
One British record, from
Cornwall, Nanquidno,
14–23 November
1982.

Wood Thrush *Hylocichla mustelina*
– North America.
One British record, from the Isles of Scilly,
St Agnes, 7 October 1987.

Naumann's Thrush *Turdus naumanni*
– Asia.
Two British records, the most recent from
Essex/Greater London, South Woodford,
6–11 January 1997.

Red-throated Thrush *Turdus ruficollis*
– Asia.
One British record, from Essex, the Naze,
29 September–7 October 1994.

Moussier's Redstart *Phoenicurus moussieri*
– North Africa.
One British record, from Pembrokeshire,
Dinas Head, 24 April 1988.

White-crowned Black Wheatear
Oenanthe leucopyga – North Africa
and the Middle East.
One British record, from Suffolk,
Kessingland, 2–5 June 1982.

WHITE-CROWNED
BLACK WHEATEAR

Rock Sparrow *Petronia petronia* –
Mediterranean, North Africa,
the Middle East and Asia.
One British record, from Norfolk,
Cley next the Sea, 14 June 1981.

Evening Grosbeak *Hesperiphona vespertina*
– North America.
Two British records, the most recent
from Highland, Badenoch and Strathspey,
10–25 March 1980.

Citril Finch *Carduelis citrinella*
– mountain regions of southern Europe.
One British record, from Shetland,
Fair Isle, 6–11 June 2008.

Summer Tanager *Piranga rubra*
– North America.
One British record, from
Caernarfonshire, Bardsey
Island, 11–25 September
1957.

Indigo Bunting *Passerina cyanea*
– North America.
Two British records, the most recent from
Anglesey, Menai Bridge, 20 May 2013.
One Irish record, from County Cork,
Cape Clear Island, 9–19 October 1985.

Eastern Towhee *Pipilo erythrophthalmus*
– North America.
One British record, from Devon, Lundy,
7 June 1966.

Lark Sparrow *Chondestes grammacus*
– North America.
Two British records, the most recent
from Norfolk, Waxham, 15–17 May 1991.

Chestnut-eared Bunting *Emberiza fucata*
– Asia.
Two British records, the most recent from
    Shetland, Mainland, 23–25 October
        2012.

   Golden-winged Warbler
    Vermivora chrysoptera – North America.
    One British record, from Kent,
    Maidstone, 24 January–10 April 1989.

   Hooded Warbler *Setophaga citrina*
    – North America.
 Two British records, the most recent
from the Outer Hebrides, St Kilda,
10 September 1992.

Cape May Warbler *Setophaga tigrina*
– North America.
Two British records, the most recent from
Shetland, Unst, 23 October–2 November
2013.

CITRIL FINCH

Magnolia Warbler *Setophaga magnolia*
– North America.
Two British records, the most recent from
Shetland, Fair Isle, 23 September 2012.

Bay-breasted Warbler *Setophaga castanea*
– North America.
One British record, Cornwall, Land's End, 1
October 1995.

Chestnut-sided Warbler *Setophaga
pensylvanica* – North America.
Two British records, the most recent from
Devon, Prawle Point, 18 October 1995.

Wilson's Warbler *Cardellina pusilla* – North
America.
One British record, from Cornwall,
Rame Head, October 1985.
One Irish record, County Cork, Dursey
Island, 18–21 September 2013.

RAREST OF THE RARE RECORDED IN IRELAND
BUT NOT BRITAIN (AS OF SEPTEMBER 2014)

Bulwer's Petrel *Bulweria bulwerii*
– central Atlantic Ocean and Pacific Ocean.
One Irish record, from County Cork,
Cape Clear Island, 3 August 1975.

Thayer's Gull *Larus thayeri*
– North America.
Up to eight have been recorded in Ireland,
the most recent from County Donegal,
Killybegs, 16 December 2013. The species'
status on this side of the Atlantic is still
the subject of discussion. Birds have been
reported in Britain but the species has not
been accepted onto the British List by the
BOU as yet.

Little Blue Heron *Egretta caerulea*
– North America.
One Irish record, from County Galway,
Letterfrack, 24 September–22 October
2008.

Bald Eagle *Haliaeetus leucocephalus*
– North America.
Two Irish records, the most recent from
County Kerry, Ballymacelligott, 17

November 1987. Caught and returned to
USA.

Griffon Vulture *Gyps fulvus*
– southern Europe, North Africa,
and southwest and Central Asia.
One Irish record, captured in Cork Harbour,
1842.

Northern Flicker *Colaptes auratus*
– North America.
One Irish record, seen to fly ashore
from a ship in Cork Harbour, October
1962.

Eastern Kingbird *Tyrannus tyrannus*
– North America.
One Irish record, from County
Galway, Inishmore, 5 October 2012.

Ruby-crowned Kinglet *Regulus calendula*
– North America.
One Irish record, from County Cork,
Cape Clear Island, 27–28 October 2013.

Blue-winged Warbler *Vermivora cyanoptera*
– North America.
One Irish record, from County Cork,
Cape Clear Island, 4–10 October 2000.

Canada Warbler *Cardellina canadensis*
– North America.
One Irish record, from County Clare,
Loop Head, 8–13 October 2006.

Fox Sparrow *Passerella iliaca*
– North America.
One Irish record, from County Down,
Copeland Island, trapped and ringed,
3 June 1961.

THE BRITISH AND IRISH LISTS

The official list of wild birds recorded in Great Britain (England, Wales and Scotland) is maintained by the British Ornithologists' Union and is referred to by birdwatchers as the 'British List'; it can be downloaded from the BOU's website (www.bou.org.uk). Species considered to be valid contenders for the list either must have occurred here in an apparently natural state or, although introduced, have self-sustaining populations. Birds that have escaped from captivity are not included in the list. At the time of writing (September 2014), the most up-to-date version was one published in June 2013 (Harrop *et al.* 2013).

The Irish List is compiled by the Irish Rare Birds Committee and can be downloaded from their website (www.irbc.ie).

GLOSSARY

Alula Group of four small feathers at the bend of the wing; also known as the 'bastard wing'. Used to control airflow over the wing.
Axillaries The group of feathers that form the 'armpit' of the bird.
Bill The beak.
Carpal The 'wrist' of a bird, forming the bend of the wing.
Cere Coloured bare skin at the base of the upper mandible containing the nostrils; typically found on raptors.

Cetaceans Collective word for whales and dolphins.
Coverts Small contour feathers found on the upperwing, underwing, uppertail and undertail.
Culmen The upper ridge of the bill.
Digiscope A digital camera attached to a spotting scope, used to take zoomed-in photographs of distant birds.
Eastern Palaearctic Eastern part of the Palaearctic, including Asia with the

exception of India, Southeast Asia and southern China.

Eclipse Cryptic plumage gained by male wildfowl undertaking post-breeding moult.

Exposed tertials The visible extent of the three feathers found between the primaries and coverts on the folded wing.

Eye-ring Coloured ring of feathers that surrounds the eye (cf. orbital ring).

First-winter A description of the plumage acquired by a bird during its first winter after hatching.

Fourth-winter A description of the plumage acquired by a bird during its fourth calendar winter after hatching, the next plumage being adult.

Gape The soft mouth of a bird, between the upper and lower mandibles.

Gonys Angular part of the bill on the lower mandible, forming a noticeable bulge; typical on gulls.

Iris The coloured part of the eye surrounding the pupil.

Irruptive A species that irregularly moves to an area in which it is not usually found.

Jizz The feel of a species gained from the general impression, size and shape.

Lores The area between the bill and the eye.

Malar The area in front of and below the sub-moustachial stripe.

Mandible The bill is made of two mandibles, the upper and the lower.

Mantle The back.

Moustachial stripe A stripe that runs from the bill to below the eye, forming a 'moustache'.

Nape The hind neck.

Nearctic North America.

Orbital ring Ring of bare skin around the eye, often brightly coloured (cf. eye-ring).

Passerines The family containing all perching birds, such Robin, Blackbird, etc.

Pectoral band Well-demarcated band of breast feathering.

Primaries The main flight feathers found on the outer half of the wing and forming the 'hand'.

Primary projection The visible extent of the primary feathers beyond the tertials on the folded wing.

Scapulars A group of feathers that form the shoulder of the bird between the back and folded wing.

Second-winter A description of the plumage acquired by a bird during its second calendar winter after hatching.

Secondaries A group of relatively large flight feathers that form the inner part of the wing.

Speculum The coloured 'square' on the innerwing of a duck.

Sub-adult Adult-like plumage, but retaining some immature features.

Sub-moustachial The area of feathers below the moustachial stripe.

Supercilium The stripe that runs above, but not through, the eye.

Tertials The three feathers that can be seen on the folded wing between the small coverts and the primaries.

Third-winter A description of the plumage acquired by a bird during its third calendar winter after hatching.

Tibia The area of the leg above the 'knee'.

Topography Description of the external features of a bird.

Vent The area underneath the tail, formed by the undertail coverts.

RECOMMENDED READING

Archer, M., Grantham, M., Howlett, P. and Stansfield, S. (2010). *Bird Observatories of Britain and Ireland*. T & AD Poyser.

Cramp, S. et al. (1978–94). *Handbook of the Birds of Europe, the Middle East and North Africa. The Birds of the Western Palearctic. Vols 1–9*. Oxford University Press.

Duivendijk, N. (2011). *Advanced Bird ID Handbook: The Western Palearctic*. New Holland.

Flood, B. and Fisher, A. (2011). *Multimedia Identification Guide to North Atlantic Seabirds. Storm-petrels and Bulwer's Petrel*. Pelagic Birds and Birding Multimedia Identification Guides.

Flood, B. and Fisher, A. (2013). *Multimedia Identification Guide to North Atlantic Seabirds.* Pterodroma *Petrels*. Pelagic Birds and Birding Multimedia Identification Guides.

Garner, M and Scally R. (2014). *Birding Frontiers Challenge Series: Autumn*. Birding Frontiers.

Harrop, A.H.J., Collinson, J.M., Dudley, S.P., Kehoe, C. and the British Ornithologists' Union Record Committee (BOURC). (2013). 'The British List: A Checklist of Birds of Britain and Ireland (8th edition)'. *Ibis* 155: 635–76. doi: 10.1111/ibi.12069.

Mullarney, K., Svensson, L. and Zetterström, D. (2009). *Collins Bird Guide*. 2nd edn. HarperCollins.

Newton, I. (2010). *Bird Migration*. Collins New Naturalist 113. HarperCollins.

Porter, R. and Aspinall, S. (2010). *Birds of the Middle East*. 2nd edn. Christopher Helm.

Sibley, D. (2000). *The North American Bird Guide*. Pica Press.

Vinicombe, K., Harris, A., and Tucker, L. (2014). *The Helm Guide to Bird Identification*. Christopher Helm.

USEFUL WEBSITES

Bird Observatories Council
www.birdobscouncil.org.uk

BirdGuides
www.birdguides.com
Website dedicated to bird news and with a database of articles about birds.

British Birds Rarities Committee (BBRC)
www.bbrc.org.uk

British Ornithologists' Union (BOU)
www.bou.org.uk

British Trust for Ornithology (BTO)
www.bto.org

Irish Rare Birds Committee (IRBC)
www.irbc.ie

Surfbirds
www.surfbirds.com
International birding site, focusing on both sides of the Atlantic.

Xeno Canto
www.xeno-canto.org
Website dedicated to bird sounds.